Riding With Sheridan

Irving Waterman and Stanton Allen

Riding With Sheridan

The Recollections of a Young Cavalryman of
the 1st Massachusetts Cavalry Volunteers
During the American Civil War

Stanton P. Allen

Including

A Short History of the Service of the
1st Massachusetts Cavalry Volunteers
by Benjamin W. Crowninshield

Riding With Sheridan
The Recollections of a Young Cavalryman of the 1st Massachusetts Cavalry Volunteers During the American Civil War
by Stanton P. Allen
Including
A Short History of the Service of the 1st Massachusetts Cavalry Volunteers
by Benjamin W. Crowninshield

First published under the title
Down in Dixie

Leonaur is an imprint of Oakpast Ltd

Copyright in this form © 2017 Oakpast Ltd

ISBN: 978-1-78282-630-9 (hardcover)
ISBN: 978-1-78282-631-6 (softcover)

http://www.leonaur.com

Publisher's Notes

The views expressed in this book are not necessarily those of the publisher.

Contents

Going to School in Uniform	9
The War Fever Again	19
Helped Out of Trouble	29
A New Hand's Experience on Post	34
Missing in the Wilderness	38
A Special Artist at the Battle of Bull Run	50
Soldier Life at Camp Stoneman	62
Lincoln, Grant and Meade	70
The Bull Run Battlefield	85
A Fatal Post	96
The Overland Campaign	108
Breaking up Winter Quarters	116
The Night Before the Battle	125
Battlefield Experiences	130
Sheridan at the Head of the Cavalry	136
The Second Day in the Wilderness	144
The Baptism of Fire	152
Sheridan Ordered to Cut Loose	158
Custer's Brigade at Beaver Dam	162

Sheridan's Raid	170
A Christian Father's Sacrifice	182
Sheridan at the Front	186
Jeff Davis rides out to see the Yankees Whipped	192
Butler's Advance on the South Side	201
The Rebels Routed	214
Ghastly Sights in the Trenches	219
The Rebels Fall Back	226
Holding on to Save the Wagons	232
Operations South of the James	236
Sent to the Hospital	240
On the Picket Line	246
A Furlough for Twenty Days	254
Home on Furlough	261
President Lincoln's Visit to the Front	265
How Jeff Davis faced the Yankees	270
The Return March	280
Discharged From the Service	287
A Regimental Reunion	289
A Short History of the First Massachusetts Cavalry Volunteers By Benjamin W. Crowninshield	299

To My Daughter
Annie Adeline Allen
Wife of William H. Edwards
This Book is Affectionately Dedicated

Gen. Warren Receives a Dispatch From Gen. Meade.

Chapter 1

Going to School in Uniform

In the local columns of the Troy (N.Y.) *Daily Times* of September 1, 1863, the following news item was published:

A few days ago one Stanton P. Allen of Berlin, enlisted in Capt. Boutelle's company of the Twenty-First (Griswold) Cavalry. We are not informed whether it was Stanton's bearing the same name as the Secretary of War, or his mature cast of countenance that caused him to be accepted; for he was regarded as nineteen years of age, while, in reality, but fourteen summers had passed over his youthful, but ambitious brow. Stanton received a portion of his bounty and invested himself in one of those 'neat, but not gaudy' yellow and blue suits that constitute the uniform of the Griswold boys. A few days intervened. Stanton's 'patients,' on the vine-clad hills of Berlin, heard that their darling boy had 'gone for a sojer.'
Their emotions were indescribable. 'So young and yet so valiant,' thought his female relatives. 'How can I get him out?' was the more practical query of his papa. The ways and means were soon discovered. A writ of *habeas corpus* was procured from Judge Robertson, and as the proof was clear that Stanton was only fourteen years old, he was duly discharged from the service of the United States. But the end was not yet. A warrant was issued for the recruit, charging him with obtaining bounty and uniform under false pretences, and a release from the military service proved only a transfer to the civil power. Stanton found that he had made a poor exchange of 'situations,' and last evening gave bail before Judge Robertson in the sum of five hundred dollars.

In order that the correctness of history may not be questioned, the subject of the above deems it expedient to place on record an outline of the circumstances leading up to the incident related by the *Times*.

At the breaking out of the war my father resided in Berlin, N.Y., on the Brimmer farm, three miles or so from the village. I was twelve years old, but larger than many lads of sixteen. I was attacked by the war fever as soon as the news that Fort Sumter had been fired on reached the Brimmer farm. Nathaniel Bass worked for my father that year. The war fever got hold of Nat after haying was over, and one night along in the latter part of August, he said to me:

"I'm going to war."

"You don't mean it, Nat?"

"Yes, I do. The fall's work won't last long, and they say they're paying thirteen dollars a month and found for soldiers. That's better'n doing chores for your board."

"If you do go I'll run away and enlist."

"No; you're too young to go to war. You must wait till you're an able-bodied man—that's what the bills call for."

"O, dear! I'm afraid you'll whip all the rebels before I can get there."

I cried myself to sleep that night.

How I envied Nat when he came home on a three days' furlough clad in a full suit of cavalry uniform! He enlisted September 20, 1861, in the Second New York cavalry. The regiment was known as the Northern Black-horse cavalry. Nat allowed me to try on his jacket, and I strutted about in it for an hour or so. I felt that even in wearing it for a short time I was doing something toward whipping the Southerners. But Bass's furlough came to an end, and he returned to his regiment.

Nat came back in time to help us plant in the spring of 1862. The regiment went as far as Camp Stoneman, near Washington, where it remained in winter quarters. It was not accepted by the United States Government, and was never mounted. The reason given was that the government had more cavalry than it could handle, and the Northern Black-horse cavalry was disbanded. The regiment was raised by Colonel Andrew J. Morrison, who subsequently served with distinction at the head of a brigade.

Nat came home "chock-full" of war stories. He was just as much a hero in my estimation as he would have been if the rebels had shot him all to pieces. I never tired of listening to his yarns about the experiences of the regiment at Camp Stoneman. He had not seen a rebel, dead or alive, but that was not his fault. Nat was something of a singer, and he had a song describing the adventures of his regiment. The soldiers were referred to as "rats." I recall one verse and the chorus:

> *The rats they were mustered,*
> *And then they were paid;*
> *'And now,' says Colonel Morrison,*
> *'We'll have a dress parade.'*
> *Lally boo!*
> *Lally boo, oo, oo,*
> *Lally bang, bang, bang,*
> *Lally boo, oo, oo, Lally bang!*

I would join in the chorus, and although I did not understand the sentiment—if there was any in the song—I was ready to adopt it as a national hymn.

I was the proudest boy in the Brimmer district at the opening of school the next winter. I fairly "paralysed" the teacher, George Powell, and all the scholars, when I marched in wearing Nat's cavalry jacket and forage cap. He had made me a present of them. I was the lion of the day. The jacket fitted me like a sentry-box, but the girls voted the rig "perfectly lovely." Half a dozen big boys threatened to punch my eyes out if I did not "leave that ugly old jacket at home." I enjoyed the notoriety, and continued to wear the jacket. But one day Jim Duffy, a boy who worked for Tom Jones, came into the school with an artillery jacket on. It was of the same pattern as the jacket I wore, but had red trimmings in place of yellow. The girls decided that Jim's jacket was the prettier. I made up my mind to challenge Jim at the afternoon recess, but my anger moderated as I heard one of the small girls remark:

"But Jim ain't got no sojer cap, so he ain't no real sojer—he's only a make-b'lief."

"Sure enough!" chorused the girls.

Then I expected Duffy to challenge me, but he did not, and there was no fight.

That same winter Thomas Torrey of Williamstown came to our house visiting. Tom was one of the first to respond to the call for volunteers to put down the rebellion. He was in the Western army, and fought under Grant at Shiloh. He received a wound in the second day's fight, May 7, 1862, that crippled him for life. He had his right arm extended to ram home a cartridge, when a rebel bullet struck him in the wrist. The ball shattered the bone of the forearm and sped on into the shoulder, which it disabled. Tom's good right arm was useless forever after.

Tom was a better singer than Bass, and as we claimed him as our cousin, it seemed as if our family had already shed blood to put down the rebellion. While the wounded soldier remained at our house and told war stories and sang the patriotic songs of the day, my enthusiasm was kept at one hundred and twenty degrees in the shade. I made up my mind that I would go to war or "bust a blood vessel." I assisted in dressing Tom's shattered arm once or twice, but even that did not quench the patriotic fire that had been kindled in my breast by Bass's war stories and fanned almost into a conflagration by Tom's recital of his experiences in actual combat.

I discarded Nat's "Lally boo" and transferred my allegiance to a stirring: song sung; by Tom:

At Pittsburg Landing
Our troops fought very hard;
They killed old Johnston
And conquered Beauregard.

Chorus: *Hoist up the flag;*
Long may it wave
Over the Union boys,
So noble and so brave.

I laid awake nights and studied up plans to go to Pittsburg Landing and run a bayonet through the rebel who shot "Cousin Tom."

The summer of 1862 was a very trying time. Charley Taylor of Berlin, opened a recruiting office in the village and enlisted men for Company B, One Hundred and Twenty-Fifth New York Volunteers. I wanted to go, but when I suggested it to my father he remarked:

"They don't take boys who can't hoe a man's row. You'll have to wait five or six years."

When the Berlin boys came home on furlough from Troy, to show themselves in their new uniforms and bid their friends goodbye, it seemed to me that my chances of reaching the front in time to help put down the rebellion, were slim indeed. I reasoned that if Nat Bass could have driven the rebels into Richmond alone—as he said he could have done if he had been given an opportunity—the war would be brought to a speedy close when Company B was turned loose upon the Confederates in Virginia. It seemed that nearly everybody was going in Company B except Bass and I. I urged Nat to go, but he said it would be considered "small potatoes for a man who had served in the cavalry to reenlist in the infantry." If I had not overlooked the fact that Nat had never straddled a horse during his six months' service in Colonel Morrison's regiment, I might have questioned the consistency of Bass's position.

The One hundred and Twenty-Fifth left Troy Saturday, August 30, 1862, and on the same day the second battle of Bull Run was fought, resulting in the retreat of the Union Army into the fortifications around Washington.

"I told you so," said Bass, when the news of the battle reached Berlin. "The boys in Company B will have their hands full. They will reach the front in time to take part in this fall's campaign. I shall wait till next summer, and then if there's a call for another cavalry regiment to fight the rebels, I'll go down and help whip 'em some more."

When the news of Grant's glorious capture of Vicksburg, and Meade's splendid victory at Gettysburg, was received in Berlin, I made up my mind that the crisis had arrived. I said to Bass:

"Nat, our time's come."

"How so?"

"We've waited a year, and they've called for another regiment of cavalry."

"Then I believe I'll go."

"So'll I."

"Where's the regiment being raised?"

"In Troy."

"Will your father let you go?"

"Of course not—don't say a word to him. But I tell you, Nat, I'm going. The Union armies are knocking the life out of the rebels east and west, and it's now or never. I can't stand it any longer. I'm going to war."

I was only a boy—born February 20, 1849—but thanks to an iron constitution, splendid health and a vigorous training in farm work, I had developed into a lad who would pass muster for nineteen almost anywhere.

Bass got away from me. My father drove to Troy with Nat, who enlisted August 7, in Company E, of the Griswold cavalry. The regiment was taken to the front and into active service by the late General William B. Tibbits of Troy.

About the first of August a circus pitched its tents in Berlin. Everybody went to the show. While the acrobats were vaulting about in the ring, a lad in a cavalry uniform entered the tent and took a seat not far from where I was sitting. The circus was a tame affair to me after that. A live elephant was nowhere when a boy in blue was around.

"Who's that soldier?" I asked my best girl.

"That's Henry Tracy; I wish he'd look this way. He's too sweet for anything."

"Where's he from?"

"Off the mountain, from the Dutch settlement near the Dyken pond. Isn't he lovely! What a nobby suit!"

When the circus was out, I managed to secure an interview with the "bold sojer boy," who informed me that he was in the same camp with Bass at Troy.

"How old are you?" I asked Tracy.

"I'm just eighteen," he answered, with a wink that gave me to understand that I was not to accept the statement as a positive fact.

"Do you think they'd take me?"

"Certainly; you're more'n eighteen."

"When are you going back

"Shall start tonight. Think you'll go along?"

"Yes; if you really think they'll take me."

"I'm sure they will; you just let me manage the thing for you."

"All right; I'm with you."

I went with Tracy that night—after he had seen his girl home. As we climbed the steep mountain, I expected every minute to hear the footsteps of a brigade of relatives in pursuit. We reached the Tracy domicile about midnight, and went to bed. I could not sleep. The frogs in the pond near the house kept up a loud chorus, led by a bull-frog with a deep bass voice. I had heard the frogs on other occasions when fishing in the mountain lakes, and the boys agreed that the burden of the frog chorus was:

You'd better go round!
You'd better go round!
We'll bite your bait off!
We'll bite your bait off!

Somehow the chorus seemed that night to have been changed. As I lay there and listened for the sound of my father's wagon, the frogs sang after this fashion:

You'd better go home!
You'd better go home!
They'll shoot your head off!
They'll shoot your head off!

And, oh! how that old bullfrog with the bass voice came in on the chorus:

They'll shoot your head off!"

We got up at daylight, and walked over to the plank road and waited for the stage from Berlin to come along, *en route* to Troy. When the vehicle came in sight, I hid in the bushes until Tracy could reconnoitre and ascertain if my father was on board. He gave a signal that the coast was clear, and we took passage for the city.

"You're Alex Allen's boy?" the driver—Frank Maxon—said, as we took seats in the stage.

"What about it?"

"I heard 'em say at the post-office this morning that you'd run away."

"False report," said Tracy; "he's just going to Troy to bid me good-bye."

"Well, he must be struck on you, as they say he never set eyes on you till yesterday."

The stage rattled into Troy about half-past ten o'clock. There was considerable excitement in the city over the draft. Soldiers were camped in the court-house yard and elsewhere. They were Michigan regiments, I think. There was a section of artillery in the yard of the hotel above the tunnel. I could not understand how it was that the government was obliged to resort to a draft to secure soldiers. To me it seemed that an able-bodied man who would not volunteer to put down the rebellion, was pretty "small potatoes."

But I was only a boy. Older persons did not look at it in the same light as I did. By the way, the draft euchred our family out of three hundred dollars. When I enlisted in the First Massachusetts, after the failure of my plan to reach Dixie in the Griswold cavalry, I was paid three hundred dollars bounty. I sent it home to my father. The draft "scooped him in," and the government got the three hundred dollars back, that being the sum the drafted men were called on to pay to secure exemption.

Tracy escorted me to Washington Square, where there were several tents in which recruiting officers were enlisting men for the Griswold

First Enlistment

cavalry. A bounty of two dollars was paid to each person bringing in a recruit. Tracy sold me to a sergeant named Cole for two dollars, but he divided the money with me on the way to camp. As we entered the tent where Sergeant Cole was sitting, Tracy said:

"This young man wants to enlist, sergeant."

"All right, my boy; how old are you—nineteen, I suppose?"

"Of course he's nineteen," said Tracy.

I did not contradict what my soldier friend had said, and the sergeant made out my enlistment papers, Tracy making all the responses for me as to age. After I had been "sworn in" for three years, or during the war, I was paid ten dollars bounty. Then we went up to the barracks, and I was turned over to the first sergeant of Captain George V. Boutelle's company. I drew my uniform that night. The trousers had to be cut off top and bottom. The jacket was large enough for an overcoat. The army shirt scratched my back—but what is the use of reviving dead issues!

One day orders came for Capt. Boutelle's company to "fall in for muster." The line was formed down near the gate. I was in the rear rank on the left. The mustering officer stood in front of the company with the roll in his hand. Just at this time, my father with a deputy sheriff arrived with the *habeas corpus*, which was served on Capt. Boutelle, and I was ordered to "fall out."

Then we went to the city, to the office of Honourable Gilbert Robertson, Jr., provost judge, and after due inquiry had been made as to "the cause of detention by the said Capt. Boutelle of the said Stanton P. Allen," the latter "said" was declared to be discharged from Uncle Sam's service. My father refunded the ten dollars bounty, and offered to return the uniform, but Capt. Boutelle refused to accept the clothes, charging that I had obtained property from the government under false pretences. Under that charge I was held in five hundred dollars bail, as stated in the *Times*, but the court remarked to my father that "that'll be the end of it, probably, as the captain will be ordered to the front, and there will be no one here to prosecute the case."

As we were leaving Judge Robertson's office, a policeman arrested me. He marched me toward the jail. Pointing to the roof of the prison he said:

"My son, I'm sorry for you."

"What are you going to do with me?" I asked.

"Put you in jail."

"What for?"

"Defrauding the government. But I'm sorry to see you go to jail. They may keep you there for life. They'll keep you there till the war is over, any way, for people are so busy with the war that they can't stop to try cases of this kind. You are charged with getting into the army without your father's consent. Maybe they won't hang you, but it'll go hard with you, sure. I don't want to see you die in prison. If I thought you'd go home and not run away again, I'd let you escape."

That was enough. I double-quicked it up the street and hid in the hotel barn where my father's team was until he came along. I was ready to go home with him. I did not know at that time that the arrest, after I had been bailed, was a put-up job. It was intended to frighten me. And it worked to a charm. It was a regular Bull Run affair.

Chapter 2

The War Fever Again

I returned to Berlin very much discouraged. There had not been anything pleasant about our camp life in Troy—the food was poorly cooked, the camp discipline was on the go-as-you-please order at first, and sleeping on a hard bunk was not calculated to inspire patriotism in lads who had always enjoyed the luxury of a feather bed. Yet the thought that I was a Union soldier, and a Griswold cavalryman to boot, had acted as an offset to the hardships of camp life, and after my return home the "war fever" set in again. The relapse was more difficult to prescribe for than the first attack. The desire to reach the front was stimulated by the taunts of the wiseacres about the village who would bear down on me whenever I chanced to be in their presence, as follows:

"Nice soldier, you are!"

"How do the rebels look?"

"Sent for your father to come and get you, they say."

"Did they offer you a commission as jigadier brindle?"

"When do you start again?"

Quite a number of the boys about the village and from the back hollows interviewed me now and then in respect of my army experience. I was a veteran in their estimation. After several conferences, a company of "minute-men" was organised. We started with three members—Irving Waterman, Giles Taylor and myself. I was elected captain, Waterman first lieutenant and Taylor second lieutenant. We could not get any of the other boys to join as privates. They all wanted to be officers, so we secured no recruits. It was decided that we would run away and enlist at the first opportunity. Taylor was considerable of a "boy" as compared with Waterman and myself, as he was married and a legal voter. Waterman was nearly two years my senior, but as I had "been to war" they insisted that I should take the lead and they would follow.

We finally fixed upon Thanksgiving Day in November, 1863, as the time to start for Dixie. Waterman had scouted over around Williamstown, and he came back with the report that two Williams College students were raising a company of cavalry. Thanksgiving morning I informed my mother that I was going to a shooting match. It proved to be more of a shooting match than I expected. The minute-men met at a place that had been selected, and started for Dixie.

At the Mansion House, Williamstown, we introduced ourselves to Lieutenant Edward Payson Hopkins, son of a Williams College professor. The lieutenant was helping his cousin, Amos L. Hopkins, who had been commissioned lieutenant and who expected to be a captain, to raise a company.

"As soon as he secures his quota, I shall enlist for myself," said the lieutenant, who added, that we could put our names down on his roll and he would go with us to North Adams, at which place we could take cars for Pittsfield, where Captain Hopkins's recruiting office was located. We rode to North Adams in a wagon owned by Professor Hopkins and which was pressed into service for the occasion by the professor's soldier son. The lieutenant handled the lines and the whip, he and I occupying the seat, and Taylor and Waterman sat on a board placed across the wagon behind.

At North Adams we were taken into an office where we were examined by the town war committee.

One of the committee was Quinn Robinson, a prominent citizen. I was called before the committee first, and having been through the mill before, I managed to satisfy the committee that I was qualified to wear a cavalry uniform and draw full rations. I remember that in canvassing the question of age—or rather what we should say on that subject—we had agreed to state that we were twenty-one. I was not fifteen until the next February. The examiners did not question my age.

"We won't say twenty-one years," said Waterman, "and so we won't lie about it."

After I had been under fire for some time I was told to step aside, and Waterman was brought before the examiners.

"He looks too young," said Mr. Robinson to Lieutenant Hopkins.

"Well, question him," suggested the lieutenant.

"How old are you?" inquired the committee man.

"Twenty-one, sir," replied Waterman.
"When were you twenty-one?"
"Last week."
"I think you're stretching it a little."
"No, sir; I'm older than Allen, who has just been taken in."
"I guess not; you may go out in the other room by the stove and think it over."

Our married man Taylor was next called in.
"We can't take you," said Robinson.
"What's matter?" exclaimed Giles.
"You're not old enough."
"How old've I got to be?"
"Twenty-one, unless you get the consent of your parents."
"Taylor's a married man," I whispered to Lieutenant Hopkins.
"Don't tell that, or he'll be asked to get the consent of his wife," said the lieutenant, also in a whisper.

The committee contended that Taylor would not fill the bill. Waterman was recalled, and Mr. Robinson said:
"Well, you've had time to think it over. Now how old are you?"
"Twenty-one, last week."
"I can't hardly swallow that."
"See here, Mr. Quinn" (I had not heard the committee man's other name then), I interrupted. "We three have come together to enlist. You have said that I can go. Taylor may be a trifle under age, but what of it? If you don't take the three of us none of us will go."

There was more talk of the same kind, but finally the war committee decided to send us on to Pittsfield and let the recruiting authorities of that place settle the question of Taylor and Waterman's eligibility.

There was no trouble at Pittsfield, and we were forwarded to Boston in company with several other recruits. The rendezvous was at Camp Meigs in Readville, ten miles or so below the city. Arriving at the camp we were marched to the barracks of Company I, Third Battalion, First Massachusetts cavalry, to which company we had been assigned.

When we entered the barracks we were greeted with cries of "fresh fish," etc., by the "old soldiers," some of whom had reached camp only a few days before our arrival. We accepted the situation, and were ready as soon as we had drawn our uniforms to join in similar greetings to later arrivals. The barracks were one storey board buildings. They would shed rain, but the wind made itself at home inside the structures when there was a storm, so there was plenty of ventilation. The bunks were double-deckers, arranged for two soldiers in each berth.

"I'm not going to sleep in that apple bin without you give me a bed," said Taylor to the corporal who pointed out our bunks.

"Young man, do you know who you're speaking to?" thundered the corporal.

"No; you may be the general or the colonel or nothing but a corporal"—

"'Nothing but a corporal!' I'll give you to understand that a corporal in the First Massachusetts Cavalry is not to be insulted. You have no right to speak to me without permission. I'll put you in the guard house and prefer charges against you."

"See here," said Taylor. "Don't you fool with me. If you do I'll cuff you."

"Mutiny in the barracks," shouted a lance sergeant who heard Giles's threat to smite the corporal.

The first sergeant came out of a little room near the door, and charged down toward us with a sabre in his hand.

"What's the trouble here?" he demanded.

"This recruit threatened to strike me," replied the corporal.

"And he threatened to put me in the guard house for saying I wouldn't sleep in that box without a bed," said Taylor.

"Did you ever hear the articles of war read?" asked the sergeant.

"No, sir."

"Well, then, we'll let you go this time; but you've had a mighty narrow escape. Had you struck the corporal the penalty would have been death. Never talk back to an officer."

"Golly! that was a close call," whispered Taylor, after he had crawled into his bunk.

We each had a blanket issued to us for that night, but the next day straw ticks were filled, and added to our comfort. Waterman and I took the upper bunk, and Giles slept downstairs alone until he paired with Theodore C. Horn of Williamstown, another new-comer.

One of the most discouraging experiences that a recruit was called upon to face before he reached the front was the drawing of his outfit—receiving his uniform and equipments. I speak of cavalry recruits. If there ever was a time when I felt homesick and regretted that I had not enlisted in the infantry it was the morning of the second day after our arrival at Camp Meigs. I recall no one event of my army life that broke me up so completely as did this experience. I had drawn a uniform in the Griswold cavalry at Troy before my father appeared on the scene with a *habeas corpus*, but I had not been called on to take charge of a full set of cavalry equipments. If I had been perhaps the second attack of the war fever would not have come so soon.

A few minutes after breakfast the first sergeant of Company I came out from his room near the door and shouted:

"Attention!"

"Attention!" echoed the duty sergeants and corporals in the barracks.

"Recruits of Company I who have not received their uniforms fall in this way."

A dozen "Johnny come Latelys," including the Berlin trio, fell in as directed. The sergeant entered our names in a memorandum book. Then we were turned over to a corporal, who marched us to the quartermaster's office where we stood at attention for an hour or so while the requisition for our uniforms was going through the red-tape channels. Finally the door opened, and a dapper young sergeant with a pencil behind his ear informed the corporal that "all's ready."

The names were called alphabetically, and I was the first of the squad to go inside to receive my outfit.

"Step here and sign these vouchers in duplicate," said the sergeant.

I signed the papers. The sergeant threw the different articles of the uniform and equipments in a heap on the floor, asking questions and answering them himself after this fashion:

"What size jacket do you wear? No. 1. Here's a No. 4; it's too large, but you can get the tailor to alter it.

"Here's your overcoat; it's marked No. 3, but the contractors make mistakes; I've no doubt it's a No. 1.

"That forage cap's too large, but you can put paper in the lining.

"Never mind measuring the trousers; if they're too long you can have 'em cut off.

"The shirts and drawers will fit anybody; they're made that way.

"You wear No. 6 boots, but you'll get so much drill your feet'll swell so these No. 8's will be just the fit.

"This is your bed blanket; don't get it mixed with your horse blanket.

"I'll let you have my canteen and break in the new one; mine's been used a little and got jammed a bit, but that don't hurt it.

"This is your haversack; take my advice and always keep it full.

"This white piece of canvas is your shelter tent; it is warranted to shelter you from the rain if you pitch it inside a house that has a good roof on it.

"These stockings are rights and lefts.

"Here's your blouse. We're out of the small numbers, but it is to be worn on fatigue and at stables, so it's better to have plenty of room in your blouse.

"You will get white gloves at the sutler's store if you've got the money to settle. He'll let you have sand paper, blacking, brushes, and other cleaning materials on the same terms.

"Here's a rubber poncho.

"Let's see! that's all in the clothing line. Now for your arms and accoutrements!"

I appealed to the sergeant:

"Let me carry a load of my things to the barracks before receiving my arms and other fixings?"

"Can't do it—take too much time; and if you did go over with part of your outfit, somebody'd steal what you left in the barracks before you returned with the rest."

"Go it, then," I exclaimed in despair, and the sergeant continued:

"This carbine is just the thing to kill rebels with if you ever get near enough to them. It's a short-range weapon, but cavalrymen are supposed to ride down the enemy at short range.

"The carbine sling and swivel attaches the carbine over your shoulder.

"This cartridge box will be filled before you go on the skirmish line; so will the cap pouch.

"This funny-looking little thing with a string attached is a wiper with which to keep your carbine clean inside.

"The screw-driver will be handy to take your carbine apart, but don't do it when near the enemy. They might scoop you in before you could put your gun together.

"Your revolver is for short-range work. You can kill six rebels with it without reloading, if the rebels will hold still and you are a crack shot. You can keep the pistol in this holster which attaches to your waist-belt, as does also this box for pistol cartridges.

"These smaller straps are to hold your sabre scabbard to the waist-belt, and this strap goes over the shoulder to keep your belt from slipping down around your heels.

"This is your sabre inside the scabbard. I've no doubt it's inscribed 'Never draw me without cause or sheathe me with dishonour,' but we can't stop to look at it now. If it isn't inscribed, ask your first sergeant about it. The sabre knot completes this part of the outfit. The sabre is pretty big for you, but we're out of children's sizes. The horse furniture comes next."

"Will you please let Taylor and Waterman come in here and help me?" I petitioned to the sergeant.

"Everybody for himself is the rule in the army," said the sergeant. "Tie up your clothing and arms in your bed blanket. You can put your horse furniture in your saddle blanket."

Section 1,620 of the "Revised United States Army Regulations of 1861, with an Appendix Containing the Changes and Laws Affecting Army Regulations and Articles of War to June 25, 1863," reads as follows:

"A complete set of horse equipments for mounted troops consists of 1 bridle, 1 watering bridle, 1 halter, 1 saddle, 1 pair saddle-bags, 1 saddle blanket, 1 surcingle, 1 pair spurs, 1 curry-comb, 1 horse brush, 1 picket pin, and 1 lariat; 1 link and 1 nose bag when specially required."

The section reads smoothly enough. There is nothing formidable about it to the civilian. But, ah me! Surviving troopers of the great conflict will bear me out when I say that section 1,620 aforesaid, stands for a great deal more than it would be possible for the uninitiated to comprehend at one sitting. The bridle, for instance, is composed of one headstall, one bit, one pair of reins. And the headstall is composed of "1 crown piece, the ends split, forming 1 cheek strap and 1 throat lash billet on one side, and on the other 1 cheek strap and 1 throat lash, with 1 buckle, .625-inch, 2 chapes and 2 buckles, .75-inch, sewed to the ends of cheek piece to attach the bit; 1 brow band, the ends doubled and sewed from two loops on each end through which the cheek straps and throat lash and throat lash billet pass."

So much for the headstall. It would take three times the space given to the headstall to describe the bit, and then come the reins. The watering bridle "is composed of 1 bit and 1 pair of reins." The halter's description uses up one third of a page. "The saddle is composed of 1 tree, 2 saddle skirts, 2 stirrups, 1 girth and girth strap, 1 surcingle, 1 crupper." Two pages of the regulations are required to describe the different pieces that go to make up the saddle complete, and which include six coat straps, one carbine socket, saddle skirts, saddle-bags, saddle blanket, etc. The horse brush, curry-comb, picket pin, lariat, link and nose bag all come in for detailed descriptions, each with its separate pieces.

Let it be borne in mind that all these articles were thrown into a heap on the floor, and that every strap, buckle, ring and other separate piece not riveted or sewed together was handed out by itself, the sergeant rattling on like a parrot all the time, and perhaps a faint idea of the situation may be obtained. But the real significance of the event can only be understood by the troopers who "were there."

As I emerged from the quartermaster's office I was a sight to behold. Before I had fairly left the building my bundles broke loose and my military effects were scattered all around. By using the loose straps and surcingle I managed to pack my outfit in one bundle. But it was a large one, just about all I could lift.

When I got into the barracks I was very much discouraged. What to do with the things was a puzzle to me. I distributed them in the bunk, and began to speculate on how I could ever put all those little straps and buckles together. The more I studied over it the more complicated it seemed. I would begin with the headstall of the bridle. Having been raised on a farm I had knowledge of double and single harness to some extent, but the bridles and halters that I had seen were not of the cavalry pattern. After I had buckled the straps together I would have several pieces left with no buckles to correspond. It was like the fifteen-puzzle.

As I was manipulating the straps Taylor arrived with his outfit. He threw the bundle down in the lower bunk, and exclaimed:

"I wish I'd staid to home."

"So do I, Giles."

"Where's Theodore?"

"I haven't seen him since I left him at the quartermaster's."

"He got his things before I did and started for the barracks."

Taylor left his bundle and went in search of Horn who was found near the cook-house. His pack had broken loose, and he was too much disgusted to go any further. Taylor assisted him, and they reached the bunk about the time Waterman arrived. We held a council of war, and decided to defer action on the horse furniture till the next day.

"We'll tog ourselves out in these soldier-clothes and let the harness alone till we're ordered to tackle it," said Taylor, and we all assented.

"Attention!"

The orderly sergeant again appeared.

"The recruits who have just drawn their uniforms will fall in outside for inspection with their uniforms on in ten minutes!"

There was no time for ceremony. Off went our home clothes and we donned the regulation uniforms. Four sorrier-looking boys in blue could not have been found in Camp Meigs. And we were blue in more senses than one. My forage cap set down over my head and rested on my ears. The collar to my jacket came up to the cap, and I only had a "peek hole" in front. The sleeves of the jacket were too long by nearly a foot, and the legs of the pantaloons were *ditto*. The government did not furnish suspenders, and as I had none I used some of the saddle straps to hold my clothes on. Taylor could not get his boots on, and Horn discovered that both of his boots were lefts. He got them on, however. When Waterman put on his overcoat it covered him from head to foot, the skirts dragging the floor. Before we had got on half our things the order came to "fall in outside," and out we went. Taylor had his government boots in his hands, as a corporal had informed him that if he turned out with citizen's boots on after having received his uniform he would be tied up by the thumbs. So he turned out in his stocking feet.

We were "right dressed" and "fronted" by the first sergeant, who reported to the captain that the squad was formed. The captain advanced and began with Taylor, who was the tallest of the squad, and therefore stood on the right.

"Where are your boots?"

"Here," replied the frightened recruit, holding them out from under the cape of his great coat.

"Fall out and put them on."

"I can't."

"Why not?"

"I wear nines and these are sevens."

"Corporal, take this man to the quartermaster's and have the boots changed."

Taylor trotted off, pleased to get away from the officer, who next turned his attention to Hom.

"What's the matter with your right foot; are you left-handed in it?"

"No, sir; they gave me both lefts."

"Sergeant, send this man to the quartermaster's and have the mistake rectified."

Waterman was next in line.

"Who's inside this overcoat?" demanded the captain.

"It's me, sir—private Waterman."

"Couldn't you get a smaller overcoat?"

"They said it would fit me, and I had no time to try it on."

"Sergeant, have that man's coat changed at once. Fall out, private Waterman."

Then came my turn. The captain looked me over. My make-up was too much for his risibility.

"Where did you come from?" he asked, after the first explosion.

"Berlin."

"Where's that?"

"York State."

"Well, you go with the sergeant to the quartermaster and see if you can't find a rig that will come nearer fitting you than this outfit."

I was glad to obey orders, and after the captain's compliments had been presented to the quartermaster, directions were given to supply me with a uniform that would fit. Although the order could not be literally complied with, I profited by the exchange, and the second outfit was made to do after it had been altered somewhat by a tailor, and the sleeves of the jacket and the legs of the trousers had been shortened.

The captain did not "jump on us" as we had expected. The self-styled old soldiers had warned us that we would be sent to the guard house. The captain had seen service at the front, and had been through the mill as a recruit when the First Battalion was organised. He knew that it was not the fault of the privates that their clothes did not fit them. This fact seemed to escape the attention of many commissioned officers, and not a few recruits were censured in the presence of their comrades by thoughtless captains, because the boys had not been built to fill out jackets and trousers that had been made by basting together pieces of cloth cut on the bias and every other style, but without any regard to shapes, sizes or patterns.

CHAPTER 3

Helped Out of Trouble

I do not know whether Robert J. Warren, who served in Company I, Third Battalion, First Massachusetts cavalry, is living or not, (as at time of first publication), I trust that he survives, and that he is prosperous. I shall never forget his kindness to me when I was a raw recruit at Camp Meigs.

Warren was a sergeant, and had seen service at the front. I think he had also served in the regular dragoons on the frontier before the War of the Rebellion broke out. Bob, as he was familiarly known, was a soldier from heels up. As already stated, I was unable to put my saddle equipments together when they were issued to me. I was sitting on my bunk, completely discouraged, when Sergeant Warren came along.

"What's the trouble here?"

"O, colonel! I can't put these things in shape—they won't fit at all."

"I'm not a colonel."

"Well, captain, then?"

"No."

"Lieutenant?"

"No. I'm only a sergeant. You'll know these things after a little. Let me see what I can do for you. All these straps and buckles are necessary to complete your saddle kit."

In less than five minutes the sergeant had "used up" that big pile of leather straps. And it was a revelation to Taylor, Hom, Waterman and myself. We stood and looked on as Warren buckled the equipments together and briefly explained the uses of the different pieces. We adopted a vote of thanks to the sergeant for his assistance.

"I don't think we should have answered roll-call tomorrow morning if you hadn't come to our help," said Taylor.

"Why not?"

"Because we were so downhearted we might have run away."

"I guess not," said the sergeant; "you boys are made of better stuff. Don't you know that the penalty of desertion is death?"

"Is it?"

"Yes."

"We didn't know it before."

A young man dressed in a brand-new uniform that fitted him to perfection came into the barracks. He had stripes on his arms and legs, and he strutted so proudly that I thought he must be the general.

"Is that the commander-in-chief.?" I asked Sergeant Warren.

"O, no!" laughingly replied the sergeant. "He may feel bigger than the general, but he's only a corporal. His name is Timothy Pelton."

Sure enough, the new-comer was only a corporal. But he proved to be a splendid fellow upon closer acquaintance. Tim left us, however, to accept a commission as lieutenant in the Fifth Massachusetts (coloured) cavalry that was organised in 1863. He was residing in Troy in 1871. Later he studied law at Northampton, Mass., where he died.

Sergeant Warren did me another good turn, after he had assisted me to become reconciled to my saddle kit. He explained to me the insignia of rank of commissioned and non-commissioned officers. In a few minutes he gave me more information on the subject than I could have obtained in a year's service had not some one taken the pains to personally enlighten me. The information will be of use to the civilians of this day and generation as it holds good now, and probably will remain the same for generations to come. By observing the directions given me by Sergeant Warren any one can tell at a glance the rank of officers of the regular army or national guard when meeting them in uniform.

"Is a corporal higher'n a sergeant?" I inquired after Pelton had gone by.

"No; a corporal's only one grade above a private. I will describe the insignia of rank so that you will have no difficulty in distinguishing any officer you may meet hereafter.

"In the first place bear in mind that there are only eight grades, or eight classes of grades, rather. Promotion in the army is like going up a pair of stairs. You are a private, and I suppose you will be surprised when I tell you that you have only eight steps to go up to be a general, but it's a fact.

"The first step makes you a corporal. Now observe that a corporal wears chevrons on the sleeves of his jacket. The corporal has two bars on each sleeve. They are sewed on above the elbow, from the outer and inner seams of the sleeve, running obliquely down and toward the centre, coming to a point and forming a V.

"The colour of the chevron will indicate the branch of service—yellow for cavalry, red for artillery, blue for infantry.

"The next grade is that of sergeant—the rank I hold. The chevrons are the same, except the sergeant wears three stripes or bars instead of two.

"The first or orderly sergeant has a lozenge or diamond in addition to the three stripes. Some call it a letter O, as O stands for orderly.

"The quartermaster-sergeant wears three stripes and three bars across the top.

"The sergeant-major's chevrons have three stripes above, forming an arc over the sergeant's stripes.

"A hospital steward has a green half-chevron with a caduceus embroidered in yellow.

"An ordnance sergeant has three stripes and a star in red.

"The next in rank above the sergeant-major, who is the highest sergeant, is the second lieutenant. Commissioned officers wear shoulder-straps. The straps are alike in each branch of service, except the ornaments inside the border which indicate the rank of the officer. The second lieutenant has a plain shoulder-strap.

"The first lieutenant's strap is the same as the junior lieutenant's except there is one gold or silver embroidered bar of the same width as the border near each end of the strap.

"The captain has two bars near each end of the strap.

"The major wears a gold embroidered leaf at each end of the strap.

"The lieutenant-colonel has a silver embroidered leaf.

"The colonel has a silver embroidered spread eagle in the center of the strap.

"The brigadier-general's strap is the same as a colonel's, except a star in place of the eagle.

"The major-general wears two stars.

"The general in command of the army has three stars.

"The ground work of the shoulder-strap indicates the branch of service—yellow for cavalry, red for artillery and blue for infantry.

"Officers of the medical department have the letters M. S. on their shoulder-strap; officers of the pay department the letters P. D.; officers of the quartermaster's department Q. D,, and officers of the commissary department C. D.

"Now don't forget there are but eight steps; in coming down they are general, colonel, lieutenant-colonel, major, captain, lieutenant, sergeant, corporal. Of course, if you go through the different promotions in each grade it takes a few more steps. But even were you to serve in every grade given in the army regulations it would take only fifteen steps to make you a major-general."

In March, 1864, a bill was passed by Congress reviving the rank of lieutenant-general, which was created in 1798 for Washington, and had been abolished after the death of the Father of his Country. Winfield Scott was breveted lieutenant-general for services in the war with Mexico. Grant's commission as lieutenant-general was handed him by President Lincoln at the White House, March 9, 1864. The lieutenant-general wore three stars on each shoulder. In 1866 the rank of "General of the armies of the United States" was revived by an act of Congress, and Grant was promoted to that rank. This title was also originally created for Washington, but had been abolished. The general wore four stars on each of his shoulder-straps. Sherman succeeded Grant as lieutenant-general of the army and also as general, March 4, 1869, upon the inauguration of the "Hero of Appomattox" as president. Sheridan was made lieutenant-general at the same time, and upon Sherman's retirement Little Phil took command of the army. He was made general of the army while on his death bed.

There was a good deal of kicking at Camp Meigs over the bill of fare. It seemed to be characteristic of recruits to growl about their rations. Had they known what was before them they would not have turned up their noses at boiled ham, potatoes, bread, vegetables, fresh meat, coffee, etc., that constituted the menu of the Bay State troops at the Readville rendezvous. Major-generals at the front saw many occasions when they would have given a month's pay for a square meal such as recruits at Camp Meigs found fault with. We had plum duff now and then, and other extra fixings on state occasions. Milk and sugar were supplied for our coffee, and boys with delicate stomachs could have tea and toast if they desired it. And then there was the sutler's store, where the boys in blue who could not live on army grub could buy home-made bread and other extras sent to the camp daily from Boston.

Yet the chronic growler was around. It was observed—and it was so all through the army—that the recruits who had had the poorest fare at home were loudest in their protestations against the rations issued at the rendezvous. I noticed that Bob Warren and the soldiers who had been to the front seemed to relish their food. The non-commissioned officers dined at side-tables. Their rations were the same as the privates', but the cook showed them favours. Sometimes they "chipped in" and purchased extras—butter, etc.

Taylor had a way of speaking his mind and thinking aloud that occasioned him no little trouble. The first breakfast we had after reaching camp consisted of bread and beef and coffee. Taylor was near the table at which the sergeants and corporals were seated. He saw a dish of butter on their table, and as there was none handed out to him, he elbowed the ranking duty sergeant and exclaimed:

"Pass the butter!"

Old soldiers will understand what a grave act of impropriety the Berlin recruit committed. Such a breach of military etiquette would have consigned the offender to the guard-house had Taylor been in uniform, but as he had not donned his suit of blue he was allowed to go with the admonition that if he ever again attempted such familiarity with a sergeant he would be bucked and gagged.

CHAPTER 4

A New Hand's Experience on Post

Heels on the same line, as near each other as the conformation of the man will permit."

In the instruction of the recruit the drill sergeant or corporal, or whoever might have the squad in hand, always began with the heels—starting from the ground and building upward. This may have given rise to the expression, common in the days of the war, when speaking of a comrade who had shown more than ordinary fitness for some position to which he had been promoted, "He's a soldier from heels up." But one could not be a soldier in any other way—according to tactics.

I have no means of knowing to whom the American soldiers are indebted for the concluding part of the sentence quoted at the opening of this chapter—"as near each other as the conformation of the man will permit." In the first volume of Hardee's tactics, which were in use when the war broke out, I find this explanatory clause referring to the latitude allowed in respect of the recruit having his "heels more or less closed:"

> Because men who are knock-kneed, or have legs with large calves, cannot, without constraint, make their heels touch while standing.

I want to say in all seriousness that if this explanation and the proviso to which it refers had been omitted or overlooked when Hardee's tactics were reissued under another name at the beginning of the war—Hardee having gone with the Confederates—there would have been bloodshed at the rendezvous where recruits were given their initiatory lessons in the school of the soldier.

There were a few men in Company I who came under the class

of knock-kneed, and one who could not make his heels touch while standing, constraint or no constraint. But no matter how much of a physical impossibility it might have been for him to put his heels together on the same line, there was one drill sergeant at Camp Meigs who would have made him do it or die, I verily believe, if the tactics had said so. The attempts of the unfortunate recruit to make his heels touch were ludicrous in the extreme. After he had done his level best, the sergeant would insist that the recruit could do better.

"Now, bring them heels together!"

"I can't!"

"Silence in the ranks! bring them heels together, I tell you! Your conformation will permit them heels to come nearer together."

And then the knock-kneed, bow-legged recruit, stimulated to extraordinary exertion by the close proximity of the drill sergeant's sabre, would go through the contortion act again. When the instructor finally got through, some of the stiffness had been taken out of the recruit's legs, but bow-legged he was when he enlisted, and bow-legged he remained till he was mustered out; so much so that large-sized cannon balls could have been fired between his legs without injury to his limbs, if the gunner had been a good marksman, and had aimed at some object in plain view through the opening. Take two capital K's, turn one bottom side up and put them together—KⱯ—the inner lines give something of an idea, on a small scale, of the "gates ajar" opportunity the cannoneer would have had.

Taylor was the tallest recruit in the squad, and he was placed on the right. It seemed to be impossible for the man in his rear, as the squad was marched by the right flank, to keep off Taylor's heels. I observed that Taylor was "getting hot in the collar," and I knew there would be an outbreak. Finally the recruit barked the right guide's ankle, and Taylor "broke ranks" in a hurry. The high-stepper fled as Taylor rushed toward him, and took refuge behind the drill sergeant.

"Halt, or I'll tierce-point you through the body!" yelled the sergeant as Taylor advanced.

"Don't you stick that cheese knife into me!"

"Keep back, then!"

"Get out of the way and let me choke that fellow that walked on my legs."

But the sergeant managed to keep the point of his sabre on a line with the third button of Taylor's blouse, so that should the latter press forward he would be sabred in a very tender spot. A compromise was effected after some parleying. It was stipulated that another recruit should march next to Taylor, and that after retreat the offender should meet Taylor over back of the stables to "have it out." As a result of the meeting, Taylor's antagonist answered sick call the next morning.

We soon mastered the heel-and-toe movements, as one recruit designated the first lessons in squad drill. The position of the trooper dismounted was pretty well understood, theoretically and practically, by nearly all the boys before we had been in camp a week. There were a good many movements that I could not get at the philosophy of, but we came to understand that these things had been prescribed for us, and, like a dose of bitter medicine, we must swallow them and make the best of it.

Guard duty at Camp Meigs was a good deal of a farce in many respects. Yet there was no serious breach of discipline. There was a chain of sentinels reaching entirely around the camp. The post of honour—the boys called it the post of horror—was at the entrance to the camp, down near the station at the railroad. Here it was that the poor recruit was almost compelled to confess that life was not worth living. I think it was Post No. 2. No. 1 was at the guard house, and the posts were numbered in succession all the way around the camp. The orders at Post No. 2 were as follows, whispered by one sentinel to another:

"This is Post No. 2—take charge of this post and all government property in view; salute all officers according to rank; in case of fire give the alarm; allow no one to pass in or out without permission from proper authority; challenge all persons approaching your post between retreat and reveille; let none pass without the countersign; repeat all calls from posts farther from the guard house," etc.

The sentinels were instructed to call the corporal of the guard in case of disturbance or trouble of any kind. There were detachments of several infantry regiments at Camp Meigs, and there was no scarcity of officers.

The first time I was put on Post No. 2, it seemed to me that there was a procession of shoulder-straps marching by without let-up. If the sentinel stopped to read the passes in the hands of enlisted men as they poured out of camp during the day, he had no time to "salute all officers according to rank," as required by the orders. Anybody who came along holding up a piece of white paper was allowed to pass, for the reason that the sentinel was kept busy saluting officers.

The regulations directed that "sentinels will present arms to general and field officers, to the officer of the day and to the commanding officer of the post. To all other officers they will carry arms." To the recruits it was a difficult task to distinguish a field officer from a line officer. But we soon discovered that it was safer to give the junior second lieutenant of a regiment a general's salute than it was to carry arms to a major who was entitled to a present. Human nature would crop out in the army the same as elsewhere.

One of our boys was posted on No. 2 the first time he went on guard. He got all mixed up over his instructions, and was taken to task by several officers for not giving them the proper salute. But his intentions were all right. He wanted to show his loyalty. After making many dismal failures in determining the rank of officers who crossed his beat, he gave it up in despair. So he simply stood with his carbine in his hand, and as an officer approached, the sentinel, with a significant nod of the head toward his carbine, would sing out:

"Say, Mister, which'll you have, field or line salute? I'll give you whichever you say, but I'm a new hand, and I don't want to make a mistake."

Most of the officers appreciated the "new hand's desire to do them justice, and the sentinel was not punished.

CHAPTER 5

Missing in the Wilderness

Although Fort Independence and the other fortifications in Boston Harbour were strongly garrisoned, and equipped with heavy ordnance, and Camp Meigs was at so remote a point from Dixie, it was impossible for the recruit now and then, when receiving his instructions on post at night, to shake off the feeling that the rebels were prowling around the camp, ready to dash in and destroy us should any of the sentinels relax their vigilance in the least degree.

The sentinels at Camp Meigs were armed with old muskets, with here and there a sabre, before the regulation equipments had been issued to the recruits. There were not weapons enough to go around, so the sentinel on post would turn over his musket or sabre to the sentinel relieving him. This mixing up of the arms of two branches of the service frequently caused confusion in the mind of a recruit in respect of the good faith of the corporal in charge of the relief.

I was on guard over toward the camp of the Fifth Massachusetts cavalry, across the railroad track, one night. When I went on post I relieved a man who was armed only with an old sabre. He turned over the sabre to me, as well as the instructions. After the sentinel had given me a long string of orders, the corporal capped the climax by quoting for my benefit the following paragraphs from the revised regulations pertaining to grand guards and other outposts:

A sentinel should always be ready to fire. A sentinel must be sure of the presence of the enemy before he fires. Once satisfied of that, he must fire, though all defence on his part be useless, as the safety of the post may depend on it."

It is not necessary to point out the inconsistency of such orders to a sentinel armed only with an old sword.

During the night the grand rounds would be made by the officer of the day. The regulations prescribed that sentinels should challenge the rounds.

It was about midnight when the grand rounds advanced on my post. The moon was shining, so that I could distinguish the officer of the day, the sergeant and the privates in the escort, even when they left the guard house. They marched down upon me in regulation order, slackening their pace as they drew near. I did not challenge the party, because, as I thought, it was all nonsense to call down anyone that I knew. But when within a half-dozen paces of my post, the officer halted, and directed the escort to halt.

"Why don't you challenge?" the officer demanded.

"Because I don't want to fight."

"Why don't you call out, 'Who comes there?'"

"I know 'who comes there,' and what's the use of asking when I know who you are?"

"What are your orders?"

I repeated the instructions as near as I could recall them. I was relieved at once, as the officer of the day declared that a sentinel who would allow the grand rounds to walk up to his post without halting them ought to be court-martialled and shot. I discovered that I had made a mistake, and I received a severe reprimand from the officer of the day in the presence of the guard. The sergeant of the guard interceded and saved me from more condign punishment. The officer said:

"I will let you off this time, you pumpkin head, as you are inexperienced. But never again allow any person to approach your post without challenging and carrying out your orders to the very letter. No one but a 'pumpkin head' would do such a thing."

Several months later our battalion joined the regiment in winter quarters at Warrenton, Va. The officer who had called me a "pumpkin head" at Camp Meigs was field officer of the day soon after we reached Warrenton, and I was on picket. My post was on the edge of a marshy strip of land through which ran a cow-path. Several days' rain had caused the water to cover the ground, and the path was submerged. The orders were to challenge all persons approaching the pickets, day or night, and the Camp Meigs instructions were enlarged, as will be seen by what followed the visit of the field officer of the day to my post. He had inspected the pickets to my right, and was riding the line toward the left. He kept a little too far outside the line as he

GETTING EVEN WITH THE OFFICER OF THE DAY.

came down toward me, and when he arrived within challenging distance, he was about midway the marsh.

"Who comes there?"

"Officer of the day."

"Halt, officer of the day. Dismount, hold up your hands, advance and give the countersign."

The officer threw back the cape of his overcoat, displaying his sash. "It's all right—you know who I am. It isn't necessary for me to dismount in this water. It's over my boot tops in places."

"Dismount, bold up your hands, advance and give the countersign."

"But the water"—

"Dismount, hold up your hands, advance and give the countersign."

As he got down into the mud and water, the officer muttered something to himself that sounded like "dough-head." He violated the third article of the war several times before he reached *terra firma*. After he had advanced and given the countersign, we exchanged compliments something like this:

Officer—"You knew who I was. What made you dismount me in that mud hole?"

Picket—"You know what my orders are, Captain."

Officer—"But you are supposed to take orders from the officer of the day."

Picket—"But I am not supposed to recognise the officer of the day until he has given the countersign. No one but a 'pumpkin-head' would do such a thing."

The officer took a good look at me, and seemed to grasp the situation.

"I have seen you before."

"Yes, sir; on post at Camp Meigs."

He rode on to inspect the next vidette.

The Fifth Massachusetts cavalry, a coloured regiment, was in camp just across the railroad track from our quarters.

It was an interesting and novel sight to see the coloured cavalrymen on dress parade. White collars were not allowed to be worn in the Fifth, so the only relieving features of the darkness were the white gloves and the whites of the eyes of the troopers. How proud they were, and how straight they stood, with heads erect—perfect machines, so to speak! And when the command, "Right dress!" was given, and that long line of coloured men turned their eyes to the right as one man, it was like a flash of lightning darting horizontally across an inky sky.

The second week after our arrival at Camp Meigs, Waterman and I were detailed to extra duty, he to carry the mail between Camp Meigs and Boston, and I to act as letter-carrier between the rendezvous and Dedham, a village only a few miles from Readville, on a branch road.

The mail for Dedham was gathered by orderlies from the camp, and left at department headquarters down at the railroad station. I received it at headquarters and carried it to Dedham on the cars. The mail that I brought back from the village post-office was sorted at headquarters, letters for each company being made up in separate packages, which I delivered throughout the camp.

The mail-carrier was the most popular man in camp.

Old soldiers will recall how they watched for and welcomed the mail-carrier, and how their hearts would leap for joy when the first sergeant would call out their names in reading the addresses on the letters.

And how a letter from home would stir the heart of the soldier boy! Father's kindly admonitions, mother's prayerful, blessed messages, sister's loving, cheerful letters—with all the news for her "hero brother"—and then the tender missives from some other fellow's sister, breathing the prayer that the rebellion might soon be put down and the boys in blue might come marching home.

Letters from our sweethearts always contained a verse or two of some ballad or war song expressive of the dear girls' undying love, and urging us to prove true—to them and to the flag of the Union. Here is a sample:

Dearest love, do you remember,
When we last did meet,
How you told me that you loved me,
Kneeling at my feet?
Oh! how proud you stood before me,
In your suit of blue,
When you vowed to me and country
Ever to be true.

Chorus:

Weeping, sad and lonely,
Hopes and fears, how vain;

Yet praying
When this cruel war is over,
Praying that we meet again.

Of course the answer to everyone received was freighted with pledges of unswerving devotion and loyalty, and something like the following was very apt to close the letter:

Heart-broken since I left you, dear—
May the heavens above me guide me,
And send me safe back home again.
To the girl I left behind me.

In one of the companies of the First Massachusetts cavalry, there was a recruit who could neither read nor write. He was from somewhere up in the mountains of New Hampshire. He had drifted down to Boston and enlisted. He was always looking for a letter, but the days and weeks rolled on without bringing him any news from home.

"Anything for me, Sergeant?" he would ask every time the mail was distributed.

"Nothing for you this time, Joe."

"Well, it'll come next mail, sure."

"I hope so, Joe."

We all hoped so, for it was evident that Joe's heart would break if somebody up in the wilds of the Granite State did not come to the rescue, and that right speedily.

One day Joe said to me:

"Will you write a letter to my girl?"

"Certainly, Joe."

I took him over to the barracks of Company I, and wrote the following at his dictation:

(Union Forever!)
Camp Meigs, Dec. 15, 1863.

My Own Sweet Mary:

I've waited till my heart bleeds, and there's no letter from you. All the other boys get letters from their true loves, but poor Joe he's left out in the cold. I can't believe you've so soon forgotten me. Don't you remember the apple paring at Jeff Taylor's, and I saw you home? You said you couldn't be the sweetheart of any stay-at-home when the flag was in danger, and I said, "Mary, I'll go if you'll promise to be mine when I come back." And you promised; yes, you did, Mary. Now, what am I to think of you? Who is the scoundrel that's come between me and you? I can lick him out of his boots. What's the matter with Mary? If you have anything to say to one you've treated in this way, write to your own

Poor Joe.

Down with traitors! Union forever!

P. S. The rose is red,
The violet's blue,
'But thoroughbred's
My love for you.'
J

"That ought to fetch her," said Joe.

It did "fetch her." I addressed the letter as directed by Joe. The return mail brought Mary's answer, which explained why her soldier lover had been so long kept in ignorance of what was going on at home. It read something after this fashion:

Stratford, N. H., Dec. 17, 1863.

My Darling Long-lost Joe:

How could you treat your own dear Mary so? I have been dying to hear from you. I was afraid you had gone straight on to Richmond and got into Libby Prison. You seem to overlook the fact that you never sent me a line telling me where you were or in what regiment, or company, or anything else. I didn't know where to direct to you. But I suppose you were too busy preparing to fight the rebels to think of that. Yes, Joe, I remember my promise, and I'll keep it. You are my own precious soldier boy. Nobody has come between us—how could you dream of such a thing.' So you've got nobody to lick but the rebels. All your folks are well, but they worried themselves nearly to death about you. Don't do so any more. Nobody around here had any idea where you were, and some of the gossips started the story, just to spite me, I believe, that you had run away to Canada to get out of the draft. Wasn't it mean, and you doing your duty in the army at the same time? If you had told me where you were I would have written every day. That's what's the matter with Mary.

P. S. My pen is poor,
My ink is pale,

> My love for you
> Will never fail,
> 	M.

"Kick me—kick me hard, so hard I can't set in my saddle for a month," exclaimed Joe. "Here I've been blaming that dear girl, and it's all my fault. I believe I'm an idiot. Of course she couldn't write till I let her know where I was."

Joe picked up wonderfully after that, and I had my hands full writing his letters to Mary, and reading hers to him. They kept up the correspondence till the opening of the campaign of 1864; the last letter came the day we left Warrenton, Va., for the Wilderness. There was no time to answer it then. It never was answered at Joe's dictation. "Missing in the Wilderness" was written opposite his name on the first company muster-roll made out after that battle. It was believed he was killed, as nothing was ever heard of him again.

When we reached the James River on Sheridan's raid, and had a breathing spell, I wrote to Joe's Mary and informed her of the poor boy's probable fate. There was a hope that he had been taken prisoner and that he would be exchanged, and all that. But he never was seen again by his comrades, and a letter from Mary to me, written just before we were mustered out at the close of the war, stated that she had abandoned all hope of ever seeing her darling Joe again. She had written to me occasionally, begging me to make every possible effort to find out something definite about Joe. I did my best in complying with her request, but I was satisfied that Mary's soldier lover filled an unknown grave—with thousands of other noble young men—in the Wilderness.

In making my daily trip to Dedham with the mail, I had about an hour to wait in the village for the return train. Patriotism was at fever heat, and the good people made my stay among them pleasant. Nothing was too good for a soldier at that time. Mothers, sisters and sweethearts of some of the boys in blue at Camp Meigs resided at Dedham. They made me their special messenger to carry knickknacks to the boys, and I was also the bearer of tender expressions of affection to their loved ones. Such of these as were written or verbal I sacredly delivered. But when blooming young ladies entrusted me with a genuine New England kiss to deliver to their sweethearts, I could not be expected to work both ways, so to speak. The osculation was perfect at the Dedham end of the line, but (telephonically speaking) the trans-

JOE DICTATES HIS LETTER TO MARY.

mitter failed to work at the point of delivery. When it is stated that I invariably reported to the lasses who sent kisses by me that the soldier boys had returned the compliment fourfold, it will be understood that my time did not hang heavy on my hands in that charming village. That special delivery business is among the pleasantest recollections of my military experience.

But something happened one day that caused me to be relieved from extra duty. There was a woman in the case, of course. As I was going from the post-office in Dedham to the depot, a woman for whom I had carried several packages to her son in Camp Meigs handed me a bottle wrapped in paper, saying:

"Please take that to Jamesy."

"What is it?"

"It's a bit of cough medicine. Me poor boy has caught his death a cold sleeping with no feather bed, and he can't get the medicine he needs in camp, at all, at all. Sure, Jamesy will die if he don't get the medicine."

"All right; I'll see that he gets it."

I put the bottle in the mail bag. When I reached headquarters at Readville and went into the office, several officers were there discussing the question of intoxication among soldiers.

"I can't understand how they manage to smuggle the liquor into camp," said the general in command.

"One of the recruits put in the guard house last night for being drunk and making a disturbance in the barracks after taps, stated that his whiskey came by mail," said the officer of the day from Camp Meigs, who had been summoned to headquarters to confer with the department commander on the liquor question.

"But they can't send bottles through the mail."

Then the officer of the day, noticing my mail bag, exclaimed:

"Maybe the mail-carriers know something about it."

"I'll vouch for this one," said the acting assistant adjutant-general. "He's as straight as a string. The general has some doubts about Waterman, but this lad's all right."

Turning to me, the A. A. A. G. directed me to empty my mail bag on the table, as was the custom.

The bottle was the most conspicuous thing among the contents.

The officers cast significant glances at one another.

"Aha!" exclaimed the officer of the day.

"How's this?" demanded the A. A. A. G.

"IT IS GIN, SIR," SAID THE ORDERLY

"I thought you could vouch for this letter-carrier," said the department commander.

"What's in this bottle?" thundered the A. A. A. G., frowning upon me.

"Cough medicine, sir."

"Who's it for?"

"Jamesy O'Donnell."

"Who gave it to you?"

"His mother."

"Where?"

"At Dedham."

The A. A. A. G. shouted to an orderly to bring a corkscrew—a rather strange piece of furniture to have at a temperance station, it seemed to me—and he pulled the cork out of the bottle. But it was evident that the A. A. A. G. did not wish to be recognized as a sampler, so he handed the bottle to the headquarters' orderly, a rollicking Irishman.

"What is it?" asked the general.

The orderly held the bottle up to the light, and said:

"It looks like gin, sir."

He put it to his nose, and continued:

"It smells like gin, sir."

Then the bottle went to his lips, and after a long swig the orderly said:

"It tastes like gin, sir."

Another long swig and the expert added:

"And it is gin, sir."

"It's a contraband article, and we'll confiscate it," said the A. A. A. G. as he rescued the bottle from the orderly.

The officer of the day smacked his lips, prematurely, however, as the A. A. A. G. carried the bottle into his private office with the remark that he would hold it as "evidence against the smuggler."

At first the officers would listen to nothing but a general court-martial for me, but I protested my innocence so strenuously that they finally concluded to give me the "benefit of a doubt," as the officer of the day suggested. I was relieved at once from duty as mailcarrier and sent to report to my company commander.

CHAPTER 6

A Special Artist at the Battle of Bull Run

Should there be living today, (1888), a survivor of Sheridan's Cavalry Corps of the Army of the Potomac who can, without shuddering, recall the buglers' drill, his probationary period on earth must be rapidly drawing to a close. I do not mean the regular bugle calls of camp or those sounded on company or battalion parade. I refer to the babel of bugle blasts kept up by the recruit "musicians" from the sounding of the first call for reveille till taps. A majority of the boys enlisted as buglers could not at first make a noise—not even a little toot—on their instruments, but when, under the instruction of a veteran bugler, the} had mastered the art of filling their horns and producing sound they made up for lost time with a vengeance. And what a chorus! Reveille, stable call, breakfast call, sick call, drill call retreat, tattoo, taps—all the calls, or what the little fellows could do at them, were sounded at one time with agonizing effect.

The first sergeant of Company I said to me one day while we were in Camp Meigs:

"The adjutant wants more buglers, and he spoke of you as being one of the light weights suitable for the job. You may go and report to the adjutant."

"I didn't enlist to be a bugler; I'm a full-fledged soldier."

"But you're young enough to bugle."

"I'm twenty-one on the muster-roll. I want to serve in the ranks."

"Can't help it; you'll have to try your hand."

I reported to the adjutant as directed, and was sent with a half-dozen other recruits to be tested by the chief trumpeter. After a trial of ten minutes the instructor discovered that there was no promise of my development into a bugler, and he said with considerable emphasis:

"You go back *mit* you to *de* adjutant and tell him dot you no got one ear for de music."

I was glad to report back to the company, for I preferred to serve as a private.

The recruits soon became familiar with the sound of the bugle. The first call in the morning was buglers' call—or first call for reveille. The notes would be sounding in the barracks when the first sergeant, all the duty sergeants and the corporals would yell out:

"Turn out for reveille roll-call!"

"Be lively, now—turn out!"

As a result of this shouting by the "non-coms" the boys soon began to pay no attention to the bugle call, but naturally waited till they heard the signal to "turn out" given by the sergeants and corporals. And in a very short time they ceased to hear the bugle when the first call was sounded.

In active service in the Army of the Potomac so familiar with the calls did the soldiers become that when cavalry and infantry were bivouacked together, and the long roll was sounded by the drummers, it would not be heard by the troopers, and when the cavalry buglers blew their calls the foot soldiers would sleep undisturbed. In front of Petersburg troops would sleep soundly within ten feet of a heavy battery that was firing shot and shell into the enemy's works all night. But let one of the guards on the line of breastworks behind which they were "dreaming of home" discharge his musket, and the sleepers would be in line ready for battle almost in the twinkling of an eye. And let the cavalry trumpeter make the least noise on his bugle, and the troopers would hear it at once.

A few weeks before our battalion left Camp Meigs for the front Mrs. E. L. Waterman of Berlin, mother of Irving Waterman, paid us a visit. She brought with her a basket full of goodies. Home-made pies, bread, butter, cheese, cookies and fried cakes were included in the supplies. She took up her quarters at the picture gallery of Mr. Holmes, the camp photographer, and we went to see her as often as our duties would permit. She brought us socks knit by our friends at home, and many articles for our comfort. About the first thing she said was: "My boys, what do they give you to eat?"

"Bread and meat and beans and coffee," we answered.

"No butter?"

"No."

"I thought not. I had heard the soldiers had to eat their bread without butter, with nothing but coffee to wash it down, so I brought you a few pounds of butter."

And the dear woman remained at the gallery, and Irving and I would drop over and eat the good things she fixed for us. If we had taken our commissary stores to the barracks they would have been stolen.

Mrs. Waterman asked Irving and myself to have our pictures taken. Neither of us had ever been photographed or tintyped, but we took kindly to the idea. We sat together, and the picture, a tintype, was pronounced an excellent likeness. What a trying performance it was, though! We were all braced up with an iron rest back of the head, and told to "look about there—you can wink, but don't move." Of course the tintype presented the subject as one appears when looking into a mirror. The right hand was the left, and our buttons were on the wrong side in the picture. But Mrs. Waterman declared the tintype to be "as near like them as two peas," and we accepted her verdict. The dear old lady has kept that picture all these years.

The soldier boys resorted to all sorts of expedients to "beat the machine." That is, to so arrange their arms and accoutrements that when the tintype was taken it would not be upside down or wrong end to. To this end the sabre-belt would be put on wrong side up so that the scabbard would hang on the right side—that would bring it on the left side, where it belonged in the picture. I tried that plan one day and then stood at "parade rest," with the sabre in front of me. I put back my left foot instead of my right to stand in that position, and when the picture was presented, I congratulated myself that I had made a big hit. But when I showed it to an old soldier in the company he humiliated me by the remark:

"It's all very fine for a recruit, but a soldier wouldn't hold his sabre with his left hand and put his right hand over it at parade rest."

Sure enough. I had changed my feet to make them appear all right, but had forgotten the hands. But recruits were not supposed to know everything on the start.

We had photographs taken as well as tintypes. But the art of photography has greatly improved since the war. Most of the photographs of that day that I have seen of late are badly faded, and it is next to impossible to have a good copy made. Not so with the tintypes. They remain unfaded, and excellent photographic copies can be secured. In many a home today, (1888), hang the pictures of the soldier boy, some of them life-sized portraits copied from the tintypes taken in the days of the war.

I know homes where the gray-haired mothers still cling to the little tintype picture—the only likeness they have of a darling boy who was offered as a sacrifice for liberty. How tenderly the picture is handled! How sacredly the mother has preserved it! The hinges of the frame are broken—worn out with constant opening. The clasp is gone. The plush that lined the frame opposite the picture is faded and worn. But the face of the boy is there. Surviving veterans understand something of the venerable lady's meaning when she puts the picture to her lips and with tears in her eyes says:

"Yes, he was only a boy. I couldn't consent to let him go, and I couldn't say no. I could only pray that he would come back to me—if it were God's will. He didn't come back. But they said he did his duty. He died in a noble cause, but it was hard to say '*Thy will be done,*' at first, when the news came that he'd been killed. I'm so thankful I have his picture—the only one he ever had taken. He was a Christian boy, and they wrote me that his last words as his comrades stood about him under a tree where he had been borne, were, that he died in the hope of a glorious resurrection, and that mother would find him in Heaven to welcome her when she came. There's comfort in that. And I'll soon be there. I shall meet my boy again, and there will be no more separation. No more cruel rebellions."

The early war-time pictures are curiosities today, particularly to veterans who study them. Not a few of the special artists of the first year of the war seemed to have gained whatever knowledge of the appearance of troops in battle array that they had from tintype pictures. I have before me as I write, a battle scene "sketched by our special artist at the front." The officers all wear their swords on the right side, and in the foreground is an officer mounting his horse from the off side—a feat never attempted in military experience but once, to my knowledge, and then by a militia officer on the staff of a Troy general, since the war. In some of these pictorial papers of the early war-days armies are represented marching into battle in full-dress uniform and with unbroken step and perfect alignment.

One thing, however, always puzzled me in these pictures—before I went to war—and that was how the infantry could march with measured tread—regulation step of twenty-eight inches, and only one hundred and ten steps per minute—and keep up with the major-generals and other officers of high rank who appeared in front of their men, and with their horses on a dead run in the direction of the enemy! These heroic leaders always rode with their hats in one hand and their swords in the other, so there was no chance for them to hold in their horses. But the puzzle ceased to be a puzzle when I reached the front. I found that the special artists had drawn on their imagination instead of "on the spot," and that it was not customary for commanding generals to get in between the contending lines of battle and slash right and left and cut up as the artists had represented. In the majority of cases, great battles were fought by generals on both sides who were in position to watch, so far as possible, the whole line of battle, and to be ready to direct such movements and changes as were demanded by the progress of the fight. To do this they must necessarily be elsewhere than in front of their armies, riding down the enemy's skirmishers, and leaping their horses over cannon.

It is possible, however, that the special artists did not fully understand the danger to which a commanding general would be exposed, galloping around on his charger between the armies just coming together in a terrible clash. At any rate, the specials were willing to take their chances with their heroes—on paper. I have in my possession a picture of the "Commencement of the Action at Bull Run—Sherman's Battery Engaging the Enemy's Masked Battery." In this picture, sketched by an artist whose later productions were among the best illustrations of actual warfare, the officers are, very considerately, placed in rear of the battery. But in front of the line of battle, in advance of the cannon that are belching forth their deadly fire, stands the special artist, sketching "on the spot."

There was a good deal of stir in Camp Meigs the day that horses were issued to the battalion. The men were new, and so were the horses. It did not take a veteran cavalryman but a day or two to break in a new horse. But it was different with recruits. The chances were that their steeds would break them in.

I had had some experience with horses on a farm—riding to cultivate corn, rake hay and the like—but I had never struggled for the mastery with a fiery, untamed war-horse. Our steeds were in good condition when they arrived at the camp, and they did not get exercise enough after they came to take any of the life out of them. The first time we practiced on them with curry-comb and brush, the horses kicked us around the stables *ad libitum*. One recruit had all his front teeth knocked out. But we became better acquainted with our chargers day by day, and although we started for Washington a few days after our horses had been issued, some of us attained to a confidence of our ability to manage the animals that was remarkable, considering the fact that we were thrown twice out of three times whenever we attempted to ride.

One day orders came for us to get ready to go to the front. None but old soldiers can appreciate the feelings of recruits under such circumstances. All was bustle and confusion. There was a good deal of the hip, hip, hip, hurrah! on the surface, but there was also a feeling of dread uncertainty—perhaps that expresses it—in the breasts of many of the troopers. They would not admit it, though. The average recruit was as brave as a lion to all outward appearances, and if he did have palpitation of the heart when orders came to go "On to Richmond"—as any advance toward the front was designated—the fact was not given out for publication.

The first thing in order was a general inspection to satisfy the officers, whose duty it was to see that regiments sent out from the Old Bay State were properly armed and equipped, that we were in a condition to begin active service. After all our belongings were packed on our saddles in the barracks, before we took them over to the stables to saddle up, the department commander with his inspecting officers examined our kits. As originally packed, the saddles of a majority of the troopers were loaded so heavily that it would have required four men to a saddle to get one of the packs on the horse's back. When the inspection was completed, each trooper could handle his own saddle.

The following articles were thrown out of my collection by the inspectors:—

Two boiled shirts; one pair calfskin shoes; two boxes paper collars; one vest; one big neck scarf; one bed quilt; one feather pillow; one soft felt hat; one tin wash basin; one cap—not regulation pattern; one camp stool—folding; one blacking brush—extra; two cans preserves; one bottle cologne; one pair slippers; one pair buckskin mittens; three fancy neckties; one pair saddle-bags—extra; one tin pan; one bottle hair oil; one looking-glass; one checker-board; one haversack—extra—filled with home victuals; one peck bag walnuts; one hammer.

Some of the boys had packed up more extras than I had, and it went against the grain to part with them. But the inspectors knew their business—and ours, too, better than we, as we subsequently discovered—and we were made to understand that we were not going on a pleasure excursion. It is hardly necessary to say that there was scarcely an article thrown out by the inspectors that the soldiers would

IN THE SADDLE

not have thrown away themselves on their first expedition into the enemy's country.

After we had been inspected and trimmed down by the officers, we were reviewed by Governor John A. Andrew. He was attended by his staff, the department commander and other officers. Each company was drawn up in line in its barracks—it was sleeting outside. As the governor came into our quarters, the captain gave the command, "Uncover!" and the company stood at attention as the chief executive of the Old Bay State walked slowly down the line, scanning the faces of the men.

I remember that the governor looked at me with a sort of "Where-did-you-come-from, Bub?" expression, and I began to fear that my time had come to go home. The governor said to a staff officer:

"Some of the men seem rather young, colonel!"

"Yes, sir; the cavalry uniform makes a man look younger than he is."

"I see. They are a fine body of men, and I have no doubt we shall hear of their doing good service at the front."

A few words of encouragement were spoken by the governor, and he passed on to the barracks of the next company.

It strikes me that Governor Andrew reviewed us again as we were marching from the barracks to the railroad station, but I am not clear on this point. I know there was a good deal of martial music, waving of flags, cheering and speech-making by somebody. Our horses claimed our undivided attention till after we had dismounted and put them aboard the cars. On the way down to the railroad an attempt was made somewhere near the barracks to form in line, so that we could be addressed by the governor or some other dignitary. It was a dismal failure. Our steeds seemed to be inspired by "Hail to the Chief," "The Girl I Left Behind Me," and other patriotic tunes played by the band, and they pranced around, stood upon their hind legs and pawed the air with their fore feet, to the great terror of the recruits and the delight of all the boys in the neighbourhood who had gathered to witness our departure. How the boys shouted!

"Hi, Johnny, it's better'n a circus!"

"Guess 'tis—they don't fall off in a circus; they just make b'lief."

"Well, these fellows stick tight for new hands."

It was fun for the boys—the spectators—but just where the laugh came in the recruits failed to discover. I was told that the governor—or somebody—gave us his blessing as we rode by the reviewing officer, but I have no personal knowledge on the subject.

After we had put our horses on board we waited a few minutes before entering the cars while the other companies were boarding the train. There was a chain of sentinels around us, and Mrs. Waterman was outside the line. She caught sight of us as we stood there, and she advanced toward us.

"Halt—you can't go through here!" commanded one of the sentinels.

"I must go through."

"But my orders"—

"I don't care; my boys are there, and I'm going to speak to them again."

She came through and gave us her parting blessing once more.

"Boys, I'll pray God to keep you and bring you both back to your mothers—God bless you; goodbye." The mother's prayers were answered. Her son and his tent-mate were spared to return at the close of the war.

There was a scramble to secure seats when orders were given to board the cars. Goodbyes were said. Mothers, wives and sweethearts were there, and with many it was the last farewell. The whistle blew, the bells rang, the band played, the troops remaining at Camp Meigs cheered and we cheered back. The train moved away from the station, and we were off for the front.

I never saw Governor Andrew again, but I recall his appearance as he reviewed our company in the barracks very distinctly. I observed that while inspecting officers paid more attention to the arms and accoutrements of the men the governor was particular in looking into the faces of the recruits, to satisfy himself, no doubt, that they could be trusted to uphold the honour of the State when the tug of war should come.

John A. Andrew was one of the "war governors" whose loyal support of President Lincoln's emancipation programme held the Northern States in line when the time came for the president to issue the proclamation that freed the slaves of the States in rebellion against the government.

The proclamation was promulgated September 22, 1862, a few days after the Battle of Antietam. It is on record that Lincoln had made the draft of the document in July, and had held it, waiting for a Union victory, that he might give it to the country at the same time that a decisive defeat of the rebels was announced. The Second Battle

"Halt—You can't go through here!"

of Bull Run came, and Pope's shattered army retreated into the works around the national capital. Lee, with his victorious followers, crossed the Potomac into Maryland. The Confederate chief hoped to rally the disloyal element in that State and along the border under the rebel flag. It began to look as though the victory Lincoln was waiting for would never come. It was one of the darkest hours of the conflict. What would have been the effect of issuing the Emancipation Proclamation at that time? The rebels had invaded the North! The Union army had been defeated—everything seemed to be going to destruction!

Lincoln is credited with saying in respect of the rebels crossing the Potomac just before the Battle of Antietam:

> I made a solemn vow before God, that if General Lee were driven back from Maryland, I would crown the result by a declaration of freedom to the slaves.

September 24, 1862, two days after the proclamation was issued, Governor Andrew, with the governors of other loyal States, at a meeting at Altoona, Penn., adopted an address to the president that must have set at rest any doubts the chief magistrate may have had that his policy was the policy of the loyal people of the North. The document was inspired and executed by patriots in whom the citizens of the loyal States reposed unbounded confidence. They declared:

> We hail with heartfelt gratitude and encouraged hope the proclamation of the president, issued on the 22nd inst., declaring emancipated from their bondage all persons held to service or labour as slaves in rebel States where rebellion shall last until the first day of January ensuing.
>
> Cordially tendering to the president our respectful assurances of personal and official confidence, we trust and believe that the policy now inaugurated will be crowned with success, will give speedy and triumphant victories over our enemies, and secure to this nation and this people the blessing and favour of Almighty God. We believe that the blood of the heroes who have already fallen and those who may yet give up their lives to their country will not have been shed in vain.
>
> And now presenting to our chief magistrate this conclusion of our deliberations, we devote ourselves to our country's service, and we will surround the president in our constant support, trusting that the fidelity and zeal of the loyal States and people

will always assure him that he will be constantly maintained in pursuing with vigour this war for the preservation of the national life and hopes of humanity.

CHAPTER 7

Soldier Life at Camp Stoneman

It was a long train that conveyed our battalion from Readville. Our horses were placed in box cars. The troopers were packed into the passenger coaches, three deep. The skirmishing for position assisted in drying the tears of those who were nearly heartbroken over parting with "the girl I left behind me" and mother dear.

In this connection it may be remarked, that during the last two years of the war, some railroad and other corporations engaged in the transportation business—and which were getting rich from the proceeds of government contracts—came to look upon the soldiers as so many common cattle. It was not the fault of the government. Money enough was paid for transporting men and material to have provided the best accommodation for the boys in blue. But it was pleaded by the railroad and steamboat officials that the capacity of their lines was totally inadequate to meet the demands of travel.

"*A soldier is a citizen, but a citizen is not a soldier,*" was a common saying during the war. Politicians in making stump speeches delighted to assert the fact. While the sentiment was all right, theoretically, it "didn't work," as the boys found when they attempted to put it into practice, and presumed upon their rights as citizens while clad in the faded coat of blue.

On our way to Washington, one of our boys, very tired, and anxious to find a place to sit down, attempted to go into a passenger coach next forward of the first car that was set apart for the soldiers. There were three or four officers, and about a dozen men in citizen's dress in the car. As the soldier reached the rear platform of the coach and opened the door, he was met by a broad-shouldered train hand, who said:

"This car is reserved for citizens."

"A soldier is a citizen," exclaimed the trooper.

"Not on this railroad," asserted the brakeman.

"But every seat in the other cars is full, and there isn't standing room. There are plenty of vacant seats in this car. I'm tired, and I want to sit down."

"Can't help it—orders are orders. This car is reserved for citizens."

"But there are officers in the car—they are soldiers."

"Yes, an officer is a soldier, but a soldier is not an officer. That's what we are given to understand by our superiors. You're only a soldier, and you can't come in."

But the rough treatment of the soldiers was not so noticeable in the New England States. It cropped out more on the railroads in the States bordering on Mason and Dixon's line—the very States that had the more reason to be thankful to those who fought to beat back the rebel columns. Sometimes the boys retaliated and settled old scores—scores which cost the railroad companies something when they came to pay for damages to rolling stock. Still, they put up with a great many impositions without complaining. There was truth in the statement that the railroads were unable at times to carry all the soldiers *en route* without packing them like sardines in a box. The boys never "kicked" when the exigencies of the occasion demanded such a huddling together. It was only when they were refused privileges accorded to citizens, and which could have been extended to the soldiers without trespassing upon anybody's rights, that the "citizens" in blue emphasized their protest.

As our train rolled along through the beautiful New England villages, we were given to understand that the patriotism of the ladies was unbounded. At the doors and windows of nearly every house along the line, fair damsels waved the stars and stripes. At every stopping place a battalion of young ladies boarded our train with refreshments. It was a prevailing belief among the female patriots at the North during the great rebellion that soldiers were always hungry—half-starved, and ready to eat at all hours of the day and night. It was a good thing for the soldiers. The young ladies gave us homemade bread and boiled ham, doughnuts and cheese, pumpkin pies and apples—lots and lots of home grub. And they blessed us, and said they would pray for us. Then they stuffed our haversacks with cookies and cakes, bade us God speed—music by the band, cheers, waving of tiny flags, and before the echoes of the sweet chorus of female voices singing "Hail, Columbia," or some other inspiring song, had fairly died out, we would be greeted by the cheers of the assembled residents of another village. It was grand—glorious. It was this sort of thing that nerved the untried recruits for the hardships of active service.

We left the cars at New London, Conn. When we began to comprehend the situation, and found that we were to go down to sea in a ship, some of us began to wish that we had been ordered to march to Washington. Said Taylor:

"I didn't enlist to go to sea. The boat'll go down if we put our horses on board. We can't afford to lose our horses."

"I'd be willing to lose my horse if they'd let me go by rail," said another trooper.

"Fall in, Company I; this way to go aboard," commanded our first sergeant.

It was dark when we steamed out into Long Island Sound. The water was rough, and there was much seasickness. I escaped that affliction, but if Taylor had lived to come home, he could have told all about it from experience. As he lay prostrate on the deck, he called to me between spasms:

"I'm going to die—they've murdered me—O, dear! Here I go again. Oh! get a sharp knife and cut my throat. If you won't do me this favour, call Waterman and let him do it."

It was a terrible night. The wind blew a gale, and the steamer pitched and tossed about. The deck hands laughed at us when we timidly inquired, "Is there any hope?" "It's only a light squall," they assured us, but somehow we felt that the sailors were not in sympathy with us—who ever knew a sailor to have sympathy for a seasick landlubber? None of us had any disposition to growl at our rations on the steamer. The government allowance for one platoon would have fed the whole battalion, with several basketfuls of fragments left over. A good many silent prayers for deliverance were made, and a few audible ones were heard from those who were the most frightened. Quite a number, I have no doubt, prayed something after the fashion of the Irishman who got down on his knees in the cabin, when he thought the vessel that was bringing him over to America was going to the bottom, and said:

"Lord, you know I've never asked a favour of you. And I'll promise never to ask another, if you'll only set me foot on dry land once more."

We landed at Amboy, N. J. The experiences of that night on the steamer seem to overshadow events of minor importance. But I remember that all the boys who had life enough left to cheer, lifted their voices in joy and gladness when it was announced that we were sailing into port. We disembarked, and boarded a train that brought us in due time to Philadelphia. The Quaker City was like an oasis in the desert. It was the bright spot—and is to this day—in the memory of the soldiers who were permitted to partake of the hospitalities of its citizens, when journeying to or from the front.

Three cheers for the Cooper shop! Yes, three times three, and a tiger! Our boys would have fared slim had it not been for the cordial welcome they received at Philadelphia. In the agonies of seasickness, many of the troopers had thrown overboard everything that partook of the nature of food. They never expected to be hungry again. They suffered no permanent injury, however, from the short trip on the Sound, and when they got their shore legs on again their appetites came back. And how they did eat!

As we left the cars and marched toward the building where we had been told we would be royally entertained, we caught sight of a broad banner suspended from a rope across the street. On the banner were the words; *Cooper Shop Volunteer Refreshment Saloon. Free.*

The building was a two-story structure. Over the door was the sign "William M. Cooper." The same name was inscribed on a streamer that floated from the top of a flag-pole near the building, and a second streamer bore the patriotic inscription: *Union, Now and Forever. Death to Traitors.*

Pretty girls clad in neat calico dresses, with red, white and blue aprons, served the soldiers with an abundance of substantial food and delicacies. "God bless you, ladies," was the universal verdict of the boys in blue. There was no stinting, no reserving of the best dishes for the men with shoulder-straps. Everybody was served with the best. To the left of the building were arranged sinks in which the travel-stained soldiers could wash their faces and hands, so as to be somewhat presentable when ushered into the presence of the bright-eyed matrons and maidens who presided at the tables. All were welcomed in a manner that attested the genuineness of the hospitality of the Philadelphians. Everything was in order, and the arrangements for feeding the troops were complete. There was a larger refreshment saloon on Swanson Street, and others not so large, in the city, so that all the soldiers could be fed.

Once more, three cheers for Philadelphia, the Cooper shop and the other refreshment saloons! Three cheers for the young ladies—we shall always remember them as young ladies, although so many years have come and gone since the troopers of our battalion were their guests. May the richest blessings of Heaven rest upon those of the ladies who survive, and upon their husbands and their children and grandchildren, for some of them have probably been blest along this line.

We were not molested on our passage through Baltimore, although some of the veterans had warned us that we would be assassinated in that hot-bed of secession. The veterans were always telling us of dreadful things that were to happen as we approached the rebel country. We reached the national capital without startling adventure, and were ordered to proceed to Camp Stoneman, a few miles southeast of the capital.

A few nights after our arrival at Camp Stoneman, several unsophisticated country lads in Company I were initiated into the mysteries of poker—draw poker, played after taps. I would draw the curtain over this poker business were it not for the belief that there will be another war by and by, and possibly this note of warning may put the boys who will then blossom out as recruits on their guard against this great national evil.

We were paid off just before leaving Camp Meigs. A large majority of the boys sent their money home. But there were quite a number who held on to their funds till they reached Camp Stoneman. An inventory of cash on hand in our tent brought to light a ten dollar bill in Waterman's possession, a five dollar note and a few smaller bills in the hands of Taylor, fifteen dollars retained by Hom and about the same amount in my inside pocket—nearly fifty dollars all told.

While we were comparing notes one evening a veteran poked his head in through the door and whispered:

"Any you fellows want to take a hand?"

"At what?"

"Poker."

"Where?"

"Sh —! Here comes the orderly."

After the first sergeant had passed on down the line of tents, the veteran again invited us to take a hand. I declined peremptorily. I had never played cards.

"It's wicked to gamble," I said.

"But this is only a friendly game of draw—it isn't gambling."

"I don't mind trying my luck," said Taylor.

"Well, if you'll go down back of the cook tent right after taps you'll find some of the boys there."

"All right; I'll be on hand."

I decided to accompany Taylor. A few minutes after taps—the bugle signal for lights to be put out—Taylor and I stole quietly down to the cook tent. Two of the boys were there to conduct us to the gambling den.

"This way, and don't make any noise," said the guide.

We moved out a few hundred yards just over the brow of a small hill, where we found the den. It was part dug-out and part brush-heap. Old blankets were hung up against the bushes to prevent the light from shining through. Inside we found a sergeant of Company M, who seemed to be boss of the ranch. Several non-commissioned officers, musicians and privates were there. It was a dismal enough place. I did not want to go in, but concluded I had gone too far to back out.

"It's only ten cents ante," said the veteran; "you are perfectly safe, as you needn't bet unless your hand'll stand it."

Taylor and I were paired off with the veteran and a trooper of Company K. The first hand dealt by the "poker sharp"—for that's what our veteran proved to be—did not show anything to bet on, as I was told by a "spectator," who looked over my shoulder.

"Draw to your ace," whispered the man who gave me the steer.

I drew two more aces.

"Go your pile on that hand," urged my backer.

"I go my pile on this hand," I exclaimed.

"How much's your pile?" asked the veteran.

"Fourteen dollars and fifty cents."

"I see you and go you a V better."

"But that's all I've got."

"All right, then; show your cards."

"Three aces and queen high! Think I'm a greenhorn, do you?" I repeated after my prompter.

"My money," coolly remarked the veteran as he raked in the cash, showing four kings and a ten spot.

Taylor and the other fellow had "staid out." I was broke on the first hand, and I was advised to "skoot for camp," but I declared I would not go till my partner went.

"I'll win your money back in no time," said Taylor, as another hand was dealt.

But what is the use of going on with the poker story. Taylor was penniless in a few minutes. As we crawled back to camp he insisted that if Waterman or Hom would loan him five dollars he could go back and "bust the bank." But they had sense enough to refuse him.

We had been in the hands of poker pirates. There was an organised gang of gamblers in nearly every camp around Washington. They fairly skinned the recruits. They had all sorts of games and apparatus. The soldier who was too good to play cards would be invited to throw dice "for fun," and before he knew it he was staking a month's pay on a single throw. But my first experience opened my eyes. I never visited the den again while at Camp Stoneman, and I never played cards again for money during the rest of my service in the Army of the Potomac.

Down in front of Petersburg the next winter, three soldiers ran a faro game the night after the paymaster's visit to a New York regiment to which they belonged, and it was stated in the sutler's tent the next morning that the trio had won every cent that had been left with the regiment, except the pay of the major in command, and his escape was due to the fact that he was summoned to corps headquarters to explain a discrepancy in a regimental return and the game was over before he could get around to try his hand.

There was another class of men in the army who were always on the make, though they were not gamblers. They were the company or regimental bankers and brokers. They made lots of money, but their victims were taken in with their eyes open. That is, they were given to understand the true inwardness of the transaction before they took stock in it. One or two men in each company could be found who had money between pay-days. How they managed to hold on to their cash under such great temptations as they were at times subjected to, was a mystery to the other boys.

There were times when "money was no object" to the soldier; he was ready to pay five dollars, ten dollars, twenty dollars or any sum that he could rake or scrape for a square meal or something in the line of food. Then it was that the company banker got in his work. Having no money to pay for what he wanted to eat or drink the financial wreck would apply to the man with the wealth.

"Loan me five dollars, Jones?"

"For how much?"

"Ten, pay-day."

"Can't spare it."

"I'll give you fifteen dollars, then."

"Well, I'll do it to accommodate you, but it's a big risk."

The money-lenders did take big risks when in the field. If the borrower were killed or detailed away from his company, the banker was the loser. But in winter quarters the risk was not so great, and there was no justification for charging twenty-five, fifty and one hundred *per cent*, interest for two months or forty days, as was frequently the case. Still there was no getting around the saying of the Shylocks that "if you don't want to pay the price you can let my money alone."

CHAPTER 8

Lincoln, Grant and Meade

Soldiers who were attentive to duty and promptly responded to details at Camp Stoneman were given passes now and then to visit Washington. Taylor and I applied for an all-night pass, mounted. It was approved, and soon after guard-mount one day we started for the national capital, bent on having a good time. We concluded that we could see the sights to better advantage on foot, so we paid one dollar each for the privilege of putting our horses in a stable on one of the side streets near the Capitol. Then we started to explore the city.

Hanging over the door of a restaurant on the north side of Pennsylvania Avenue, midway the Capitol and the treasury building, was a picture—an oil painting—which caused a good deal of controversy among visitors. On our way up the avenue Taylor and I ran across one of the Berlin boys who belonged to the One hundred and twenty-fifth New York. He said he was stopping at the hospital, awaiting transportation to his regiment. He had been wounded at Gettysburg, I think he said. As we approached the picture our infantry friend exclaimed:

"That's a splendid picture of General Meade. I fought with him at Gettysburg—it's so lifelike."

We stopped and admired the portrait. The gallant commander of the Army of the Potomac was represented in full uniform. As we moved on and were directly in front of the building I chanced to look again at the picture.

It was not Meade—it was Lincoln! "See here!" I remarked to the comrade from the One hundred and twenty-fifth, "you couldn't have been very close to General Meade at Gettysburg if you don't know his picture from that of Uncle Abe."

"I guess I know Meade's picture when I see it."

You didn't fight at Gettysburg. If you had been there

He had been wounded at Gettysburg

you might be qualified to pass judgment on the picture."

"Well, we'll leave it to you. Take another look—whose picture is it?"

"Jimmynetty! Sure enough that's Lincoln! I didn't know, boys, that Washington whiskey would affect one like that. But I haven't got entirely over my sickness yet. If I had been put on the stand I would have sworn that it was General Meade."

Taylor and I had a big laugh at the expense of our friend from Gettysburg. As we walked up the street we met a trooper from Camp Stoneman, who said:

"Boys, tell me what you're laughing at?"

"We were laughing at the queer effect of Washington whiskey on this doughboy. He was trying to make us believe that that picture of Lincoln was a portrait of General Meade," I replied.

"You wouldn't swallow it, of course?"

"Not much. I'm green enough, but I guess I know the picture of President Lincoln when I see it."

"Well, I guess you don't if you call that Lincoln's picture."

"It's old Abe's picture, all the same," said Taylor.

"You're mistaken, my boy."

"Bet you ten dollars it's Lincoln."

"I'll take it."

"Leave it to Allen?"

"All right."

"Well, whose picture is it?" the new-comer asked.

"It's—Lincoln's," I started to say, but just then I looked at it again. It was a life-size portrait of the hero of Vicksburg!

"That's General Grant's picture," said I. "Taylor, you're ten dollars out."

"You boys ought to wait till you get acquainted in Washington and know the president's picture from Grant's before you stake your money," said the winner of the wager. "They don't look a bit alike. But come on, it's my treat."

As we were about to enter the door over which the picture was suspended Taylor seized the man who had won his money by the arm, and exclaimed:

"Give me back my ten dollars!"

"What for?"

"That's not Grant's picture—it's Abe Lincoln's."

"Guess not!"

"Look and see, then!"

"You're right, old boy; here's your money. But it's strange—I was sure it was Grant."

"Well, I'll treat as I'm ten dollars better off'n I thought I was," said Taylor.

As we started for "a soldiers' retreat" near the Capitol, our infantry friend yelled out:

"If that isn't Meade's picture, I never saw Meade, and I never was at Gettysburg!"

We all looked at the picture again. The doughboy was right. There was no mistaking the features of the hero of Gettysburg. Taylor whispered to me:

"Let's get our horses and go to camp—another drink will make us all crazy."

"Hold on; I'm going to find out about this picture," I replied.

Then we began an inspection. We found that it depended entirely on where we stood in respect of whose picture we saw. From the Capitol side it was Meade; in front of the picture it was Lincoln, and from the treasury side it was Grant. We continued our investigation, walking along with our eyes fixed on the picture, and we found that at a certain point Meade's picture faded out and Lincoln's began to appear in the frame.

At last the secret came out. The pictures were painted on slats, and arranged like the soap advertisements one sees in front of groceries. As you approach the sign it tells you the name of the soap, as you are in front of it you are assured that "It floats," and as you look back at the slat-sign you are reminded that "It is the best and cheapest." It was a revelation to us, as we had never seen nor heard of anything like it before. Old soldiers will recall the picture. It was amusing to get three persons standing so that each saw a different face in the frame, to "name the picture." Each would be ready to "bet his pile" on his man. Then they were called on to change positions and the fun began.

The soldier who visited Washington on pass was called upon every few minutes, if he kept moving about the city, to show his papers to the provost guard. There were mounted guards and foot guards. Their only object in life seemed to be to allow no enlisted man to breathe in the capital of the Union he had volunteered to defend unless he could show that his permit had been duly approved through all the red-tape channels. Taylor and I were obliged to show our pass a dozen times during the day. If a soldier lost his permit, or if he was found in

Washington without a document of that sort, the patrol would rush him to the guard house and notify the commanding officer of the regiment to which the "stray" belonged.

But Yankee ingenuity was too much for the provost guard at times. On one occasion I was out exercising my horse with a veteran of company I. It was about ten o'clock a. m. We had both come off guard that morning, and were not required to report for ordinary duties till stable-call in the afternoon. We were on high ground near one of the forts north of Camp Stoneman, and we could see the Capitol and a considerable portion of the city.

"Let's go to Washington," suggested my companion.

"Haven't got a pass."

"We don't need a pass. I know how to beat the provo', and we can get back by two o'clock and have a good time."

"But how can we work it?"

"I'll show you. Wait here till I come back."

The veteran rode into camp, and in a few minutes he returned with our waist belts and white gloves. He wore a neat-fitting blouse and a "store cap." After we had covered half the distance to the city he produced a pair of captain's shoulder-straps which he fastened on his blouse with clasp-pins made for that purpose. Then he said, with mock sternness:

"Orderly, you will fall back, and ride a few paces behind your superior officer."

"All right, Cap'n," I replied, as I began to comprehend the situation.

We reached the city without molestation, and had a good time. We were back in camp before stable-call sounded, and as the "captain" reduced himself to the ranks by taking off his shoulder-straps on the way from the city, no one suspected that we had been masquerading in the capital.

Another "racket" worked by some of the troopers was successful nine times out of ten when the boys kept sober and put on a bold front. Having permission to exercise their horses in the vicinity of Camp Stoneman, they would tog out in their parade clothes and side arms—sabre and revolver. Then they would address a large envelope to some officer of high rank in Washington, write "official business" in big letters in the upper left hand corner, put a make-believe letter inside, seal the envelope and stick it in the waist belt. With the envelope conspicuously displayed, the trooper would ride boldly into the city.

If he did not run into the provost guard there was no necessity to play the role of a dispatch bearer. But if the guard were met the trooper was generally equal to the emergency. He would make no attempt to evade the provost, but riding straight for the officer in charge of the guard he would hold his "O. B." envelope in his hand, and ask:

"Where will I find the office of Adjt.-Gen. E. D. Townsend?"

This would throw the guard off his guard, so to speak, and he would give the information asked for to the supposed dispatch bearer, who would salute and thank the officer and gallop away in the direction indicated.

One of our boys had a narrow escape from arrest by the provost guard one day. He visited Washington as the bearer of a fictitious dispatch to the adjutant-general. The provost guard—the cavalry patrol—had been instructed to be very particular in examining passes of mounted men, as it was stated rebel spies in the uniform of Federal cavalrymen had been about the city. The Massachusetts trooper was riding up Pennsylvania Avenue when he was halted by the provost guard.

"Show your pass," said the officer.

"This is all the pass I have," replied the trooper, pulling the "O. B." envelope from his belt.

"Who's the letter from?"

"Major Sargent, commanding the third battalion of the First Massachusetts cavalry at Camp Stoneman."

"What business has a major to send letters to the adjutant-general direct? They ought to be forwarded through the regular channels."

"All I know about it is that I was sent with the letter. Open it if you don't think it's all right."

"I won't open a sealed letter addressed to the adjutant-general, but I'll send a guard with you to see that it's all right. If it isn't you'll have a general court-martial. Sergeant, take two men and go with this fellow to the adjutant-general's office and see if the dispatch is genuine."

Here was a condition of things. The trooper understood that nothing but military strategy of high order could save him from arrest and punishment. When the adjutant-general's office was reached he dismounted, and handing the rein of his horse's bridle to one of his escort, he walked boldly into the outer office. The sergeant remained outside, supposing that no private soldier would go into the adjutant-general's office except on official business. As the trooper entered he shoved the "O. B." envelope under his jacket.

"Can I see the adjutant-general?" the trooper inquired of the clerk nearest the door. "I want to ask him about a transfer to the infantry."

The clerk was evidently a new hand or, more likely, he thought the cavalryman was too green to know better than to apply personally to the adjutant-general on any such business. Said the clerk:

"He'll be busy all the forenoon. I don't believe he would see you if he were not busy."

"Well, then, I'll come again. Will you let me have a sheet of paper?"

The clerk complied with this cheeky request, and the cavalryman after going through the motions of writing a letter asked for an envelope.

"I have none but official envelopes," replied the clerk.

"That'll do just as well. Will you please direct it for me?"

This request was also complied with, as the clerk seemed to think it the quickest way to get rid of an unwelcome visitor. The next minute the trooper was outside with a big official envelope addressed to "Major L. M. Sargent, commanding third battalion First Massachusetts cavalry. Camp Stoneman."

The provost sergeant examined the envelope. There was the official office mark of the adjutant-general's office. The sergeant said apologetically:

"I'm sorry we bothered you, but I had to obey orders."

"I don't blame you, sergeant, but the lieutenant ought to know better than to interfere with a courier to the adjutant-general."

The "courier" enjoyed the freedom of the national capital till he was ready to return to camp. He took dinner at a restaurant at the expense of the lieutenant of the provost guard, who assured the trooper:

"Our orders are so strict now that we are obliged to halt everybody."

"It's all right. I didn't say anything to the adjutant-general about it. But I must go back to camp with the letter to Major Sargent."

Washington was crowded with soldiers and civilians connected with the army as contractors and the like. New regiments and recruits for old organisations were pouring in from the loyal States. Some two-year men were on their way home, having served their time out. Washington was the lay-over station for troops *en route* to the front or on the way back to the States. Everything seemed to be run on the go-as-you-please order, but back of it all there was a good deal more

INTERCEPTED BY THE PROVOST GUARD

system and regularity than appeared on the surface.

In the midst of all this confusion the enlisted men swore at their officers, and the officers found fault with the higher authorities. As an illustration of the condition of things and how, at times, the fault-finding was premature, the trials of a New Jersey regiment passing through Washington on the way home may be instanced. The hungry heroes marched over the Long Bridge from Arlington Heights, arriving in the capital late in the afternoon. They did not care anything about a place to camp. The sidewalk was better than the Virginia mud which they had wallowed in for the last six months. But they did want something to eat.

"Where's our rations?" the men demanded of the officers as soon as they were marched into the soldiers' retreat near the Baltimore and Ohio depot.

"A requisition was made out and sent on in advance," was the answer made by the regimental commissary.

"The government don't care anything about our stomachs, now our time's out," chorused the hungry Jerseyites.

The boys growled a good deal, raking over the authorities from the president down.

"We could have found hard-tack and coffee at the front," they said, "and right here under the shadow of the Capitol we can't get as much as a smell of a camp kettle. And they even ask us to come back for three years more!"

The government was voted a fraud by a large majority. About this time—half an hour after the regiment had reached the retreat—a staff officer appeared at the door and asked for the commanding officer. When the colonel, who was in command, responded, the staff officer said:

"Colonel, please fall in your regiment and bring them to supper. I will show you the way."

The growlers were marched to a coffee house, where they were given a big feed—hot coffee with plenty of milk and sugar, cold boiled ham and soft bread, with pickles and potatoes. The boys sang another tune after supper, for there is nothing like a square meal to take the growl out of an old soldier. While stuffing themselves remarks like the following were made:

"This is a regular feast—the government does look after its soldiers."

"And milk and potatoes and other side dishes—hurrah for Father

Abraham!"

"Bring on the enlistment papers; I'll go back for three years or during the war!"

It was a feast for the veterans. And it showed that back of the hubbub and uproar and all that there was a system—call it red tape or what you will—that was looking after the stomachs of the nation's defenders. To be sure, mistakes were made now and then, but so far as the government was concerned every possible step was taken to provide for the soldiers. The latter were frequently victims of rascally contractors, but it can be said that Uncle Sam paid enough to furnish the soldiers with an abundance of food.

The Jersey regiment was breakfasted at the same place the next morning, and then marched to the depot to take the cars for home. Here the growls came to the surface again.

"Your train will be here right away," said the staff officer, who had been detailed to look after the regiment.

The soldiers stacked arms, and in a few minutes a train of cattle cars was backed in.

"I thought there was some mistake," exclaimed one of the chief growlers. "They are going to make us ride in these nasty cattle cars to make up for the two square meals they have given us."

"I'll never ride into New Jersey in a cattle car!"

"Nor I; I'll walk home first."

"It's too bad, boys," assented the colonel.

But it proved another case of premature growling. The cattle train had only backed in to clear a switch. A few minutes later a regular passenger train with reserved cars for the Jersey boys made its appearance. After the regiment had boarded the train—there were seats enough for all; cushioned seats, too—the staff officer said:

"Have your men all got seats, Colonel?"

"Yes; thank you."

"Well, goodbye."

Then the boys cheered the staff officer. They cheered President Lincoln and all the authorities, civil and military. They left the national capital in excellent spirits, well-pleased with their treatment, and the majority of them returned within a month, enlisted again, and this time for three years or during the war. There is no question that the special attention shown them at Washington had an influence in respect of their re-enlistment. And some old soldiers—chronic growlers—asserted that the Jerseyites were sweetened up to get them to re-enlist. If that was the reason, it worked to a charm. But the boys enjoyed the viands and cushioned seats, all the same.

Everything in Washington seemed to be in an unfinished state. There was staging all around the dome of the Capitol, where preparations were being made to place the Goddess of Liberty. Down in the bottom lands north of the Long Bridge, the unfinished monument to the Father of his Country stuck up like a sore thumb. There were tackle and pulley blocks and staging on top of it. Government teams were mired every day on the principal streets, and in the rainy season the mud was knee-deep in many places on Pennsylvania Avenue. There was an army bakery in the basement of the Capitol, and here and there throughout the city rough board shanties had been erected for storehouses, corrals, barracks, etc.

Much has been written and told in story around the camp fire since the war about the army mule. Little if any credit has been given to the animal. Mule-whackers seemed to feel that they were compelled to swear at their teams—that the mules could not understand any language that was not made up entirely of oaths and execrations. In support of this theory the drivers declared that the mules never buckled down to business and took a heavy load out of a mud-hole till they had been cursed with all the oaths in the mule-whacker's vocabulary. True enough. But let it be remembered that the mule-whacker's swear was set on a hair-trigger, and went off many times before he had mounted his saddle-mule and given the signal to "get out of this." Nothing but electricity, and fifty mule power at that, could have started the load in advance of the driver's blasphemous outbreak.

It was charged against the government mule that he was in league with the Devil. A Virginia contraband who drove a six-mule team in our brigade supply train, was a firm believer in this theory. When spoken to about it, the runaway slave replied:

"Can't help b'l'evin' it, sah. De mule is de debbil's fren,' shuah's yo' born. De debbil heself get in de mule and say, 'Don't yo' move one step till de driber he swar and swar and swar.' De mule mind de debbil, sah. And de driber know nuffin else'll start de mule, so he jes swar and swar. Den de debbil say: 'Go 'head, mule, dat driber's mine!' Yes, sah, de mule and de debbil understan' each udder, dar's no mistake 'bout it."

Yet there are some things to be said in defense of the army mule. As stated above, mighty quick work would have been necessary to start a loaded wagon—or an empty one, either—in advance of the driver's preliminary discharge of profanity. No one seemed to ever think of giving the mule a chance. In anticipation of the controversy, drivers would crack their whips and swear an oath or two when starting for the corrals to harness their teams. As a rule the drivers were educated up to this. It was the popular way in which to deal with a mule. Now and then a driver was found who managed to handle a six-mule team without violating the third commandment, but it required as much grace as it did to nerve the soldier to participate in a charge on the enemy's batteries—and more. Not but that the mules were capable of appreciating kind treatment. But mule cursing was contagious, and few drivers had courage to resist it.

In answer to the charge, that the army mules could not understand any language but the "code" of the drivers, it may be said that the mules seldom heard any other language after they were drafted into the army. The driver rode the "nigh boss" of the wheelers, and drove the swing team and the leaders with a jerk line.

If the mule must be condemned, it is but a simple act of justice to produce the testimony upon which the verdict is given. Yet it must be admitted that the boys could not have marched and fought and slept on the around in rain and sleet had it not been for the rations that were brought to the front, even to the skirmish line, on pack mules and in Government wagons drawn by six-mule teams through mud and mire and swamp and fields and forests where roads had never been made. Stubborn, but no more so than his driver; vicious, perhaps, but receiving ten times as many kicks as he gave; given to foraging around for grub, but did not the soldiers themselves set the example? The army mule is entitled to no small share of credit for his part in knocking the bottom out of the Southern Confederacy.

Many a time at the close of a day which had been one of severest trial to the footsore doughboys and saddle-blistered troopers composing the rear guard of the supply train, the glad tidings of great joy that camp had been reached were telegraphed back from the head of the column to the rear by the keen-scented mules, who, snuffing the water and oats, would join their voices in sounding "quartermaster's call."

Boys, when you come to remember all these things—and also the occasions when in the heat of battle, you suddenly discovered that you were loading with your last cartridge and the day would have been won by the boys in butternut but for the providential arrival of ammunition packed on the back of the army mule—is it not about time to concede that our four-footed comrades deserve a kind word for their services in defence of the stars and stripes?

ODE TO THE MULE.

The shades of night were falling fast,
As through "Virginny" mud-holes passed
A mule who bore upon his back
The soldiers' rations of hard tack
And salt pork!

"Make way!" the hungry soldiers cried.
"Make way!"—they surely would have died
But for the coming of the beast,
Who brought the boys a royal feast
From way back!

"E-yah-hah! yah-hah!" brayed the mule.
The soldiers cursed him, as a rule,
But when the grub came they would say:
"Hurrah! the mule has saved the day.
God bless him!"

Then in the thickest of the fight
The mule was brought both day and night,
With ammunition in his pack
To save our boys from falling back
For cartridges!

The mule amid the fire and smoke
Stood firm—sometimes the mule was "croaked"
By rebel bullet—in that hell;
He faced the fire and rebel yell
Unflinching!

The years roll on, but strange to say,
While every dog must have his day,
The army mule no praise receives.
He's dying with old age and heaves,
A veteran!

A quarter century has gone
Since Boys in Blue have heard the song
Of army mules—but all will say.
The mule helped whip the Boys in Gray—
"E-yah-hah!"

Taylor and I rode up Pennsylvania Avenue, took a look at the White House, and continued our ride out through Georgetown and as far up the river as the chain bridge and the battery that covered it on the Maryland side of the Potomac. We could see the "tented cities" on the Virginia side of the river. A good view of Arlington Heights was had from the high ground at Georgetown. The white walls and the pillars of the porch at "Arlington," the abandoned home of General Robert E. Lee, the Confederate commander, could be plainly seen. The line of fortifications on the Virginia side of the river from above the chain bridge away down to Alexandria, was outlined before us, and the glorious old flag of the Union floated proudly above the forts and camps.

It was a grand sight. Martial music was heard from the camps nearest the river, as the calls for dress parade were sounded. We could see the boys in blue falling in and marching to the parade grounds.

While we were taking observations, we saw a soldier standing on top of a log structure on Georgetown Heights and waving a flag. Our curiosity was aroused, and we rode up close to the signal station, for such we found it to be. A detachment of the signal corps was camped on the Heights. We were much interested in the talk across the river that the signal boys had with another station over at Arlington. One of the men was seated, with a big telescope in front of him. He was the receiver, and read the signals made by the flagman at Arlington, and reported the same to the officer. The latter gave direction to the signal man at the Georgetown station, who waved his flag up and down and sideways, a certain movement indicating a certain letter or cipher of the signal code.

We were made acquainted with the importance of the services of the signal corps after we reached the front and saw active service. Messages were telegraphed by the means of signals—flags being used by day and torches by night—all along the front, and from outposts back to headquarters, in a few minutes.

In this connection one can but think of the wonderful possibilities for communication that have been opened up by the introduction of the telephone and other electrical improvements since the war. Telegraph wires were strung—and here the army mule rendered excellent service, as the wires were let out from a coil carried on the back of a mule—between different headquarters when the army was on the move. Telephone wires could now be run out in the same way, and the commanding general could call up and talk with his subordinates.

Orders could be given personally by telephone. The outposts could alarm the reserves by simply ringing up the machine as follows:

"Halloo, reserve!"

"Halloo?"

"The enemy's breaking camp and moving toward our line."

"All right; we'll be ready for them. We'll call up the camps and headquarters, and the troops will be under arms in a minute. Don't let on that you see the enemy till they approach close to your post—then fall back without firing and let them come after you. Goodbye!"

"Goodbye!"

Chapter 9

The Bull Run Battlefield

The recruits at Stoneman looked upon the camps on the other side of the Potomac as the "front"—we found later on that the front was down near Culpepper Court House—and veterans from the other side came over and filled us so full of their exploits on the picket lines and in the battles of the campaign of 1863 that some of us envied the old soldiers the proud distinction of having smelled powder in the face of the enemy. We felt grateful to these old heroes that they had thus far saved the nation, and also that they still stood between the rebels and the national capital—and between the rebels and the recruits at Camp Stoneman. They borrowed all the money we had saved from our first pay. They induced us to part with our extra blankets and other articles that went to make the boys comfortable. They traded their old leaky canteens and rotten haversacks for ours, which were new. And in many other ways these revered warriors familiarized themselves with our property and made themselves at home in our camps.

I have no doubt that our comrades from the Army of the Potomac would have robbed us of our last change of government linen if Sergeant Warren, who had been on duty in Washington, had not arrived in camp. As soon as he was informed of the visits of the soldiers from the south bank of the Potomac, he said to us:

"You deserve to be skinned of everything you've got!"

"But, Sergeant, how could we help sharing things with the men who have fought so bravely at the front all summer?"

"Some of those fellows never saw a live rebel, and never will see one unless they get a glimpse of a Johnny that's brought in a prisoner."

"Then they've been lying to us."

"Well, I shouldn't wonder. Three of the 'veterans' who were here

Trading Canteens

laying in grub and supplies when I came this morning, belong to a regiment that's camped on this side of the river. They were in Readville when we came on to Washington. They have taken the cue from other regiments that have been fleecing you, and they'll skin you alive if you don't keep your eyes open. If you've got any sense left at all, you'll shoot every mother's son of them that shows his face in this camp hereafter."

We held an indignation meeting, and determined to act on the sergeant's suggestion. But the matter had been brought to the attention of the major in command, and he issued orders for a chain of sentinels to be posted around our camp. Then the major gave us extra drill. I suppose he intended to have us make up in drill what we lacked in knowledge of the "amenities of army life," as a good-natured recruit from Berkshire County styled the wicked acts of the alleged old veterans who had robbed us.

How my wrist ached when I came in after two hours' sabre exercise!" Until the command guard, right and left *moulinet!*" was what took the tuck out of me. It seemed that the drill sergeant would never sing out "Guard!" Oh! how they did drill us! One poor private was marched to the guard house and made to carry a log for simply shouting out while doing the *moulinet* and against-infantry-cut act:

"If they would only let me have a 'doughboy' to cut—just a stray rebel now and then—it wouldn't seem so foolish. I'm getting awful tired of all this nonsense."

So was I, but after the example made of the private that audibly sighed for a live rebel to carve, I deemed it expedient to keep my mouth shut. The memory of those busy days of preparation is with me yet. Once in awhile even now—more than a quarter of a century after my soldier life at Camp Stoneman—I go through the "right and left *moulinet*" and "cut and parry" movements in my sleep. And the old pain in the wrist and shoulder is there, too. What a relief it is to have the scenes shifted—to be shaken by my wife and brought down to the present by the admonition:

"My dear, you've been sleeping on your back again, and had the nightmare."

Then the cuts and parries and *moulinets* seem all mixed up, and the sabre—how heavy it was then!—whirls through the air, putting to flight the drill sergeant and scores of troopers in blue and infantry in gray. I open my eyes to find that it is but a dream; that the pain in the wrist and shoulder is caused by rheumatism, and all the rest is but a reminiscence.

Our horses were as green as the men, and yet they acquired a knowledge of cavalry drill in a remarkably short period. A majority of the animals became familiar with the bugle calls, and would "halt" and "march" and "wheel" at the sound of the trumpet without direction from their riders. All the animals recognized stable call as readily as the soldiers did dinner call. The cavalryman and his horse became deeply attached to each other, and it was no uncommon thing for the trooper, when forage could not be had, to share his last hard-tack with his four-footed companion.

Occasionally we were sent on patrol, a company at a time, down on the Maryland side of the Potomac. We enjoyed these trips, and began to gain confidence in ourselves as cavalrymen. The slipping back of our saddles, causing our horses to run away and throw us off, was an interesting feature of our initial expedition. But we soon discovered that the average horse was averse to tight lacing, and the animals would swell out when we buckled the saddle girths. Then, after we had mounted, the horses would materially reduce their circumferences, so much so at times that the saddle would turn when the rider was jolted to one side on the trot or gallop, and there would be fun all along the line.

Once we ran down a "rebel spy," only to find him a genuine Yankee bearing dispatches to a fort opposite Alexandria. He had the laugh on us; more so than he would have had if the captain had not restrained a set of fours near the head of the column, that bore down on the "suspect" with drawn sabres, determined to end the rebellion then and there, by tierce-pointing the stranger through the body.

We lost our first comrade by gunshot wounds at Camp Stoneman. The circumstances were the most distressing of any that came under my observation during the war. It was a case of didn't-know-it-was-loaded. We had been out on drill. Joe Homer, a private in Company I, had been doing some duty that excused him from drill. Before turning out for drill, Joe's tent-mate, a sergeant in the company, had drawn the cartridges from his revolver and oiled the weapon preparatory to cleaning it after drill. He left the pistol on a little shelf over the fireplace in the tent. When Joe returned to the tent, he cleaned his own revolver and the sergeant's pistol and reloaded them, as was the custom. Homer was sitting on a cracker box near the door of the tent, when our company returned from drill. The sergeant entered the tent, picked up his revolver, and turning to Homer he said:

"Look out, Joe! I'm going to shoot you!"

The weapon was pointed directly at Homer's forehead, and the sergeant pulled the trigger. There was a loud report. Homer fell a corpse almost at the sergeant's feet. The ball entered the brain, just as Joe raised his hand and opened his lips to warn his comrade that the revolver was loaded. Poor Joe was dead. His relatives came on and returned with his body.

That evening the company was drawn up in line, and the sergeant stepped to the front. Standing beside the captain he faced the company, and with broken voice he told the facts of the shooting. The boys all assured the sergeant that there was not the least suspicion that the shooting was intentional, and he had our heartfelt sympathy.

Upon returning from patrol one evening, we found that orders had been received for the battalion to go to the front. We were to join the other companies at Warrenton, Va. It was stated that Mosby's guerrillas were operating out that way, and we expected to come face to face with the armed forces of the Confederacy right speedily. We had become tolerably proficient in drill, and had attained to a remarkable confidence in our ability to engage in mortal combat with the butternut-clad troopers. The fear that the war would be ended before an opportunity should come for our battalion to have at least one chance to cross sabres with the rebels, was not so great as it had been when we left the Old Bay State, yet we were glad to cross the Potomac and enter upon the sacred soil of Virginia,

One of the heaviest mails that ever left Camp Stoneman was carried into Washington the morning we broke camp and started for the front. Letters were written by the light of candles, shaded under cracker boxes, after taps. Parents and wives, brothers and sisters and sweethearts were informed that the regiment had been ordered into battle, and that the immediate capture of Jeff Davis and the Southern Confederacy was likely to follow our attack upon the enemy.

We marched into Washington and down to the Long Bridge, where the column halted till the wagons closed up. Then we crossed the bridge and found ourselves on the sacred soil of Virginia.

"I don't see why they sent for us when there are so many regiments of 'veterans' over here," said a private in Company I.

And surely it did seem that there were troops enough in camp and in the line of breastworks and forts on Arlington Heights to destroy the Confederate army before breakfast. Up the river toward Georgetown and down the river in the direction of Alexandria the hills and valleys were literally covered with the snowy tents of the Union forces. Guard-mounting was in progress in the camps, and the sound of the music of many bands was borne to our ears by a gentle breeze. The stars and stripes waved from hundreds of flag-poles along the line of the fortifications. It was an inspiring scene, and the music cheered us. Even the horses were influenced by it, and pranced about and held up their heads as if sniffing well-filled nosebags from afar. As we reached the top of Arlington Heights we halted to tighten the saddle girths. As we mounted again we took a look back at the city.

"I hope they'll get the Goddess up on the top of the Capitol before we come back," said Taylor.

Poor Giles! He did not come back.

At Fairfax we halted for the wagons to close up again, and also to feed our horses and cook coffee. Then we moved on and found ourselves outside the line. We were marching along a road that was not picketed except at stations several miles apart. An advance guard was thrown out, and we were told to be on the watch for bushwhackers or a sudden dash from the enemy. We met several Union scouting parties, but saw nothing of the gray-backs that day.

We camped at night in a strip of woods just off the Warrenton turnpike. Picket lines were stretched between the trees, and our horses were securely tied to the lines. Here we were treated to an unexpected experience. Snow began falling a little before dark. It came down in flakes and volume that would have done credit to the State that contained "the girl I left behind me." Sentinels were posted all around the camp, and a stable guard was detailed to watch the horses. Supper was cooked under difficulties, but the hot coffee was relished. The boys were instructed "to sleep with their eyes open," and be ready to fall in with their carbines and pistols loaded, at the first sound of the bugle.

"See here, is this the sunny South we've read and heard so much about?" inquired a youthful corporal.

"It is," said a sergeant.

"I came down here to get shed of a cold winter," remarked a private.

"Sergeant, where'll we sleep?"

"Crawl under the brush heaps."

The snow kept coming down, and soon the ground was covered. The officer of the day dispersed a crowd of loud-mouthed growlers gathered about a coffee-kettle by saying:

"Men, we are in the enemy's country, and the guerrillas are apt to fire into a crowd. You had better crawl under the bushes and go to bed.", They crawled under.

There were piles of pine boughs and brush that had been cut from trees felled by soldiers, who had camped in the vicinity. Under these brush heaps the boys spent a portion of their first night in "Ole Virginny." It was a most distressing experience. The storm was one of the heaviest ever known in that latitude.

I was one of the detail for stable guard on the second relief. The first relief was posted right after supper, about seven o'clock. The man on the first relief was to call me at nine o'clock, and at eleven o'clock I was to wake up the private who was on the third relief. Corporal Goddard of Great Barrington, was in charge of the stable guard of our company.

About ten o'clock the boys had become quiet for the night. Except for the horses at the picket lines and the sentinels, no one in passing would have suspected that soldiers were stored away under the brush heaps.

"I'll be under this pile of brush if you want the corporal of the guard," said Goddard, as he got down on all-fours ready to burrow beneath a brush heap.

"This claim's already pre-empted," shouted some one from under the bushes.

"Don't talk to a corporal in that way, or I'll put you in the guard house."

Goddard was, I think, the tallest man in the regiment, something like six feet two or three inches in his stocking feet. He could not make a brush heap only three feet in diameter serve as covering for his entire body.

"You can't get in here, only by sections, anyway," said the man who was curled up under the brush.

But Goddard succeeded in burrowing his head and shoulders, and spliced out his bedclothes by using a blanket, a shelter tent and a rubber poncho. He then subsided, as did the man who had previously taken refuge under the same brush heap.

About an hour after the corporal had turned in, I went to wake up the man who was to go on at eleven o'clock. I routed out the men under several brush heaps, and brought down upon myself the indignation of all whom I disturbed. Still the third relief did not hear me, or hearing did not heed. It would tax the patriotism of any soldier to respond to an invitation to turn out and go on post under such circumstances.

As a last resort, I concluded to rouse the corporal. I did not intend to stay on post all night if I could obtain relief in the camp. By this time all the brush heaps looked so near alike in their snowy coverings, that I could not locate the particular pile where Goddard was sleeping. I had no desire to arouse the battalion, and possibly the guerrillas, by shouting "corporal of the guard." As I was passing between two brush heaps in my search, I stumbled upon the toes of a pair of boots protruding above the snow.

"What fool left his boots out here in the snow?" I muttered, giving the nearest one a whack with my sabre.

There was a smothered shout under one of the brush heaps. I had found the corporal of the guard, or at least had struck his trail. The boots moved toward the brush heap. I followed the boots and found that the corporal's feet were in them. We hunted up the third relief, and I was given a chance to rest by turning in where the third relief turned out. It was a dismal night, but our spirits revived the next day, after we had dug ourselves out and got a warm breakfast.

At the time of our march to Warrenton, that part of Virginia lying between the Federal capital and the advanced Union lines was practically a barren waste. Buildings and fences had disappeared, and hundreds of acres of timber had been cleared away by the axes of the two armies. Rain—how easy it rained in the Old Dominion whenever the troops were on the march!—and mud made the picture all the more gloomy. Now and then we passed the ruins of soldiers' huts. Pieces of old knapsacks, split canteens and shreds of Government clothing, water-soaked and half-buried in the mud, were seen on either side of the road. It was a dreary, comfortless outlook.

We crossed Bull Run, an insignificant stream as compared with our previous ideas of its size and appearance.

"There's the Henry hill where we fought the rebels hand-to-hand, and blood flowed like water," exclaimed a veteran, who had participated in the first battle of Bull Run while serving in the infantry. "Our regiment was nearly all cut to pieces out there."

"How did you get away?"

I never could make it clear to my own mind. We were holding our ground when orders came to fall back. Then it was a race for life. The roads were blocked with army wagons and vehicles of all sorts, for you know everybody came out from Washington to see us exterminate the rebels. Major-generals and other officers of high degree were neck and neck with rear-rank privates in that race for the capital. Civilians, some of them Members of Congress I'm told, demonstrated that they could run as fast as the soldiers. I don't know how I got away, but when I reached a place where I deemed it safe to bivouac for the night, I found myself north of the Potomac."

Although we were on a road that was travelled more or less by Union soldiers every day, it was understood that a visit from the enemy's scouting parties might be expected at any time. Our battalion marched with advance and rear guards and with flankers well out from the column. Instructions were given to report promptly the appearance of any troops that might be seen on the march.

The advance guard of a cavalry column is composed generally of a platoon of troopers commanded by a lieutenant or sergeant. One man—or two or three, as the officer in command shall direct—rides in advance one hundred yards or so. He has his carbine at the "advance" and ready for use, should he be fired at by an enemy from behind bushes or bowlders along the way. If he spies out the enemy, he halts and awaits the arrival of the reserve under the officer. The commanding officer of the column is notified, and preparations are made for the attack if it be decided to go on and the enemy hold his ground. The soldier in the advance is in a position which calls for lots of backbone, particularly when moving through a wooded country known to be occupied by the enemy.

The rear guard's duties are frequently as dangerous as those of the soldiers in advance. It is always a trick of the enemy to look after straggling soldiers. Supply wagons, pack mules and soldiers whose horses are nearly played out are required to keep ahead of the rear guard. This naturally brings the guard quite a distance behind the main column, and a sudden dash from the enemy now and then results in a lively skirmish, and sometimes the rear guard is routed and compelled to close up on the column, leaving the wagons and stragglers at the mercy of the attacking party. Contrary to the prevailing idea among civilians, the rear of an army is not always a place of absolute safety.

Flankers ride on either side of the road, far enough removed from the column to discover any approach of the enemy indicating an attack upon the flank of the troops *en route*. The flankers nearest the advance guard ride closer in toward the column, forming with the advance something; like a half-circle to the front. The flankers ride one behind another, so that the second flanker can see the one ahead of him, and so on to the rear of the column, where the flankers close in to connect with the rear guard. Flanking in a hostile country is dangerous and difficult. The flankers must ride on through jungles and swamps, up hill and down dale, through briers and brambles, making their way through almost impenetrable labyrinths; scratched and bruised and bleeding, on they go. There is no time to deplore the situation.

Keep your eyes and ears open, boys! Behind that large rock to your right may lurk a foe with rifle ready to send a fifty calibre ball through your heart. Hark! There is a noise out there. The bushes are moving. Draw back the hammer of your carbine and ride on. The noise grows louder, and there is more of a stir—here they come; now for it! The carbine is brought up to the shoulder with the right hand, the finger on the trigger, and a tighter hold of the reins is taken with the left; the trooper is prepared to face the enemy, to sell his life dearly, determined to fire at least one shot, that his comrades may know of the presence of the foe. The bushes sway back and forth a little, and the enemy emerges from his hiding-place.

A Virginia razor-back—a hog that has escaped the forages of both Union and Confederate armies—faces the flanker. As the trooper lets back the hammer of his carbine to a half-cock, he regrets that he cannot shoot the porker—must not fire except at a rebel, as it would alarm the column. Time after time the nerves of the soldiers were thus taxed, and the boys were brought face to face—in expectation—with death itself. The ante-conflict experience was just as real as it could have been had the razor-back been a bushwhacker or the advance guard of the enemy coming in to attack our flank.

But the flankers' fears were not always unfounded. Behind rock and tree the enemy waited the approach of the troopers, and a score or more of flankers went down at the first volley. This generally preceded an attack on the flank.

At other times the flankers were startled by the report of a single rifle or shotgun, and some poor Yankee boy fell a victim to the bushwhacker's hatred of the "vandal horde." Men who were enrolled in no regiment or military organisation, stay-at-homes who managed to escape the rebel conscripting officers, would steal up on a Federal picket and shoot him down without warning. If this was not murder in cold blood, what was it?

Not far from the Bull Run battlefield, our advance guard sent back word that a body of troops was approaching on the Warrenton turnpike. Preparations were made to fight. In a short time the troops came within hailing distance. They proved to be a detachment of cavalry *en route* to Washington, as escort to a paymaster. We exchanged greetings with them and marched on, reaching Warrenton without encountering Mosby or any of the enemy's scouting parties.

Chapter 10

A Fatal Post

It rained the day the third battalion of the First Massachusetts cavalry arrived at Warrenton, Va., and it rained for three days, almost without a let-up, after we reached our destination.

Recruits always received a hearty welcome at the front—the less the old soldiers had to do in the way of picket duty, the better they liked it. The recruits were—at first—ready to do all the duty, and the veterans were willing to let the new arrivals have their own way along this line. But after a few weeks of wear and tear at the front, the raw recruits could generally give the old soldiers points on dodging duty and feigning sickness, so as to have "excused from picket," or "light duty" marked opposite their names on the sick book. These peculiarities of soldier-life were characteristic of camp and winter quarters. As a rule, when the troops were brought face to face with the "business of the campaign," there was a sort of freemasonry among them. Then the veteran was ready to share his last cracker with the recruit, and they drank from the same canteen. An engagement with the enemy was sure to place all who stood shoulder to shoulder on a level. In the jaws of death, with comrades dropping on every hand, all were "boys," and all were soldiers—comrades.

Our first night's experience at Warrenton was not calculated to inspire us with love for the place. When we arrived we were drawn up in line in front of headquarters.

"You will camp your men just south of that row of tents," a brigade staff officer said to the major in command of our battalion. "You can pitch tents till such time as you can build winter quarters. Stretch your picket lines so as to leave proper intervals between your camp and the regiment next to it."

The staff officer hurried back into his log-house, to get out of the rain. We broke into columns of fours, and were marched to the ground on which we were to build our winter quarters. The outlook was discouraging. The camp was laid out on a side hill, down which good-sized brooks of water were flowing. And the ground! It was like a bed of mortar. Next to prepared glue, Virginia mud is entitled to first prize for its adhesive qualities.

"See here," exclaimed Taylor, "they're only just making fools of us. No general could order us to get off our horses and make camp in this mud-hole."

Taylor's indiscretion was always getting him into trouble, and his talking in ranks this time secured him another tour of double duty.

Down came the rain, and we were in for it. In due time the horses were picketed and their nosebags put on. As soon as the animals were taken care of and fed, the weary troopers, drenched to the skin, were directed to "pitch tents!" The tents with which we were provided were known as shelter, or dog tents, the latter name being most popular, as they often failed to afford anything but a poor apology for shelter. Each soldier had half a tent—till he lost it. The half-tent was a piece of canvas about five feet by four, or something-like it. Along one edge was a row of buttonholes, and a little further back a row of buttons. Two pieces buttoned together were put over a ridge-pole, supported by two crotches, and the bottom edges of the tent were fastened to the ground by little cord loops through which sticks were driven. Both gable ends of the tent were open to the weather, but sometimes a third "bunkey" would be taken in, and one end of the tent closed up with his piece. The shelter tents were always too short at both ends. Think of a man like Corporal Goddard of our company, who was an inch or two over six feet, trying to "shelter" himself under such a contrivance. A man of medium height could find cover only by doubling himself up in the shape of a capital N, and it was necessary to "spoon it" where two or three attempted to sleep under one dog tent.

Waterman and I continued as bunkies. At Camp Stoneman, Taylor and Hom had occupied the upper bunk in our log-house, and the same quartet had decided to go together when we should build winter quarters at our new location. Hom was detailed for stable guard as soon as we dismounted, and Taylor, Waterman and myself concluded to pitch tents together.

The ground was so soft that the sticks would not hold, and the tent was blown down several times. All our blankets were wet. Long after dark, however, we made fast the tent as best we could, and crawled in.

Taylor being the oldest and largest, was assigned by a majority vote of Waterman and myself, to the side from which the wind came. I took the middle. It was close quarters.

"I don't see what's the use of getting up to fix it again," said Taylor, as the dog tent was blown down the third time after we had turned in. "I'm just as wet's I can be, and I'd rather sleep than get up again."

I had managed to raise myself a few inches above the water. My saddle was under my head, and I had two canteens under my back. The water was running a stream between Waterman and Taylor.

"I'll sit up and hold the tent while you fellows sleep," volunteered the genial Taylor the next time the tent went down.

There was nothing selfish about Taylor. After we had gone to sleep he "hadn't the heart to disturb us," as he expressed it the next day, and when the wind shifted and there was a slight let-up in the deluge, he took the three pieces of tent, our rubber ponchos, saddle blankets and bed blankets and, selecting the driest spot he could find on the side-hill, he rolled himself up in them and slept till reveille. Just before daybreak Waterman and I were drowned out, and sought shelter in an old brick building up on the hill.

The erection of log huts for winter quarters at Warrenton was no "joke." We had to go on Water Mountain to cut the trees for building material. Then we waited our turn for teams and wagons to haul the logs.

It was thirteen days before we got our log-house built and our shelter tents nailed on for a roof. Two bunks, one over the other, were made of poles. Taylor and Hom had the upper bunk, while Waterman and I slept "downstairs."

"There's more of Giles than there is of us," suggested Waterman, "and we'll put him and Hom in the top bunk so that when it rains and the roof leaks they'll absorb a good deal of the water before it gets to us."

Waterman and I chuckled over our success in securing the lower bunk, but one night when the upper bunk broke, and Taylor and Hom came tumbling down upon us, we realized, indeed, that there was a good deal more of Giles than there was of us.

We went on picket in our turn. The line ran along the top of Water Mountain for some distance, and we occasionally exchanged compliments with Mosby's men. The first night we were on picket, a little down to the south of the mountain, I went on duty at nine o'clock. The post was across a creek and near an old stone mill. It rained, sleeted and snowed during the night, and the creek filled up so that the "relief" could not cross over to my post when the time came to change the pickets. As a result I remained on post till daylight. It was one of the longest nights I ever put in during my army service.

Of course, every noise made by the wind was a bushwhacker. I was so thankful to find myself alive at daybreak that I forgot to growl at the corporal for not relieving me on time. When I unbosomed myself to Taylor, and told him how nervous I felt out there by the old mill, he laughed and said:

"Don't you never feel nervous again when you're caught in such a scrape, for, mark my word, no rebel, not even a 'gorilla' would be fool enough to go gunning for Yankee recruits such a night as last night was." I found a good deal of comfort in Taylor's logical admonition after that when alone on picket in stormy weather.

Just over the divide on Water Mountain, on the side toward the rebel camp, was an old log shanty. We called it the block house. Our pickets occupied it by day, and the rebels had possession of it by night. This happened because the Union picket line was drawn in at night, and the pickets were posted closer together than during the day. Our line was advanced soon after daylight.

One morning when we galloped down to the block house from our reserve, we surprised the Johnnies. They had been a little late in getting breakfast, and their horses had their nosebags on. We were just as much surprised as they were, and we stood six to six. Carbines and revolvers were pointed, but no one fired.

"Give us time to put on our bridles and we'll vacate," said the sergeant of the rebel picket.

"All right; go ahead," our sergeant replied.

The Johnnies bridled their horses, mounted and rode down the mountain.

"We kept a good fire for you all," the rebel sergeant remarked as they left.

"And you'll find it burning when you come back tonight," was the Yankee sergeant's assuring reply.

After the rebels had got out of sight our boys began to feel that they had missed a golden opportunity to destroy a detachment of the Confederate Army. We had longed for a "face-to-face" meeting with the rebels.

"I could have killed two rebels had I been allowed to shoot," said Taylor.

"Who told you not to shoot?" demanded the sergeant.

"Well, nobody gave the order to fire. I had my gun cocked and if the rest of you had killed your man I'd killed mine."

"Bu-bu-bu-but they had si-si-six t-t-to ou-ou-our si-si-six, di-di-didn't they?" interrupted Jack Hazelet, whose stammering always caused him to grow red in the face when he wanted to get a word in in time and couldn't.

"Yes; we stood six to six, but if each one of us had killed his man they would all be dead."

"Je-je-jesso; bu-bu-bu-but di-di-didn't they ha-ha-have gu-gu-guns, t-t-too?"

"Of course they did."

"Sup-po-po-posen they ha-ha-had ki-ki-killed 's ma-ma-many 'f us a-a-as we di-di-did o-o-o-of th-th-them, wh-wh-where wo-wo-would we-we-we b-b-be n-n-now? co-co-confound you!"

As we found that only two of our party had their carbines loaded when we surprised the rebels, we concluded that it was just as fortunate for us as it was for the enemy that the meeting had resulted in a stand-off, although Taylor insisted that if anyone had given the command "fire" he would have killed his man. When his attention was called to the fact that his carbine was not loaded, he said:

"Well, I could have speared one of them with my sword before they could all get away."

"Bu-bu-bu-but wh-wh-what wo-wo-would th-th-the re-re-reb be-be-been do-do-doing; yo-yo-you in-in-infernal blockhead!" exclaimed Hazelet, and Taylor subsided.

There was one picket post halfway down Water Mountain, toward the Federal camp, that was dreaded by all the boys. It was within three hundred yards of the picket reserve or rendezvous. There was an old wagon road winding through a narrow ravine, and a stone wall crossed at right angles with the road opposite the reserve. On either side of the ravine was thick underbrush, and just back a little were woods. We were informed that four pickets had been shot off their horses near the old tree. The bushwhackers would ride to within a few hundred yards of the stone wall, dismount and while one would remain with the horses another would crawl like a snake in the grass up behind the wall and pick off the Union cavalrymen. It was cold-blooded murder, committed at night, without cause or provocation. Let it be said to the credit of the Confederate rank and file, that the boys in butternut—the regularly organised troops—discountenanced the cowardly acts of the guerrillas and bushwhackers.

A soldier was shot on picket at the old tree one night, and our company relieved the company to which he belonged the next morning. The murdered trooper was strapped across his saddle and taken to camp for burial. When our boys were counted off for picket Taylor "drew the fatal number," as it was called.

"If I'm murdered on post, boys," he said, "don't bother about taking my carcass to camp. Bury me where I fall."

Taylor made a poor attempt to appear unconcerned. But he was a droll sort of a boy. He continued:

"I've no doubt I was cut out for an avenger; so if any of you fellows want me to avenge your death just swap posts with me tonight. If any infernal gorilla steals up on you and takes your life, I pledge you that I'll follow him to Texas, but what I'll spill his gore."

"I'd rather go unavenged than to take chances on that post from eleven o'clock to one o'clock tonight," chorused several of Taylor's friends.

I had the post next to Taylor toward the reserve. The rain was falling, and it was dark down in the ravine. I could hear Taylor's horse champing his bit, and once my horse broke out with a gentle whinny, the noise of which startled me tremendously at first. And I have no doubt it operated the same on Taylor. Soon after that the rain let up and the clouds broke away so that the moon could be seen now and then. All at once there was a flash and a loud report.

"That's the last of poor Giles," I exclaimed, as the sound of the shot reverberated through the ravine.

Then I rode toward Taylor's post as cautiously as I could. I was pleasantly startled by the challenge in his well-known voice:

"Who comes there?"

The reserve came galloping down the hill. After the usual challenges and answers had been given, the lieutenant inquired:

"Who fired that shot?"

"'Twas me," replied Taylor.

"What did you fire at?"

"A bushwhacker."

"Where?"

"Over by the wall."

"Did you see him?"

"Of course I did; you don't suppose I'd fire at the moon, do you?"

The reserve rode forward to the wall and a few hundred yards beyond. It was decided that it would be useless to follow the guerrillas in the darkness. The pickets were doubled, two men on a post, for the rest of the night. I was put on the same post with Taylor, and after the reserve had returned to the rendezvous I questioned him about the alarm:

"Are you sure you saw a live bushwhacker, Giles?"

"If I hadn't seen him I'd be dead now."

"You didn't challenge him?"

"Well, I should say not. I saw him raise his head over the wall, just as the moon broke through a cloud. I first saw the glisten of his gun. Then I fired, and I believe I singed his hair, for I took good aim. If the moon had staid behind the clouds three seconds longer, the gorilla would 'a' had me sure. After I fired I heard him run, and then there were voices, followed by the noise of horses' hoofs as the bushwhackers galloped away. It was a close call for Taylor, but I tell you I sat with my carbine cocked and pointed at that wall all the time till the gorilla appeared. If my horse hadn't shied a little, that fellow would never have gone back to tell the story of his failure to murder another picket."

The next day arrangements were made to surprise the guerrillas in the event of another visit. Two dismounted troopers were stationed behind the stone wall, within easy range of the opening down the road toward the rebel lines. But the bushwhackers did not return during our tour of picket.

It was never clearly explained why the post at the old tree had been used, when the picket could be so much more safely stationed up behind the wall. There were a good many things that seemed strange to privates, but whenever an enlisted man made an effort to suggest that the plan of operations of his superiors be revised or corrected, it did not take him long to discover that he had made "one big shackass of mineself," as a recruit from Faderland expressed it when he was booted out of a sergeant's tent at Warrenton for simply informing the wearer of chevrons that in "Shermany the sergeants sometimes set up *der lager mit de* boys."

The experiences of the First Massachusetts cavalry at Warrenton during the winter were similar to those of other regiments in camp at that station. Some of us would have been fearfully homesick if we had found any spare time between calls. We scarcely had opportunity to answer letters from home, so thick and fast came the bugle blasts. One of our boys received a letter from his sweetheart, and she wondered what the soldiers could find to occupy their time—"no balls, no parties, no corn-huskings," as she expressed it. Her soldier boy enclosed a copy of the list of calls for our every-day existence in camp, and when we were not on picket duty.

I have no doubt the dear girl was satisfied that her boy in blue would suffer little, if any, for the want of something to keep his mind occupied. As near as I can remember, the list of calls for each day's programme—except Sunday, when we had general inspection and were kept in line an hour or two extra—was as follows:

Buglers' call	Daybreak
Assembly	Five minutes later
Reveille	Immediately after
Stable call	Immediately after
Breakfast call	(about) 7 a. m.
Sick call	7.30 a.m.
Fatigue call	8 a.m.
First call for guard mount	8.50 a.m.
Adjutant's call	9 a.m.
Water call	9.15 a.m.
Drill call	9.30 a.m.
Recall from drill	11 a.m.
Orderly call	11.30 a.m.
Dinner call	12 p.m.
Drill call	1 p.m.
Recall from drill	2 p.m.
Water call	2.30 p.m.
Stable call	3.30 p.m.
Dress parade	half-hour before sunset.
Retreat	Sunset
Tattoo	8.30 p.m.
Taps	9 p.m.

The roll was called at reveille, drill, retreat and tattoo. The boys had "words set to music" for nearly all the calls. The breakfast call was rather inelegantly expressed when infantry and cavalry troops were camped close together. The foot soldiers, not having horses to groom and feed, had their breakfast the first thing after reveille. Then they would stand around, and as the cavalry bugler-boys would sound the breakfast call after stables, the heroes of the knapsack would chorus:

Go and get your breakfast,
Breakfast without meat.

But a cavalry poet tried his hand, and after that whenever the infantry fellows shouted the above at us to the tune of breakfast call, we all joined in the refrain:

Dirty, dirty doughboy,
Dirty, dirty feet.

That settled it. The doughboys soon fell back. If they had not, there might have been a riot, for our poet was at work on another verse that he said would settle their hash. Judging from the result of his first effort, I can readily see that the infantry had a narrow escape.

We had inspection every Sunday morning after stables. Each company was looked over by its first sergeant. Then the captains would appear and take charge. If it were to be a regimental inspection, all the companies would be marched to the parade-ground, and the colonel or regimental commander would be the inspecting officer. Every now and then a brigade review would follow the inspection. It was fun for the brigadier, or inspector, but after the rear rank privates had been in the saddle two hours or more, sitting bolt upright, with eyes fixed square to the front while waiting to have the inspector come round to them, and go through the motions of examining their carbines, revolvers, sabres and equipments, the affair became tedious.

But our regiment was blessed with an excellent band. The members rode white horses, and on all grand reviews and parades they took position on the right of the regiment. Whenever the inspection was particularly protracted and severe, the band would play inspiring selections, and many a poor fellow who was on the point of asking permission to fall out of the ranks, would cheer up as the strains of "The Girl I Left Behind Me," or some other popular air, would reach his ear. Survivors of the Army of the Potomac—and all other armies—will recall that the playing of a single tune as the comrades rushed forward into the heat of battle, was worth more than the spread-eagle speeches of scores of generals. The soldier that could muster backbone enough to turn tail and run when his comrades were presenting a solid front to the enemy, and the bands were playing national airs, was made of queer material, indeed.

On one of these Sunday morning inspections, Taylor remarked to me in a low tone of voice:

"I'd like to know how they expect us to diligently attend divine worship when they keep us harnessed up all day after this fashion?"

"Keep still, Giles; if the sergeant hears you he'll tie you up by the thumbs."

Yet Taylor's inquiry was to the point. The articles of war had been read to us only the day before that inspection. Here is what we were given along the line referred to by Taylor:

> Article 2.—It is earnestly recommended to all officers and soldiers, diligently to attend divine service; and all officers who shall behave indecently or irreverently at any place of divine worship, shall, if commissioned officers, be brought before a general court-martial, there to be publicly and severely reprimanded by the president; if non-commissioned officers or soldiers, every person so offending shall, for his first offense, forfeit one sixth of a dollar, to be deducted out of his next pay; for the second offense he shall not only forfeit a like sum, but be confined twenty-four hours; and for every like offense, shall suffer and pay in like manner; which money, so forfeited, shall be applied by the captain or senior officer of the troop or company, to the use of the sick soldiers of the company or troop to which the offender belongs.

The boys called the regulations the army Bible. Of course, many of the articles were intended for troops in garrison.

When in active service, on the march and on the battlefield, divine services were impracticable until there was at least a temporary cessation of hostilities. Regimental chaplains exhibited remarkable fortitude, courage and self-sacrifice in administering spiritual consolation to the wounded and dying at the front, even under heavy fire from the enemy. There were services in camp in such organisations as had ministers of the gospel with them, but many regiments were without chaplains, and had to forage for religious food, if they had any.

I do not remember attending divine service in the army, except once in the Wilderness campaign. It was at night, and the congregation stood around a blazing camp-fire. The good old chaplain exhorted the boys to prepare the way, and buckle on the whole armour. It was a striking scene. Some of the boys wept as the minister alluded to the loved ones at home, who were looking to the Army of the Potomac for a victory that would crush out the rebellion. There were few dry eyes when the benediction was pronounced, after the chaplain had urged his hearers to "be prepared to stand an inspection before the

King of kings."

It was the last religious service that many who were present that night ever attended. The next day rebel bullets mowed them down by scores. They died in defence of the right—that the Union might be preserved. Of those who fell as they fell a poet has written:

> *No more the bugle calls the weary one,*
> *Rest, noble spirit, in your grave unknown;*
> *We will find you and know you,*
> *Among the good and true,*
> *When the robe of white is given*
> *For the faded coat of blue.*

I may have had many opportunities to hear the Gospel preached during the war, but I do not recall the circumstances now. Yet I am sure that if I had diligently reconnoitred the camps, I could have found faithful disciples preaching the Word of Life to such as had ears to hear. And I believe that when the general roll shall be called on the shores of eternity, the noble Christian soldiers who held aloft the banner of their Master on the battlefields of the great Civil War, will not only hear the welcome, "Well done," but they will be crowned with diadems bedecked with many stars.

The third commandment laid down in the regulations was probably violated more frequently than any of the one hundred and one articles of war. It read:

> Article 3.—Any non-commissioned officer or soldier who shall use any profane oath or execration, shall incur the penalties expressed in the foregoing article; and a commissioned officer shall forfeit and pay, for each and every such offense, one dollar, to be applied as in the preceding article.

Had this article been lived up to, the "sick soldiers" referred to would have been provided for for life, as would their children and children's children. There would have been no call for the sanitary and Christian commissions to raise money to alleviate the sufferings of the sick. All that money could have supplied would have been provided. I do not mean to convey the idea that the Union soldiers were particularly profane, but something like a half-million of men were under arms at one time, about the close of the war. Some of them swore. Even generals blasphemed before their men. The general-in-chief, however, was an exception. No soldier in the Army of the Potomac ever heard

General Grant utter an oath. There were officers and soldiers in all regiments who did not swear. But they were in the minority. Had the penalty for using profane oaths been enforced, seventy-five *per cent*, of the soldiers would have been in the guard house all the time, and at the end of a week they would have been indebted to the government more than their three years' salary would have footed up, and the guard house would have had a mortgage on them for years to come.

The third article of war was read to one company in our regiment by a first sergeant, who gave such an emphasis to the reading of the penalty for swearing that the boys began to feel that they must "swear off" on profanity. Said the sergeant:

"I want you men to understand that in this company the articles of war will be strictly lived up to. If I hear any man use profane language, be he non-commissioned officer or soldier, I'll bring him up for punishment as prescribed."

Then the sergeant swore a "blue streak" for a minute or two before he gave the order to "break ranks." Yet he did it unconsciously, as he said when his attention was called to it by a corporal, and only intended to emphasize the interdiction.

Quite a number of the articles of war enumerated offenses for which the penalty provided that the offender "shall suffer death, or such other punishment as by a court-martial shall be inflicted." In the reading the officers always emphasized the penalty "shall suffer death," and then dropped their voices till the "or such other punishment" could scarcely be heard by the soldiers standing the nearest to the reader. The death penalty was sandwiched all through the articles of war, and at the close of the reading the average recruit felt condemned, and could remember nothing but "shall suffer death," and expected to hear the captain order out a detail to execute the sentence. But the death penalty was inflicted, except in rare instances, only upon spies or men who had deserted to the enemy and been recaptured.

CHAPTER 11

The Overland Campaign

When U. S. Grant was promoted to lieutenant-general, and assigned to command all the armies of the United States, the announcement was received by the Army of the Potomac without any marked evidence of approval or disapproval. There was no enthusiasm whatever among the troops in winter quarters around Warrenton.

A few expressed the opinion that the "Western importation" would not come up to the country's expectations when brought face to face with the great rebel chief, who was personally acquainted with every inch of the ground on which the battles of Virginia must be fought. Then there was a feeling, though not out spoken to any great extent, that the new-comer, being a stranger to Lee's tactics, and unacquainted with the Eastern troops, would be placed at such a disadvantage, that the Confederate leader would be enabled to "play all around" Grant, and demoralize the Union army. The veterans of the grand old Army of the Potomac were prepared to fight—to the death, if need be—no matter who received the three stars of a lieutenant-general. They were loyal to their flag, and that carried with it loyalty to the new commander.

Probably it did not occur to a dozen soldiers in the Army of the Potomac that Grant would adopt tactics of his own, instead of following in the beaten paths of former commanders. No one suspected that the lieutenant-general would be able to knock the bottom out of the Southern Confederacy inside of twelve months after his first order for the advance of the army had been promulgated. We all believed that the Union cause would triumph. But when? Three years had rolled round since the rebels fired on Sumter. And "Uncle Robert," with his veterans in butternut, still flaunted the stars and bars as defiantly as ever, within a few miles of the national capital.

Company I, First Massachusetts cavalry, received the news at first in the same spirit that other companies in our locality received it. The new commander's qualifications were discussed in the light of what had been heard of his career in the West. How much light we had received may be inferred from a discussion around the reserve picket fire on Water Mountain, a detachment of the Sixth Ohio and First Pennsylvania cavalry being on duty with our regimental detail:

"Who's this Grant that's made lieutenant-general?"

"He's the hero of Vicksburg."

"Well, Vicksburg wasn't much of a fight. The rebs were out of rations, and they had to surrender or starve. They had nothing but dead mules and dogs to eat, as I understand it."

"Yes; but it required a good deal of strategy to keep Pemberton's army cooped up in Vicksburg till they were so weak for want of grub that they couldn't skedaddle even if they had found a hole to crawl out of."

"I don't believe Grant could have penned any of Lee's generals up after that fashion. Early, or Longstreet, or Jeb Stuart would have broken out some way and foraged around for supplies."

"Maybe so."

"Pemberton couldn't hold a candle to Lee."

"Of course not."

"What else has Grant done?"

"He has whipped the Johnnies every time they have faced him, all the way from Fort Donelson to Chattanooga."

"He's a fighter, then?"

"That's what they call him."

"Bully for Grant!"

"Where does he hail from?"

"Galena, Illinois. He was clerking in a leather store when the war broke out."

"I don't care if he was in Illinois when the war began, he was born in Ohio, graduated at West Point, and served in Mexico and out West."

"Hurrah for Ohio!" (chorus of the Sixth Ohio cavalry). "Hurrah for Grant!"

"Hurrah!" "Hurrah!" "Hurrah!"

"Tiger!"

I do not know but what the "Ohio idee" was inaugurated on our picket line away back there in 1864. At any rate the Sixth Ohio boys insisted, when they were assured that the lieutenant-general was a native of that State, that "Bob Lee's goose was as good as cooked already." It was rather a crude way of expressing a prophecy that proved as true as Holy Writ. The Ohio Volunteers were ready to cross sabres with the enemy without more ado. Grant was from Ohio, and that settled it.

The Bay State boys indorsed Grant after his record had been established. To be sure there was our own General Butler, the hero of New Orleans. Butler was then in command of the Army of the James, with Fortress Monroe as his base of supplies. Somehow we had come to associate Butler with naval expeditions, and never thought of him in connection with a campaign on land beyond the support of the gunboats. It is probable that our estimates of military men were influenced by what we read in the newspapers. One of the boys declared that in a description of the capture of New Orleans he had read, mention was made of Butler being "lashed to the maintop," while the fleet under Farragut was fighting its way up the Mississippi under fire from the guns of Forts Jackson and St. Philip. Said an Ohio trooper:

"I don't believe that story."

"Neither do I. I'm only telling you what I read."

"I think Butler had better stay in the navy."

"But he isn't a sailor; he's a major-general of volunteers."

"Well, there's no telling how he might cut up on dry land. He'd better keep his sea legs on and stay where if he gets whipped he can't run."

The veterans from the Keystone State had not lost faith in "Little Mac." They contended that McClellan had been handicapped just at a moment when he was "about to execute a *coup de main* that would prove a *coup de grace* to the Southern Confederacy!" Meade was the second choice of the Pennsylvanians. His splendid victory over Lee at Gettysburg had brought him into the front rank. He had won the gratitude of the whole North, Copperheads excepted. Checking Lee's advance Northward, whipping the rebel army and compelling the defeated Confederacy to "about face" and put for home, gave General Meade a big place in the hearts of the soldiers and the loyal people of the Keystone State. Surely the patriots of the North had good cause to rejoice on the eighty-seventh anniversary of the signing of the Declaration of Independence. On that day Grant's victorious army raised the stars and stripes over the rebel fortifications at Vicksburg, and the Mississippi was opened to the sea; and Lee's army of Northern Virginia was retreating from the scene of its unsuccessful attack on Meade's army at Gettysburg. Within forty-eight hours after the Union troops had crossed the Rapidan under the direction of General Grant, there was not a soldier in the Army of the Potomac but what felt that the lieutenant-general meant business. The official records on file at Washington show that during that two days' terrible struggle in the Wilderness—May 5 and 6, 1864—the loss sustained by the Army of the Potomac was 13,948, of which 2,261 were killed, 8,785 wounded and 2,902 taken prisoners or missing. Then came Spotsylvania, with an aggregate Union loss of 13,601. The total loss sustained by the Army of the Potomac, the Army of the James and by Sheridan's operations in the valley, from May 1, 1864, to the surrender of Lee at Appomattox, April 9, 1865, is given in official compilations at 99,772—14,601 killed, 61,452 wounded and 23,719 missing. In the meantime the Federal forces operating in Virginia captured 81,112 Confederates, and Lee's killed and wounded are believed to have been equal to Grant's, but the "scattering" of the rebels after Richmond fell, and the destruction of Confederate records, made it impossible to arrive at the exact figures.

As already stated, the veterans of the Army of the Potomac were satisfied that Grant was a fighting man. During the period beginning with the opening skirmish in the Wilderness, and continuing down to the end of the conflict at Appomattox, there was not wanting evidence of Grant's determination to "fight his men "for all they were worth whenever opportunity presented for hammering the rebels. There was no going back this time. It was "On to Richmond" in earnest. The Army of the Potomac was ready to be led against the enemy. There was general rejoicing all along the line when the command was given, "By the left flank, forward!"and the Federals moved toward Spotsylvania instead of retreating across the Rapidan, as President Lincoln said any previous commander of the Army of the Potomac would have done at the close of such a battle as that fought in the Wilderness.

In Richardson's *Personal History of U. S. Grant*, it is stated that in the rebel lines it was believed that our army was falling back at the close of the conflict in the Wilderness. The account continues:

Gordon said to Lee:
"I think there is no doubt but that Grant is retreating."
"You are mistaken," replied the Confederate chief earnestly, "quite mistaken. Grant is not retreating; he is not a retreating man."

Lee was right. The Army of the Potomac was never again marched back across the Rapidan until after the backbone of the Confederacy had been broken, and the gallant Union soldiers were *en route* to Washington to be mustered out.

I first saw General Grant while the battle of the Wilderness was going on. In changing position during the fight, our regiment was marched around by Meade's headquarters. There were a dozen or more officers grouped about General Grant and General Meade. The latter wore the full uniform of a major-general, including sword and sash. He was somewhat fussy in giving directions, and a stickler for red tape. But Meade was a soldier "from heels up." Grant was plainly dressed, and wore no sword. His coat was unbuttoned, and not until he was pointed out as the commander-in-chief was he recognized by the troopers who were riding across the field.

"There's General Grant."

"Where?"

"On the left of General Meade."

"That officer with his coat open?"

"Yes; that's Grant."

Off went our caps, and the commander acknowledged our cheer by raising his hat.

Just then there was a terrific firing along Hancock's front, and Grant galloped over in that direction after a moment's conversation with Meade. We took up the trot, and in a few minutes found plenty to do out on the road leading to Todd's tavern. When a breathing spell came, the boys had their say about the lieutenant-general.

"I expected to see him all covered with gold lace and other fixin's," said one.

"He looks as if he would stay with 'em till somebody cried enough."

"He's got good qualities, any way," remarked Taylor.

"How can you tell?"

"Because he smokes fine cigars, and rides a good hoss. I got a smell of that cigar as he cantered by to see what was going on in front of the second corps. I think"—

The discussion was cut short by another attempt of the Johnnies to hustle us back from the position held by our brigade. We protested so vigorously that the rebels retreated after making three or four dashes against our advance squadrons. It was warm work in the Wilderness. One of our boys exclaimed:

"If any of us get out of this Wilderness alive, our chances will be good to see the end of the Southern Confederacy."

"Yea, verily," groaned a corporal who had been shot in the arm.

That Grant had no suspicion of being in a tight box, as the rebel sympathizers at the North declared he was, is shown by the fact that at the very moment when his defamers asserted he was so badly crippled that had Lee attacked the Union army Grant's forces would have been destroyed, the lieutenant-general was so much on the aggressive that he was marching to renew the battle at Spotsylvania, and felt able to spare Sheridan and his splendid cavalry corps for a raid on Lee's communications.

We saw Grant again when we rejoined the army; at Cold Harbor, on the march to the south side of the James several times, and during the assaults in front of Petersburg. While in winter quarters we saw the lieutenant-general often at City Point and along the line, and the more we saw of him the higher he rose in our estimation. Then came the campaign of 1865, ending with the surrender of the rebel army at Appomattox. Grant was a modest officer, not given to display, but when the Army of the Potomac awoke to the fact that Lee's army was in the "last ditch," then, and not till then, did the soldiers begin to appreciate the true greatness of the commander-in-chief.

The downfall of Richmond and the capture of Lee's army silenced even the assistant Confederates at the North. It was a grand victory—a magnificent triumph of superior generalship combined with a patriotism that had never wavered in the face of armed rebellion.

After the surrender I next saw Grant in Washington on the grand review in May, 1865. He was on the stand in front of the White House with a large crowd of dignitaries, including President Johnson.

I saw the old commander but three times after the war closed. The first time was on the occasion of his visit to Troy, N.Y., several years ago. He attended and spoke at a public installation of Post Willard, Grand Army of the Republic, at Music Hall. He was accompanied to the city by Governor Cornell, and a grand parade was had in which all the local military organisations and veterans participated. The general and the governor occupied a carriage with General J. B. Carr and Honourable John M. Francis, and dined with Mr. Francis at his residence. I was glad of the opportunity to grasp the old commander's hand.

I had the pleasure, as a representative of the Troy *Daily Times*, to accompany the Grant family from Albany to Saratoga about the middle of June, 1885. It was, indeed, a pleasure to meet the hero of Appomattox again, but the heart of the soldier who had served under Grant from the Wilderness to Appomattox and had been present when the surrender took place, was saddened to find the old warrior only a shadow of his former self. Only once on the trip to Mount MacGregor did the general display any of that martial spirit that twenty years before had animated the commander-in-chief and inspired his gallant army. It was at Saratoga Springs during his transfer from the palace coach on which he travelled from New York to Saratoga to the car that was to convey him up the mountain to MacGregor. The Grand Army veterans and the local national guard company gave the distinguished visitor a military salute. The general raised himself on his crutches, took in the situation at a glance, and as he acknowledged the salute with his hand, the old-time light came into the eye, and the foremost general of modern times was recognized in the person of the almost helpless invalid.

Thursday, July 23, 1885, the news of the brave general and honoured ex-president's death was flashed over the wires from the top of Mount MacGregor, and a whole nation was in mourning. Old soldiers met in the streets and grasped each other by the hand. "The old commander's dead," was about all they could say; their sorrow was too deep for words. From all sections of the Union, and from across the ocean messages of condolence and sympathy were sent to the bereaved family at MacGregor.

I attended the funeral of the dead hero at Mount MacGregor, Tuesday, August 4, 1885. Of the pallbearers two, Buckner and Joe Johnston, had fought under the stars and bars, while Sherman and Sheridan had been the deceased commander's most trusted lieutenants. Never before had a funeral taken place under such circumstances. The exercises were remarkably impressive. The closing verse of the beautiful hymn which was sung before the Rev. Dr. J. P. Newman began his memorial sermon seemed particularly appropriate:

When ends life's transient dream;
When death's cold, sullen stream
Shall o'er me roll;
Blest Saviour, then in love,
Fear and distress remove;
O bear me safe above—
A ransom'd soul.

After Dr. Newman's glowing tribute came the closing hymn, led by Mrs. Whitney, soprano, of Boston, and in which the congregation joined:

Nearer, my God, to Thee,
Nearer to Thee!
E'en though it be a cross
That raiseth me;
Still all my song shall be—
Nearer, my God, to Thee I
Nearer to Thee!

As the echoes of the general's favourite hymn rang through the tall trees that surmounted the mountain top, the benediction was pronounced, and the remains of the old commander were borne to the funeral train. General Hancock was in charge. Down the mountain to Saratoga the train proceeded. At the village the casket was transferred to the funeral car in which the remains were taken to Albany and subsequently to New York. The gallant Sherman, Sheridan, Hancock and other noble heroes have since answered their last roll-call on earth—gone to swell the ranks of the great majority beyond the river. In a few years the veterans who fought under Grant will all pass over, but their deeds of valour will ever live in song and story. The name of Grant is inscribed on the nation's roll of patriots side by side with that of the martyred Lincoln. Of the hero of Appomattox it can be truly said that he was

Our greatest, yet with least pretence,
Great in council and great in war,
Foremost captain of his time,
Rich in saving common sense,
And, as the greatest only are,
In his simplicity sublime.

Note—This chapter was published in the Troy *Daily Times* at the time of General Grant's death, and it is deemed best to insert it without change, although the events are not presented in chronological order with the other chapters.—S. P. A.

CHAPTER 12

Breaking up Winter Quarters

In winter quarters kitchens were erected and men were detailed from each company to act as cooks. It was easy enough to find soldiers who would sing out "here!" when the first sergeant inquired if there was a good cook in the ranks. Thoughts of extra food and "every night in bed" sometimes prompted men who had never even fried a slice of pork to step to the front and announce themselves as experts in the culinary art. These pretenders, however, were not permitted to spoil more than one day's rations. As soon as the soldiers had sampled the mystery into which their allowance of food had been transformed by the greenhorn kettle slingers, there was trouble in the camp until a change was made in the cook house.

One day a company I boy found a piece of soap in his soup. The discovery was not made until he had stowed away nearly all the contents of his quart cup. He had felt the lump in the bottom with his spoon, and had congratulated himself on the supposed mistake of the cook in leaving a piece of beef in the broth. He raised it out of the cup and held it up on his spoon to exhibit it to less fortunate comrades, saying:

"Nothing like being on the right side of the cook, boys. How's that for beef?"

"It's rather light-coloured for government ox—let me see! If it isn't soap I'm a marine."

"Soap?"

"Yes, soap!"

"And in my soup! Boys, that cook's time has come. Who'll stand by me till I make him eat this piece of soap?"

"You'll have to go it alone; you're on the right side of the cook, you know. We've got nothing to do with it. He knows better than to give us soup with soap in it."

"But, hold on a minute; all the soup came out of the same kettle."

"Sure enough; he's soap-souped us all. Go ahead; we're with you."

The cook would have been roughly handled had he not called on the officer of the day for protection. The cook protested that the soap had not been in the soup kettle, but must have fallen off the shelf over the window as the soldier held his tin cup through the opening to receive his soup. This theory was gladly accepted by all but the trooper who had found the soap in his cup. By this time he was too sick to be aggressive.

"Boys, send my body home," he moaned.

"Soap suds," chorused the troopers who had been relieved from the terrible suspicion that they had been fed on soap also. The poor victim was given a drink of hospital brandy as soon as he could retain anything on his stomach. He was on the sick report for four or five days.

Paragraph 1,190 of the Revised Regulations for the Army (1863), fixed the soldier's daily ration as follows:

> Twelve ounces of pork or bacon, or one pound and four ounces of salt or fresh beef; one pound and six ounces of soft bread or flour, or one pound of hard bread, or one pound and four ounces of corn meal; and to every one hundred rations, fifteen pounds of peas or beans, and ten pounds of rice or hominy; ten pounds of green coffee, or eight pounds of roasted (or roasted and ground) coffee, or one pound and eight ounces of tea; fifteen pounds of sugar; four quarts of vinegar; one pound and four ounces of adamantine or star candles; four pounds of soap; three pounds and twelve ounces of salt; four ounces of pepper; thirty pounds of potatoes, when practicable, and one quart of molasses.

I have quoted the exact language of the regulations for the information of civilians who every now and then inquire of the veterans: "What did the government feed you fellows on down in Dixie?" Hard-tack, salt pork and coffee were the soldier's mainstay. The sweetest meal I ever ate consisted of crumbs of hardtack picked up out of the dirt, where the boxes had been opened to issue crackers to the troops, and a piece of salt pork that had been thrown away by an infantry soldier. I still cherish the memory of that feast.

There were two or three violinists in our battalion, and the boys

"SOAP IN MY SOUP!" HE EXCLAIMED.

occasionally induced these musicians to fiddle for a "stag dance," as they called the old-fashioned quadrille in which troopers with their caps off went through "ladies' chain" and other figures prescribed for the fair partners in the regulation dance. The dances took place by the light of the camp fires between retreat and tattoo. The boys managed to get a good deal of enjoyment out of these gatherings.

During the war a great many men made fortunes by selling goods of various kinds, including provisions, to the soldiers. The army traders took big chances after the spring campaign opened, unless they packed up and moved to the rear as the troops marched to the front. Yet there were sutlers who followed the army even on dangerous expeditions into the enemy's country. The boys contended that if a trader could sell one wagon load of goods at sutler's prices—and get his pay—he could afford to retire or to lose five or six wagon loads. There was much truth in the statement.

Among many stories current in the Army of the Potomac about "euchring the sutler," as the soldiers called any trick by which they could secure goods without coming down with the cash, was the following:

The troops were in bivouac on the James River. The boys received four months' pay, and there was no place to buy anything except at the sutler's. The trader took advantage of the situation and marked his goods up fifty *per cent*. He had just received a barrel of whiskey, which he was retailing at fifty cents a glass. The sutler's glass held a little more than a thimbleful. There was a run on the whiskey for a time. Then trade slacked up, and the sutler was at a loss to account for it, as it was contrary to all precedent, the rule being that the more liquor the boys got the more they wanted.

Finally the call for whiskey ceased.

"What's the matter with the men?" the sutler asked one of his clerks.

"I don't know—they never acted like this before."

"They're not buying our whiskey."

"No."

"And many of them seem to be getting drunk."

"That's so."

"Must be somebody else's selling in camp. I thought we had a corner on whiskey."

"So did I."

"Well, you go out and see what you can find."

The clerk was gone about five minutes.

"Have we competition?" inquired the sutler, as the clerk returned to the tent.

"Well, I should say so."

"What are they selling at?"

"Twenty-five cents a drink."

"Just half our price?"

"Yes."

"Where are they located?"

"Right outside our tent."

"Where do they keep their liquor?"

"Take hold of the barrel with me and I'll show you."

The sutler was surprised to find a faucet in the rear end of the barrel as well as in the front end from which he had been drawing.

"Somebody tapped this barrel from the outside," he exclaimed.

"Yes, and retailed your liquor at twenty-five cents a drink while you asked fifty. It's no wonder they drew all the customers," said the clerk.

"There's but a little whiskey left in the barrel—not more'n a gallon. Don't sell another drop for less than two dollars a glass."

A Down East Yankee had made the discovery that the sutler's whiskey barrel was so placed that one end of it, as it was resting on boxes, touched the canvas. He went around behind the tent, cut a hole through the canvas, and after borrowing a brace and bit from an extra-duty man in the quartermaster's department and a faucet from another comrade in the commissary department, he tapped the sutler's whiskey barrel and did a thriving business, the enterprise being advertised by word of mouth through the camp.

It never failed to be noised about that something was in the wind several days before the receipt of orders for any movement of importance. The great multitudes of citizens who bore arms under the flag of the Union to put down the rebellion, had a way of thinking for themselves, and of making observations of what transpired around them, that was exasperatingly fatal to the regular red-tape idea that a soldier was a machine and nothing more. When it became necessary to perform daring deeds in the very jaws of death, the intelligent Yankee volunteers were capable of understanding that sacrifice was demanded. And they made it, bravely and without complaint.

Whenever a big thing was on the programme it was next to impossible to keep it quiet. The old soldiers seemed to grasp the situation

TAPPING THE SUTLER'S WHISKEY BARREL.

intuitively, and the recruits generally knew more about it, or thought they did, than the generals themselves.

There were certain signs in our military existence that came to be accepted as reliable. Orders from brigade headquarters to have the horses well shod at once, meant a cavalry expedition into the enemy's country. Extra ammunition for the light batteries that belonged to the cavalry corps meant that the movement was to be a reconnaissance in force. The assembling of a division or two of infantry in battle trim near the cavalry outposts, with several days' commissary stores in transit, showed that an attempt was to be made to gobble up another slice of the Confederacy or make a break in the communications of the rebels. The issuing of dog tents, extra ammunition and commissary supplies as a rule preceded the starting of an expedition against the enemy. A sudden dashing out of camp, light saddle, and unencumbered with anything but arms and ammunition, in response to a signal from the outposts, always gave rise to the suspicion, frequently confirmed in the heat of battle, that the Johnnies were making an expedition against us.

The rumours of a general advance came thicker and faster the last week in April, and May the third the long roll was sounded by the brigade buglers. The breaking up of winter quarters was always attended with scenes that were excruciatingly funny. What a lot of worthless old plunder the soldiers would accumulate! It always required sorting over a dozen times before the boys could really determine just what to leave behind. And then it invariably happened that after the very last thing that they could spare or think of abandoning had been cast out the inspecting officers would poke around and order us to throw out the articles we prized most highly.

Railroad communication with Washington and the North had made it comparatively easy for us to secure creature comforts, and many delicacies from the homes of the boys in blue reached our camp. Waterman had received a large-sized packing box full of good things to eat, from his parents. The goodies were shared among "our four" Waterman, Taylor, Hom and myself.

The first feed we had after the cover of Waterman's box was taken off brought tears to our eyes—tears of joy, of course—but somehow the taste of the homemade pies and cake produced a longing for home and mother which was made all the more intense as the contents of the box disappeared and we came face to face with the stern reality that a return to "mule beef and hard-tack" was inevitable.

Waterman's parents resided only a short distance from where my father and mother lived in Berlin, and when his box was sent my family helped to fill and pack the box. Then when the dear people at home thought our food must be getting low another box was packed by my parents, and Waterman's family contributed some of the good things. It was sent by express, but owing to the increased demand upon the railroads and trains to forward munitions of war to the Army of the Potomac, my box did not reach Warrenton until the morning that we started for the Wilderness. The company was drawn up in line waiting to move forward when a government wagon arrived loaded with boxes and packages for the troopers. My long-expected box was thrown out of the wagon, and I obtained permission to interview it.

I pried off the cover, and as I caught a glimpse of the good things from home, I felt like annihilating the quartermaster's department that had held back my box while extra supplies of ammunition and commissary stores had been dispatched to the front. Just then the bugler at brigade headquarters sounded "forward." There was no time to waste. I did the best I could under the circumstances—filled my haversack, and invited the boys in the company to help themselves, after "our four" had stowed away all we could. The second platoon swept down on that box, and in less than a minute the boys were eating homemade pies and cookies all along the line. A picture or two, a pair of knit socks and a few souvenirs were secured by Waterman and myself.

"Attention, company!"
"Prepare to mount!"
"Mount!"
"Form ranks!"
"By fours, march!" and we were *en route* to the Rapidan. It was the last taste of home-made grub that we enjoyed till the campaign was over. We secured the makings of a square meal now and then while raiding around Richmond, but the territory had been foraged so often that it was considered mighty poor picking the last two years of the war.

As we rode forward, we found that everybody was on the march or getting ready to leave. Lines of tents were disappearing on all sides as the long roll sounded through the camps. Supply trains were moving out, and everything was headed about due south. As we rode by the bivouacs of the infantry, the foot soldiers, imitating the Johnnies, would sing out:

"Hay, there! where be you all goin'?"

"Bound for Richmond."

"But we all are not ready to move out yet."

"Then we'll drive you out."

"You all can't whip we all. Bob Lee will drive you all back as he has done before."

Then there would be a general laugh all along the line at the expression in this semi-serious way of an idea that had gained a strong lodgement in the minds of many "peace patriots" at the North. The soldiers at the front who were doing their best to crush out rebellion did not share in the feeling that the Jeff Davis government would carry the day. The veterans of Gettysburg and of Antietam knew that the Union army was in no respect inferior to the chivalry of the South—man to man. All the Army of the Potomac needed to enable it to fight Lee's army to the finish, and win, was a commander that knew what fighting to a finish meant. Would the new commander fill the bill?

President Lincoln, in presenting Grant's commission as lieutenant-general at the White House, March 9, 1864, assured the modest hero from the West that "as the country herein trusts you, so, under God, it will sustain you." A few days after the lieutenant-general remarked:

> The Army of the Potomac is a very fine one, and has shown the highest courage. Still, I think it has never fought its battles through.

The Army of the Potomac was waiting for a general who would give it an opportunity to "fight its battles through.

All eyes were fixed on the lieutenant-general. The result is recorded in history.

As we pressed toward the Rapidan there were evidences all about us that the Army of the Potomac was stripping for the fight. All superfluous baggage and trappings were left behind. The army was ready to strike a powerful blow at its old adversary, and the conflict was at hand. Sheridan was at the head of the cavalry corps. As we came in sight of the Rapidan and made preparations for swimming the river with our horses to cover the laying of the pontoon bridges, so that the infantry and artillery could cross, we felt that a few days would determine whether the Army of the Potomac would go "on to Richmond," or, bleeding and shattered from an unsuccessful onslaught upon Lee's veterans, fall back to its old quarters, as it had done on other occasions.

CHAPTER 13

The Night Before the Battle

The crossing of the Rapidan by the Army of the Potomac, May 4, 1864, was an interesting and exciting event. Gregg's division—the second—of Sheridan's cavalry corps formed the advance of the column that crossed at Ely's ford. The First Massachusetts cavalry was in the first brigade of Gregg's division.

At nightfall Wednesday the crossing had been effected by the entire army. The second corps, commanded by Gen. Hancock, and the supply train crossed on the pontoon bridge at Ely's ford. Wilson's cavalry division headed the column that crossed at Germania ford, six miles up the river, and included Gen. Warren's fifth corps and the sixth corps commanded by Gen. Sedgwick, who was killed by a rebel sharpshooter at Spotsylvania a few days later. We arrived at the ford soon after midnight, and preparations were made to swim the river.

"I never thought the army went hunting round in the night for Johnnies in this way," said one of our boys.

"We're stealing a march on old man Lee."

"Think we'll make it?"

"Don't know—tell better when daylight comes."

"Lee will miss us in the morning."

"Yes; and then look out. He'll come tearing down this way ready for fight."

The boys were not far out of the way. Lee did miss us in the morning, but he found us Wednesday night, and pitched into Grant's army bright and early the next morning. But to the river!

The Rapidan was high for that season, and the recruits were given special instructions about managing their horses while swimming the stream. The bank was steep on the north side of the river, and the opposite bank was precipitous, except the narrow cut where the road descended into the water. Old troopers declared that the only way to swim a river was to dismount, take hold of the horse's tail, urge the animal into the stream and hang on to the tail. But I noticed that the veterans did not try the experiment. They remained in their saddles. One "new hand" who accepted every thing the old soldiers said as law and gospel, essayed to swim the Rapidan "on foot." With his clothes on, including a large overcoat, the foolhardy trooper marched into the water behind his horse. His carbine was attached to the sling over his shoulder, and his sabre balanced him on the other side. Then he carried a haversack and canteen, besides wearing a waist belt and cartridge-box with pistol and holster. Heavy top-boots and spurs were included in his make-up. His body was not recovered.

Our horses were as new to this sort of thing as we were, but they carried us over after a fashion. The current was so swift that not one horse in each set of fours landed in the road on the south side. I remember that as my set took to the water, I twisted my horse's mane through my fingers and around my wrist. I was determined not to separate from my charger till we reached the other shore. We were carried down stream at a lively rate for a few minutes, but I kept the horse's head steered for the cut where the road was, and we came out not more than one hundred yards below the objective point.

We did not have metallic cartridges for our carbines and revolvers at that time. When we rode into the Rapidan and struck out for the south bank, we were admonished by the officers—in the language of a distinguished patriot—to "Trust in God and keep your powder dry."

It was stated after we had reached *terra firma* and inventoried ourselves, that the rebel cavalry pickets at the ford had opened fire on us as we were swimming the river. But my attention was so much occupied while in the water, that I did not hear the firing. The Johnnies did not remain to interview us after we had crossed. The pontoon train was soon on hand, its arrival being announced by the braying of the mules attached to the wagons.

"I hope Lee's men up around Orange Court House are all good sleepers," said a trooper, who was pouring the water out of his boots.

"Why so?"

"Because if any of them are awake and fail to hear those infernal mules, they must be mighty hard o' hearing."

The pontooners were soon at work on the bridge, which was completed by the time the head of the infantry column reached the ford.

The laying of a pontoon bridge, where the current was swift and the stream was of considerable width, required quick and skilful manipulation of the boats and the timbers and planks that went to make up the structure. Every boat and every plank was calculated to fit in a certain place. Anchoring the boats was attended with risk and difficulty. Yet so perfect was the system, and so thorough the drill of the pontooners, that an ordinary stream could be bridged in remarkably quick time. As fast as the boats were anchored, one after the other, and equidistant, the timbers were laid and the planks placed and fastened, so that as soon as the last boat was in line and made fast to the opposite shore, the bridge was completed by the placing of the timbers of its last span. Before the shore connection had been fairly planked, the soldiers were crossing.

Pickets were thrown out toward Todd's Tavern and the Wilderness as soon as we reached the south bank of the Rapidan. We knew that a battle was at hand, and although we were spoiling for a fight, some of us—two of us, anyway, for my tent-mate and I compared notes and found that we were a unit on the question—felt relieved when the advance guard of the infantry came tramping over the bridge. We suggested to each other that should Lee's army dash out of the woods that surrounded us, the Johnnies could make it hot for us with infantry, cavalry and artillery, before our foot soldiers could cross. But the rebels did not know the condition of things at the ford. We scouted out toward Todd's Tavern and connected with Wilson's cavalry pickets up toward Germania. Still the Johnnies kept shady.

In the reorganisation of the Army of the Potomac for the campaign of 1864, our regiment. Major Lucius M. Sargent commanding, was brigaded with the First New Jersey, Lieutenant-Colonel John W. Kester; the Sixth Ohio, Colonel William Steadman, and the First Pennsylvania, Colonel John P. Taylor. The brigade was commanded by Brigadier-General Henry E. Davies, Jr., formerly colonel of the Second New York, and was known as the first brigade, second division, cavalry corps. Two companies of our regiment, C and D, Captain Edward A. Flint commanding, were on duty as escort at Gen. Meade's headquarters.

The second division was commanded by Brigadier-General David McM. Gregg, a model cavalry officer. He won the star of a brigadier in 1862, and at Gettysburg he commanded the second cavalry division. At different times he was in command of the corps. In discipline he was strict, but he knew how to take care of his men. The second division always had rations for man and beast if they were to be had anywhere.

After the crossing of the Rapidan had been effected, Sheridan's cavalry thoroughly scouted the country to the front. The enemy kept well in the background, and when we bivouacked for the night Wednesday, May 4, we congratulated ourselves that we had slipped past Lee's right and would be able to head him off before he could withdraw from his lines at Orange Court House, and reach the fortifications in front of the rebel capital. Inside of twenty-four hours, however, we found that our congratulations were premature. Wednesday the Union cavalry scouted over the ground that on Thursday saw the bloodiest fighting. An old darky was interrogated by our cavalry near Todd's Tavern:

"Uncle, where are the rebels?"

"I 'clare, massa, dey don dusted 'way from heah when Massa Linkum's army cross de ribber up yondah."

"When did they leave here?"

"Fo sun up. One come ridin' 'long an' say, ' De Yanks's comin'.'"

"And then what?"

"Dey say, 'We better go'n tell Uncle Robert.'"

"Did they leave in a hurry?"

"I dunno what you all might call hurry, but 'pears as how dey wanted to see Massa Robert drefful bad."

We bivouacked on the road not far from Chancellorsville the night before the Battle of the Wilderness. The boys were in excellent spirits. Pickets were posted well out in front. Everybody was on duty. The Army of the Potomac slept that night with more than one eye open. There was something in the air that seemed to betoken a crisis. It was felt that the situation was extremely hazardous—for Lee, if not for us. But the boys would have their fun.

"I've about made up my mind to desert," said a lad who had been dubbed "Company I's titman" because of his diminutive size.

"Why so?"

"Because the quartermaster refuses to supply me with a stepladder."

"What do you want of a stepladder?"

"To climb on to my horse with. My legs are stiff after that soaking in the river, and when the command 'mount' is given I'm obliged to climb up the stirrup strap. If Taylor hadn't given me a boost the last time, I never could have got into the saddle."

There was a hearty laugh at the titman's complaint. It was, indeed, a serious matter for him to mount his horse without assistance. He was not over five feet tall, and his legs were shorter in proportion than his body. Getting into the saddle according to tactics was no easy thing for a short-legged man.

It was a physical impossibility for some of the boys to "prepare to mount" according to tactics, to say nothing about completing the movement. In active service the officers did not bother with a strict enforcement of the "times and motions." But in camp! There the stirrup climbers' lives were made miserable. It was not always safe for recruiting officers to assume that a boy's legs would lengthen out a foot or two pending the recruit's initiation into active service after enlistment. The necessity of a stepladder in some cases was more real than one would think at first blush.

At ten o'clock Wednesday night our pickets reported "all quiet" on our front. But it was the calm that preceded the storm. The general opinion among the rank and file was that Lee would hustle himself into his Richmond fortifications when he awoke to the fact that Grant was swinging the Army of the Potomac by the left flank in that direction.

But Lee was nearer at hand than we suspected!

CHAPTER 14

Battlefield Experiences

Thursday morning, May 5, 1864, found the First Massachusetts Cavalry well out on the left flank of the Union army. Grant had his troops well in hand, but the lay of the land was decidedly unfavourable to military movements. There was scarcely an open space in the Wilderness in which a single regiment could make a right wheel without breaking files to the rear to avoid obstacles in the shape of scrub-oak and other kinds of trees, with an abundance of underbrush, etc. Then the land was all cut up with gullies washed out by the rain. We had no suspicion that the rebels would attempt to bring on a general engagement in such a miserable place. If our wishes had been consulted the Battle of the Wilderness would have been postponed until we had reached the open country further toward the rebel capital. I have no doubt that surviving Confederates recall much that is unpleasant in connection with that terrible struggle. But the gray coats were responsible for it—they pitched into us before breakfast.

Bang!

A single shot down the turnpike that led to Todd's Tavern. The First New Jersey of our brigade was on picket out there.

We were a little off the road, dismounted, and cooking our coffee. Our horses were unbridled, with their nosebags on, eating their allowance of oats. Old soldiers will understand the situation exactly when I say that the water in our tin cups was just beginning to "simmer around the edge." Some of the boys had already put in the spoonful of ground coffee that constituted the ration, and were anxiously waiting for it to bubble up—the first authentic rumour of its boiling. Many a time the correctness of the saying that "a watched pot never boils" was demonstrated to the hungry soldiers.

Bang! bang! bang!

It was hard for the boys to believe that the first shot was not accidental, but when after an interval of a minute or two, three distinct reports were heard, we began to wish that we had boiled our coffee before reveille to make sure of it. Still we did not doubt the ability of the Jersey lads to take care of the picket line, but we were apprehensive that a staff officer or somebody in authority would get excited and order us into our saddles.

"She biles!" exclaimed my bunkey who was watching the two tin cups on our little fire while I was sprinkling salt and pepper into a mixture of soaked hard-tack and pork that was stewing away in my frying pan. When cooked, the amalgamation was sweetened to taste, if there was sugar in the haversack. If not, we took it without sugar. The dish was popular in the army. I never could understand why it was given the name it was known by, unless the soldier who christened it entertained well-grounded suspicions that the meat used had been cut from a canine instead of a porker.

Just as we were taking our breakfast off the fire the bugle sounded "to horse." And the call was emphasized by lively picket firing all along our front.

"You bridle both our horses, and I'll try and cool our coffee so we can drink it," said my partner.

But the order to mount came close on the heels of the first bugle call, and the effort to save the coffee resulted in the blistering of my bunkey's hands. It was impossible for him to get into the saddle with a cup of hot coffee in each hand. He was so much disgusted with the situation that he threw the coffee away, and was not thoughtful enough to hold on to the cups.

"By fours, forward, trot, march!" and we were heading for the picket line where the First Jersey was exchanging leaden compliments with the enemy. A staff officer came dashing in from the woods where the fighting had begun, and the command "gallop" was given after he had reached the head of our regiment.

In a few minutes we were at the front. The Jersey boys cheered as we came into line across the turnpike and deployed to the right and left. We cheered also, but I suppose it was because some one had suggested it. Our battalion had never been in a regular battle, and we concluded it was proper to do as the veterans did. Off at our right the rattle of musketry and the booming of cannon indicated that the battle had begun out that way also. The sharp crack of carbines told where Sheridan's troopers were holding forth. We felt that our turn had come to uphold the honour of the flag, and show the other regiments in our brigade that the Bay State boys could fight even if they were to be initiated in one of the bloodiest conflicts of the rebellion.

I believe our battalion went into and through the Battle of the Wilderness with less of concern in respect of personal safety than was felt by the veterans. The new men were not alive to the actual dangers of battle. Such things cannot be understood second hand. Old soldiers, familiar with the horrors of war, went in with their faces set as a flint toward the foe. But they knew what was coming; the recruits did not. And we had no time to speculate after we reached the skirmish line. We were kept so busy that we could scarcely take in the new features of the fight as they were brought out while the battle progressed.

Since the war I have heard old soldiers around the camp fires, tell how they lost all sense of fear after their first battle, and that the more engagements they participated in the less concern they had about it, until toward the end of the war they became so inured to the dreadful carnage on the battle field that they "had rather fight than eat." I never reached that experience. And I do not believe anybody else did.

Love of country, and a willingness to die in defence of the flag, were characteristics of the Yankee volunteers. A desire to kill somebody and be killed in return, for the mere love of killing, is another thing entirely. But if some of the comrades still insist that they got into that blood-hardened condition, I will have no quarrel with them.

This brings to mind a story about a Rensselaer county soldier who came home on furlough in 1862.

The warrior bold astonished the people of his native village by his blood-curdling accounts of the battles he had been in, and the scores of rebels he had slain. Every time he told his story he increased the number of his dead until his hearers began to question if there were enough rebels left to continue the war.

"I only came home to give the Johnnies a chance to recruit a few more regiments for me to exterminate," he said.

The volunteer's mother felt that her son had forgotten his early training, and she had within her a grieved spirit over her boy's apparent indifference to the Scriptural declaration that "All liars shall have their part in the lake which burneth with fire and brimstone: which is the second death." The mother requested the minister to labour with her soldier son, and see if something could not be done to reclaim him. The good pastor cheerfully complied, as reports of what his former Sunday-school scholar had been telling had already reached his ears. He cornered the boy in blue alone, and the following conversation was had:

"Dost thou still believe the teachings of thy youth, John? Wot ye not what the Scripture saith?"

"I do, Parson."

"And dost thou believe it is wicked to lie?"

"I do."

"Well, then, tell me honestly and truly, how many rebels have you killed?"

"Do you mean since I first enlisted, or during the last campaign?"

"I mean all—the blood of how many rebels is on your hands?"

"Now, Parson, do you want the truth?"

"Most assuredly—the truth, the whole truth, and nothing but the truth."

"Well, if I must tell it, Parson, I have killed just as many of them as they have of me—no more, no less; but don't give me away."

But to return to the Wilderness.

As our regiment came into line to support the Jersey boys, we found a high Virginia rail fence directly in our front. It was impossible to clear this obstruction mounted. The rebel fire was getting hotter, and the necessity of doing something in return was imperative. It was seen that unless we could get beyond the fence there was no chance to pay the enemy back in kind. Several of our comrades had fallen, and the command was passed along the line, "Prepare to fight on foot!" The regiment dismounted, and, passing through an opening in the fence, a line was formed to charge the rebels in our front.

A cavalryman is at great disadvantage when dismounted. He is handicapped with extra belts, boots and spurs, etc., and fighting on foot is not half as romantic as dashing upon the enemy mounted on a spirited charger. However, there was no time nor inclination for this line of reasoning.

When we came out of the tangled forest that skirted the fence on the opposite side from the place where we left our horses, we found ourselves in a ploughed field. We sank into the soft ground nearly to our knees as we charged. There was a log house on the brow of a little hill in the clearing. The Confederates were posted behind a fence a few rods beyond. We were exposed to a raking fire as we advanced. It seemed as if we would never get across. A man to my right got stuck in the mud and called for assistance. A corporal essayed to pull the comrade out. He succeeded, but the trooper's boots were left in the mud hole. Quite a number lost one boot and some both boots before they reached *terra firma*. But we came out in a zigzag sort of a line after a while. We were nearly exhausted.

There was a halt on the brow of the hill long enough to take observations of what was before us. Then we charged up to and over the fence from behind which the Johnnies skedaddled on the double quick. They rallied in the dense thicket, across a deep ravine, and returned our fire.

Orders came to "hold the line at all hazards," and we were directed to crawl back over the fence, and keep up a steady fire on the rebels. Then we began to realize that we were occupying a position it would be extremely difficult to hold should the enemy come in on our left flank. We had time to catch our breath while loading and firing from behind our rail-fence breastwork. We banged away whenever we saw a rebel in our front, and when we could not see their heads we fired into the bushes from whence came the bullets that were *ping-pinging* about our ears,

A battery over on a hill back of the line occupied by the rebels in our immediate front, soon began to feel for us, and they managed to drop shot and shell in the field behind us, and altogether too close for our comfort. Every now and then a shell would explode against our fence, shattering the rails and wounding the troopers who were in line with the course of the shell.

Soon after we took position along the line of the fence our ammunition began to run low. Each man had one hundred rounds extra in his saddle-bags, but our horses were somewhere in the woods back on the other side of the ploughed field.

"I'm loading with my last cartridge," exclaimed a trooper down toward the left.

"Keep still, you jackass," interrupted a sergeant. "Do you want to tell the rebels about it?"

"No; but we'll be in a nice fix if the Johnnies come at us again."

Several of the boys volunteered to go back to the horses and bring up a supply of ammunition. They started on a run, across the open space. Two or three reached the log house, and halted behind it, for the rebels opened such a hot fire that it would have been almost certain death for the boys to venture from behind the house. Others returned to the shelter of the fence. A man named Wilson was wounded near me, and up on the right the volunteers fared worse.

"If the Johnnies want me they'll have to come over here and take me," said a young trooper who was reserving his last round for the rebel assault which we expected would not be long deferred.

"I don't believe I could run through that mud hole again if every rebel in Lee's army was at my heels," said another.

"Look over there—they're flanking us!"

Sure enough. About three hundred yards to our left we saw rebel cavalry moving across the low ground in the direction of the woods where we had dismounted and left our horses.

To attract our attention from their flank movement the Confederates in our front kept firing away, and the battery sent over shot and shell. It was a very interesting situation. A good many felt that our first battle would end in our capture unless something in our favour turned up without delay. "I wish they'd give the command 'prepare to mount,'" said a sergeant.

"How could you 'prepare to mount' without your horse?" asked a lieutenant.

"I'd get where my horse was. Don't you see, such a command wouldn't be an order to retreat—it might amount to the same thing, but it would take the curse off."

But the command to fall back soon came. The rebels were getting well around to our rear, and our position was untenable. The boys went back over that ploughed field, every man for himself, a regular go-as-you-please. I noticed that the troopers who had expressed doubts of their ability to go through the mud again were well in advance as we fell back. As we retreated from the fence the rebels closed up on the other side of it, and our flight was stimulated by the bullets they sent after us. I fired my last round of ammunition as I reached the brow of the hill near the log house. Then I buckled down to business, and wallowed through the ploughed field to the woods in the rear.

We scattered as we fled, but all felt the importance of reaching our horses before they should be captured by the rebels on our flank. We came to the fence where we had dismounted, only to find a sergeant and two men of our regiment, who had been left to pilot us to the spot where the animals had been taken for safety. The rebel battery had shelled the woods, compelling the men in charge of the horses to fall back up the turnpike out of range. We were well-nigh winded from our race across the field, but we knew we must go on or be captured.

We went on.

CHAPTER 15

Sheridan at the Head of the Cavalry

Phil Sheridan never led his men into a ticklish place and left them to get out by themselves. He never sent his soldiers on a dangerous expedition without arranging to have assistance at hand if there was a suspicion that help would be needed. And he never asked his men to go where he was not willing to go himself. I wish I had known all this on the morning of Thursday, May 5, 1864. It would have saved me from a great deal of worry about the fate of the cavalry corps in the Wilderness, and also from no little anxiety as to what was to become of the youngest trooper in Company I, First Massachusetts cavalry. But Sheridan was new to the Army of the Potomac. He came East with Grant. The old soldiers in our brigade had' done considerable kicking because a number of cavalry generals who had raided around in Virginia, had been jumped by Sheridan.

General Grant in his *Memoirs*, says, referring to his assuming command of the Army of the Potomac:

"In one of my early interviews with the president, I expressed my dissatisfaction with the little that had been accomplished by the cavalry so far in the war, and the belief that it was capable of accomplishing much more than it had done if under a thorough leader. I said I wanted the very best man in the army for that command. Halleck was present, and spoke up, saying, 'How would Sheridan do?' I replied, 'The very man I want.' The president said I could have anybody I wanted. Sheridan was telegraphed for that day, and on his arrival was assigned to the cavalry corps of the Army of the Potomac."

Grant was right—he was always right—and Little Phil not only proved a thorough leader of the cavalry corps, but he demonstrated his ability to command an army in one of the most successful campaigns of the war.

"Where are our bosses?" demanded a Berkshire boy, who was one of the first to come up with the sergeant and two men left to guide us to the reserve, as stated in the last chapter.

"In the woods back up the turnpike about a mile."

"This is a nice way to treat American soldiers!" exclaimed a corporal, who had left both his boots in the mud in the ploughed field. "I can't run through blackberry brush barefooted!"

"I'm going to camp here till they bring back my horse and something to eat. I didn't enlist to caper around on foot in such a place as this," said another.

I volunteered to take the sergeant's steed and go and see that the horses were sent to meet us, but at that moment there was heard the noise of the rebel cavalry coming in on our flank crashing through the bushes.

"You couldn't manage my horse—he's so fiery," said the sergeant. "I can't hold him when he takes it into his head to go where the other horses are."

Away went the sergeant and the two men who had been left with him, on a gallop up the road.

"Follow me!" shouted the sergeant, as he put spurs to his charger.

We followed.

As the sergeant and his two companions turned a bend in the road, rebel cavalrymen, who had penetrated the jungle almost to the turnpike, opened fire on the three troopers. It was a race for life. The bullets whistled close to the ears of the Federals as they dashed by the Johnnies in ambush. Then the saddle girth of one of the privates gave way, and the terrified trooper was left sitting on his saddle in the middle of the road, his horse going on with the procession. He shouted, "Whoa!" The "rebel yell" went up as the Yankee went down. It stimulated him to the greatest effort of his life. Springing to his feet he held the saddle between his head and the Confederates to shield off their bullets, and darted into the bushes to the left of the turnpike. As he reached the thicket he threw the saddle back into the road and shouted defiantly at his would-be executioners:

"Take the old saddle, you infernal asses. I've got no use for it without a horse!"

Then he bounded away through the forest, keeping well to the left of the road. He was a pitiable sight when he rejoined the company that night. His clothes were literally torn off. He would not have been presentable at all if an artilleryman had not given him a spare shirt.

It may be stated that several others reported to their company commander in about the same fix.

Some of us had taken such a deep interest in what was going on up the turnpike, that we almost forgot the rebels who were looking for us. I remember that I laughed, tired and concerned for my own safety though I was. The ludicrous figure cut by our comrade as he glanced around him when he landed in the road and yelled "Whoa!"—as if a runaway horse would stop under such circumstances—was too much for my risibility. But I did not have my laugh out. It was interrupted by one of our sergeants shouting:

"Streak it, boys—here they come!"

We made nearly as good time in getting away from that place as the mounted troopers had scored, and for the same reason. The butternut-clad cavalrymen fired their carbines almost in our faces at the first round. We needed no further notice to take to the woods. It was entirely unnecessary for "our six-footer corporal" to urge us to "remember Lot's wife," as he led the retreat over the brow of the hill and bounded down the slope out of range.

As I halted after crossing the divide to catch my breath, a terrible racket broke out in the woods to the right. As near as I could judge, not having paid much attention to the points of the compass, there was trouble somewhere in the vicinity of the turnpike where we had parted with the Confederates. There was no mistaking the sounds. There was fighting out there in the woods, and the cheering of Federal cavalrymen was heard above the yell of our late pursuers.

"We're licking 'em out o' their boots!" said my bunkey, who had kept neck and neck with me through the woods.

"That's what we're doing."

"I'd go back and take a hand if I had a horse."

"So would I."

Several of our boys ventured to the top of the hill, and then along the ridge toward the turnpike. They soon came to a rail fence, and on the other side of it was a squadron of Federal cavalry drawn up in line.

It did not take us long to introduce ourselves. We ascertained from the troopers who belonged to the Tenth New York that our regiment was on the other side of the road about a quarter of a mile north. By this time the firing on our front had dwindled down to irregular skirmishing.

As we were getting over the fence to go in the direction pointed out, Sheridan rode up. He came from the front, and was greeted with a hearty cheer that was echoed by cavalry posted away to the left, and also by those of us who had breath enough left to shout. "Little Phil" waved his hat, which he was holding in his hand.

"Our line is all right, boys," and he galloped up the turnpike to report to Grant, who was at Meade's headquarters.

Sheridan had inflicted severe punishment on the rebel cavalry that had come in on our flank. He was informed of the condition of affairs at the front, and at the time our battalion was ordered to fall back, a line had been formed further up the turnpike ready to receive the rebels. The road was left clear, and as Hampton's "critter companies" followed the dismounted Union troopers, they fell into the trap. Then they went back faster than they had come. Sheridan's troopers charged, and the chagrined gray-coats were driven way beyond the ravine where our battalion had held the line of the rail fence before our ammunition failed.

As the memory of that day's events comes to me now, there is a sprinkling of regret that I was forced to "streak it" through the Wilderness. It completely destroyed my confidence in the ability of our regiment to put down the rebellion single-handed at one fell swoop. And, moreover, a good many of us were almost naked when we reached the horses after our run through the forest. Yet it was necessary that sacrifices should be made. Sheridan was fishing with live bait, and it was part of the programme that the bait should be kept moving.

When I reached my company, which was waiting orders near the turnpike leading to Todd's Tavern, I was informed that my horse had been killed by a shell while the animals were being led to the rear. I felt the loss of my horse keenly. And then my saddle-bags were gone, with the picture of my best girl and other memories of home.

Orders came for the regiment to move a little further to the left. An infantry brigade was forming on our right. There had been serious business on the other side of a strip of woods to the right of the line occupied by the cavalry. Wounded men were carried to the rear on stretchers. Several army surgeons had ventured to establish a field hospital well up to the front line. The Johnnies may have had a hankering for the medical stores in the hospital chests that were unpacked so temptingly near the enemy, for they made a dash for the wagons. But this time the Confederates made a mistake. The infantry holding the line in front of the "doctors' den" peppered the gray-coats until the would-be consumers of United States *spiritus fermenti* were glad to

Taking possession of the runaway.

turn and get back out of range as fast as their legs could carry them.

The narrow escape of the medical men showed that they had spread out their operating instruments too near the enemy, and the base of operations was removed over a hill to the rear. There was a stampede when the rebels charged to break the line in front of the field hospital, and a horse belonging to one of the surgeons dashed down the turnpike. The infantrymen made no effort to stop the animal—the average foot soldier was afraid of a horse—and it occurred to me that the horse was just about what I needed to complete my outfit. My heart beat a double tattoo as I attempted to spread myself across the road to intercept the runaway. He came on at full speed, but as he shied toward the fence to pass by me, I was fortunate enough to catch the bridle rein, and that horse was mine—till further orders.

I examined the saddle girths and found everything in good shape. After I had taken up the stirrup straps—the doctor's legs were considerably longer than mine —I mounted the prize, and once more felt there was a possibility that the Southern Confederacy might be conquered! Then I took an inventory of the contents of the doctor's saddle-bags. There was a bottle of hospital brandy in one of the bags. It was the "genuine stuff," as Sergeant Warren remarked that night when I allowed him to sample it. I investigated further and found a field glass, several boxes of pills, a few rolls of bandages and lint, with a small case of instruments. There were two six-shooters in the holsters on the pommel of the saddle, and a surgeon's regulation sword fastened on the left side. A canteen, and a haversack containing a couple of ham sandwiches, a piece of cheese and a can of condensed milk were included in the outfit. I whistled dinner call at once, and made an excellent meal on what the medical man had provided for his supper. Then I rejoined my company.

The Wilderness was full of terror when night came on and spread its mantle of darkness over the scenes of bloodshed. On every hand could be heard the groans of the wounded and dying. The gathering of the unfortunates went on all night, and the poor fellows were borne to the field hospitals. There was heavy firing at intervals. Here and there the bivouac fires lighted up the otherwise Egyptian darkness and served to make the shadows all the darker, and to give the surroundings a weird and dismal aspect. It seemed as if daylight would never return. When it did break we hailed it joyfully, although we knew that the light of the newborn day would witness a renewal of the conflict.

We did not unsaddle our horses that night, but along about midnight we were given an opportunity to feed our chargers and make coffee for ourselves. Preceding the feed the company rolls were called by the first sergeants. In Company I not more than fifty *per cent*, of the number on the roll responded—I mean of the number that had charged down the turnpike Thursday morning. A majority of the boys who failed to show up at the first roll-call in the Wilderness put in an appearance later on.

It was the same with other regiments. In a battle like that of the Wilderness there was a good deal of the go-as-you-please, especially if there were charges and retreats and frequent changes in formations. Details would be made from companies for skirmishes and other duties, and the men so detailed when they returned were unable to find their companies, their regiments having been transferred to another part of the field. I recall an incident of the Battle of the Wilderness that was the cause of a whole town going into mourning:

Company B of the One hundred and twenty-fifth New York Volunteers contained many Berlin boys. In one of the movements in the Wilderness that regiment marched past the First Massachusetts. I was on the watch for Company B. I think it was after the second day's battle. The One hundred and twenty-fifth had been fighting furiously somewhere near the Brock road, and the slaughter had been great. The ranks of the regiment were depleted, and when I spotted the Berlin boys I saw that B Company had suffered badly. There were only two or three faces that I recognised. Rube Fry was one, I think.

"Halloo, Company B!"

"Halloo!—there's Alex Allen's boy."

"Where's the rest of the company—the Berlin boys?"

"All killed but six."

"It will be sad news for Berlin."

"Yes; and it will be a wonder if any of us escape if we don't get out of the Wilderness pretty soon."

"It will indeed."

"Goodbye."

"Goodbye, Rube. I'll write home if I get a chance."

I got the chance the day that we started on Sheridan's raid—May 8. I wrote the news just as I had received it. There was mourning all over the town when that letter reached Berlin. The news from the front was contradicted, however, soon after by letters from several of the boys who had been included in the list of casualties I had sent home.

It seems that a part of the One hundred and twenty-fifth was sent on picket duty to the left, and a charge had been made by the men not included in the detail. Lieut.-Colonel A. B. Myer and thirty-four men out of one hundred and four who made the charge were killed. Somehow the report had been started that all the rest of the regiment had been killed or wounded or taken prisoners. I was rejoiced to learn when I next met the One hundred and twenty-fifth, after Sheridan's raid, that the report of the casualties in Company B sent home in my letter after the Battle of the Wilderness was exaggerated.

I find in the roster of B Company as given in the history of the One hundred and twenty-fifth New York Volunteers by Chaplain Ezra D. Simons of that regiment, that none of B Company was killed in the Wilderness, and only five were wounded.

But B Company did not escape so luckily in the battle of Spotsylvania, following close on the heels of the Wilderness. Several were killed outright and a number wounded. The company lost twenty-four men, killed and died, during its service—a number far above the average of companies throughout the army. The One hundred and twenty-fifth made a splendid record. I was always glad to run across the regiment at the front, and to compare notes with the Berlin boys in Company B.

Chapter 16

The Second Day in the Wilderness

At daybreak we expected to renew the Battle of the Wilderness—if the rebels did not pitch into us again during the night. The enlisted men of our company held a council of war before any of them availed themselves of the privilege of turning in for a snooze.

"I wonder if the Johnnies will skedaddle before morning?" said one of the boys who had been back at Ely's ford and had not participated in the first day's fight. "You had better take a sleep. We'll call you if the enemy shows up before reveille."

"All right, here goes. I can sleep one night more with a clear conscience, for my hands have not been stained with the blood of a single enemy."

Of course, these remarks were made jokingly. No matter how serious the situation might be, there was always a disposition among the soldiers to make light of it. After the "re-enforcement" had retired the council was continued.

"I don't think it's fair to ask the cavalry to fight on foot as we did yesterday."

"But what else could we do when we come to that high fence?"

"We might have stopped and waited for the Johnnies to charge us."

"Well, I guess Phil Sheridan knows how to fight his men better'n we know ourselves."

"We'll have another fight in the morning."

"Certainly."

"And there'll be more of us killed and wounded."

"Yes."

"I wonder whether we're whipped, or the rebels have got the worst of it?

"Can't tell till daylight, we're all mixed up so."

"But Grant must know."

"That's so—but where's Grant?"

"He's with Meade back near that old quartz mill where we had dinner the day we crossed the Rapidan."

"The lieutenant told me that Grant's orders are for our side to make an attack at three o'clock."

"Then we're not whipped."

"Not if we've got orders to open the ball in the morning. Let's get what rest we can."

"All right."

About three o'clock Friday morning—we were taking turns in sleeping—I called upon my bunkey to "get out of bed and let me get in."

"I haven't been asleep yet."

"That's your own fault; you've had time enough."

"I was just getting good and sleepy—but I'm not piggish. Take the bed."

I stretched myself on the piece of tent, and tried to go to sleep. But it was no easy thing to settle down. The events of the day—the attack on our picket line, charging down the turnpike, exciting experiences at the rail fence, fighting on foot, charging across the ploughed field, holding the enemy in check, falling back when flanked by the rebels, Sheridan's punishment of our pursuers—all crowded themselves to the front, and it seemed a year since we broke camp at Warrenton. I had never been in a pitched battle before, and I tried to remember the events in their order that I might be able to write them down as a basis tor a letter to friends at home. The more I tried to straighten things out the more I got mixed. I dropped to sleep, but just as I was describing the battle to a group of villagers at Berlin, I was brought suddenly back to the front by a sergeant who was poking me with his sabre scabbard.

"Private Allen, turn out for picket."

"But I've only just turned in. There's my bunkey; can't you take him? he's already turned out after a good long nap"—

"No back talk, out with you!"

I was on my feet as soon as I awoke sufficiently to realize the situation.

"Mount your horse, and report to Sergeant Murphy out there in the road. Is your cartridge box full?"

"Yes, sir."

"Hundred rounds extra in your saddle-bags?"

"Yes, sir."

"Mount at will, and go ahead."

Sergeant Murphy took charge of a detail from several companies. We rode down the road a few rods, and a staff officer then assumed command of the detachment.

"We're to go out beyond the picket line and watch the movements of the rebels at daybreak," the lieutenant informed Sergeant Murphy.

In fifteen minutes we were at the last picket post out toward Todd's Tavern.

"Detail a man to ride ahead, sergeant," the officer directed.

I had ridden close up to the officer to hear all I could about the prospects of a fight, and the sergeant detailed me.

"The object of keeping a man well to the front," the officer said to the sergeant, "is to draw the enemy's fire should we run into the rebel pickets, and thus prevent the detachment from falling into an ambush."

"Very proper, sir," assented the sergeant.

"You will ride down the road, keeping a hundred yards or so from the head of the column," the lieutenant said to me. "Load your carbine and keep it ready for use, but don't fire unless the enemy opens on you, for it is desired to secure a favourable position for watching the movements of the rebels as soon as it is light enough."

It was quite dark down there in the woods. I did not take kindly to the thought that I was to be used as a target for the rebel pickets. This riding to the front to draw the enemy's fire was a new experience to me. But I tried to comfort myself with the hope that we were so far out on the left that we would not encounter the Confederates.

The advance business was as new to the doctor's horse as it was to me. I had to use my spurs freely to induce him to go down the road ahead of the other horses. We got started after awhile, and the still hunt for Lee's right and rear was begun.

It was lonesome work for man and beast. Suddenly, and without any intimation of what he intended to do the horse began to neigh. It may have been in the animal's "ordinary tone of voice," but to me it seemed to be loud enough to be heard way back to the Rapidan. I expected the Johnnies would open fire at once. The staff officer rode up to me—after waiting long enough for me to draw the enemy's fire if they were close at hand—and said:

Detailed to draw the enemy's fire

"What's the matter?"

"Horse 'whickered,' sir."

"What made him?"

"Can't tell, sir; he broke out without any notice."

"Ever do it before?"

"Don't know. I only got him yesterday afternoon. He belonged to an infantry doctor who was shot."

"That accounts for it; a doughboy horse don't know anything about this kind of work! Take your place at the rear of the detachment, and if that horse neighs again, break his head with your carbine."

"All right, sir."

Another man was sent to the front, and we moved on. We did not run into the rebel pickets, and the officer said we must be further to the left than the right of Lee's line. We halted on the top of a hill where the road turned westward and waited for daylight.

As soon as it became light enough for the officer to take observations with his field-glass, he rode to the highest point he could find and surveyed the broken country in our front. He could not see far in any direction, as the woods were thick and there was little cleared land.

"Come here, Sergeant," the lieutenant called to Murphy, after looking off to the west for a few seconds through his glass. "Look over there."

"Rebels, sir," said the sergeant.

"Yes; cavalry moving over this way. We will return at once."

We went back up the turnpike at a gallop.

"What's up?" inquired the officer in charge of the outposts when we reached our pickets.

"The rebels are up and moving around to get on our left flank. Keep a good lookout and be ready to move at once. I will report to General Sheridan, and there will soon be lively work."

Sheridan's cavalry was in the saddle and *en route* to Todd's Tavern within twenty minutes after our return from the reconnaissance in that direction. The cavalry was to connect with the left of the infantry commanded by General Hancock. The staff officer's prediction that there would be lively work on our left was fulfilled. Sheridan was in time to intercept Stuart's advance along the Furnace road, a few miles northwest of Todd's Tavern. It was hot work.

There was desperate fighting as the troopers came together at the intersection of the Brock and the Furnace roads. Jeb Stuart's attempt to get around in our rear to make a dash on the wagon trains of the Army of the Potomac, and to smash things generally, was a complete failure. He was driven back from the Furnace road, and after a stubborn stand at Todd's Tavern the rebel cavalry leader was forced to call off his troops and fall back from Sheridan's immediate front.

In the afternoon, having been re-enforced, and after being ordered by Lee to turn Grant's left, Stuart again attacked the Federal troopers. He was assisted by infantry, but Little Phil refused to budge an inch from the position held at Todd's Tavern. The rebels were driven back with heavy loss. In the meantime the entire army was engaged, and the fighting was continued all day.

A rebel trooper of Fitzhugh Lee's division, taken prisoner the evening of May 6, inquired:

"Who's you all fightin' under this time?"

"Grant."

"I reckoned so; but who's overseer of the critter companies?"

"Sheridan."

"He's a doggoned good 'un. Fitz Lee knew what he was talkin' 'bout when he told Wade Hampton that we all would be 'bliged to take care of our own flanks this trip."

"You're right, Johnny."

"Be you all headed for Richmond, sure 'nough?"

"That's where we're going."

"But what be you all to do with me?"

"We'll send you North, and let you live on the fat of the land till we gobble up the rest of the rebel army."

"Stranger, do you mean it?"

"Certainly."

"Hallelujah! I'm ready to be fatted. Where's you all's commissary department?"

He was sent to the rear with the other prisoners.

At the close of the second day's battle in the Wilderness, the report was current among the troopers of Sheridan's cavalry corps, that the Army of the Potomac would retire from the front of Lee's army in that Virginia jungle and fall back to Fredericksburg, which would be occupied as a new base of supplies pending the reorganisation of the army to again move "On to Richmond!"

There is no denying the fact that the Army of the Potomac was seriously crippled. An order to fall back to the north bank of the Rapidan would have been accepted as a matter of course had the new commander directed such a movement. But if some of the soldiers had known Grant better, they would have spent less time that night in speculating whether the line of retreat would be by the Germania plank road or over the route to Ely's ford.

It turned out that Grant did not discover that the "Yankees were whipped in the Wilderness" until he read an account of the "rout of the Federal army" in a Richmond paper at Spotsylvania a few days later. Of course, it was then too late for the Union commander to use the information to any advantage. It may be remarked also, that Lee had not heard of Grant's defeat until he received the news *via* the rebel capital.

There was a disposition on the part of a few brigades on the Union right to get back across the Rapidan without waiting for orders Friday night. General Gordon of Georgia made a desperate effort to demoralize the Federals by charging Grant's right, coming in on the flank. He gobbled up a brigade or two, and sent a good many blue-coats flying back toward the river. But the fugitives could not find their way out of the Wilderness, and they halted before going far. for fear they would get turned around and run into the enemy. The gallant Sedgwick again demonstrated his fighting qualities. He did not intend that the colours of the sixth corps—the banner with the Greek cross—should go down. Sedgwick brought order out of chaos. He drove back the Confederates and saved the day—or the night, as Gordon's charge was made after darkness had set in.

Every hour or so during the night, the Johnnies would give us the rebel yell. These outbreaks occasioned alarm on our side at first, but after the terrible din had died out several times without the appearance of the boys in butternut, we concluded that the enemy was shouting to keep up courage for a general attack in the morning.

We had no opportunity to sleep—I mean to go into camp and stretch our weary bodies at full length on the ground for a season. About the time we would begin to congratulate ourselves on the prospects of a nap we would be ordered into the saddle, ready to repel an attack. There were any number of false alarms. Old soldiers will remember how exasperating it was to be hustled out at the dead of night, marched here and there—"up and down and through the middle"—only to find that somebody had made a bull. We marched several times during the night, sometimes going a hundred yards. When daylight came Saturday morning we found ourselves within three hundred yards of the spot where we bivouacked Friday night.

We had been moved around like men on a checker-board—one man trying to catch another in the double corner, so to speak; "hawing and geeing," as a Berkshire boy expressed it.

The Battle of the Wilderness ended Friday night, from an infantry standpoint, but Sheridan's cavalry had fighting enough Saturday to prevent them from getting rusty. We were given to understand early in the morning that the army was to go on. While the infantry were cutting the pegs out of their shoes, and burying the dead Saturday, the troopers were feeling the enemy over on the left toward Spotsylvania. There was a good deal of trouble in locating Lee's line of battle. The rebels had not felt safe outside their breastworks after Gordon had failed to double up our right. When they were found by our pickets Saturday morning, they seemed to have lost their thirst for Yankee blood so far as coming outside to rebuke our curiosity was concerned. A reconnaissance by General Warren of the Fifth Corps occasioned a suspicion that the infantry were at it again, as the firing was lively in Warren's front for a few minutes. Lee did not accept the challenge, and no general engagement was brought on.

There was a sharp set-to between Stuart's cavalry and the first brigade of the first division of Sheridan's corps, commanded by General G A. Custer, early Saturday morning. The rebels found Custer an ugly customer. They skedaddled to Todd's Tavern, after vainly trying to check the advance of the boys in blue.

General Custer was an ideal cavalry officer. He was something like six feet in height, and sat his horse perfectly. He was one of the youngest generals in the army, having won the star of a brigadier before he was twenty-four years old. His pleasant blue eye seemed to fire up with the first intimation of battle. His appearance was all the more striking because of his long wavy hair and his dashing make-up, which included a large red necktie. His brigade adopted the red tie as a part of their uniform, and Custer's troops could be distinguished at long range. It was a common saying in the cavalry corps that the rebels preferred to have nothing to do with Custer's brigade except at "long range," and therein the Confederates exhibited excellent judgment.

Custer was a favourite in the regular army after the war, and his death—in the Custer massacre in 1876—was mourned by soldiers and civilians throughout the United States.[1]

---

1. *My Life on the Plains or Personal Experiences With Indians* by George A. Custer is also published by Leonaur.

CHAPTER 17

The Baptism of Fire

To the third battalion of the First Massachusetts Cavalry the Battle of the Wilderness was the most interesting and exciting event of the war. The battalion was hustled around so lively from the time the first shot was fired in our front till the battle was over, that there was little chance for the troopers to take an inventory of themselves and their belongings. As I recall the scenes and try to pass them in review with a simple allusion to the most prominent features, it is difficult to reconcile the facts or to believe that so much could have taken place in so short a time. Yet the facts will not give way, although the events of a lifetime, as memory brings them forward, seem to have been crowded into that first day's battle, to say nothing about what took place the next day and the succeeding days of the spring campaign.

I have read accounts of the Battle of the Wilderness—and of many other leading engagements of the rebellion—in which the writers described with minuteness, and in the most graphic manner, all that was done on different parts of the field from the opening to the end of the conflict. Such description is always interesting, but when a writer requests his readers to accept the statement that he was an eyewitness to all that happened in the Wilderness or in any other large battle, the reader is justified in calling a halt. Of course, after the battle was over and corps, division, brigade and regimental commanders had submitted detailed reports, accompanied by maps, etc., giving full information of the movements of troops, a pretty accurate account of the battle as a whole could be made up.

Gen. Grant was at Meade's headquarters, one of the best points of observation on the whole field, during a good share of the time while the Battle of the Wilderness was going on, and even from that spot the general commanding could not see any of the troops in the main line of battle without going forward into the woods.

It cannot be expected, then, that a young recruit, whose personal safety was a matter of no little concern, could have had better opportunities for observation in the Battle of the Wilderness than were obtained by the Union commander. However, it was not necessary to go away from that portion of the line held by Sheridan's cavalry to gather material enough for a volume. I took in more than enough, personally, with my limited means of observation, to fill ten times the space allotted to *Down in Dixie*.

In that almost impenetrable forest it was next to impossible for one regiment to know what was going on among neighbours to the right or the left. It was a sort of touch-elbow relation that organisations had with each other. The man on the right of each regiment was supposed to keep close in to the right within a few feet at least of the man on the left of the regiment to the right, to prevent the enemy from stealing through gaps in the line and getting into our rear. This arrangement was absolutely necessary to maintain anything like a solid front.

At times when the firing was exceedingly brisk, and there were charges and counter-charges at any point, the troops so engaged could form no sort of an idea which side was getting the better of it on other parts of the battlefield. The noise of battle close at hand drowned the roar of cannon and the rattle of musketry comparatively only a short distance away. When there was a lull in the fight anywhere, soldiers who were not actively engaged for the time being could "read the sounds," if the expression will pass muster, and thus obtain a tolerably fair understanding of the condition of affairs on their right and left.

The irregular scattering discharge of rifles indicated that the skirmishers were exchanging shots. The continuous roll of musketry developing into an almost deafening roar, above which could be heard now and then the hearty cheers of the boys in blue or the rebel yell of the butternut-clad warriors, gave warning that the battle was on in earnest. When the rapid firing of artillery added to the fearful din, until an indescribable roar went up from the terrible cyclone of death, it was known that a charge had been ordered, and that desperate effort was being made for the mastery. It did not require much stretching of the imagination to hear the crash at a distance when the opposing lines came into collision. It was a moment of the greatest suspense while listening with every nerve strained to catch the sound of victory.

If there ever was a time when the North American soldiers—Federal and Confederate—pricked up their ears and listened for news from the fight, it was when a charge had been made and they were waiting the announcement of the result. At such times the cheer of the soldiers was set on a hair trigger. The participants in the hand-to-hand struggle—the victorious participants—would shout themselves hoarse as the enemy was hurled back and the banners of the conquerors were planted on the captured lines. And the cheer was contagious. It would be taken up by the comrades on the right and left, and along the line it would go until the inspiration would be felt among all the troops. Soldiers who were desperately wounded and even while undergoing operations in the hands of the surgeons, were known to join in the glad acclaim when the echo of the hurrahs reached the field hospitals.

But it made all the difference in the world to the soldiers holding the line to the right or to the left of the strategic point which side whipped. If our boys took up the shout and passed it along the line it meant that the advantage had been gained by the Union forces. And in such cases the glad tidings proved an incentive to the troops in reserve to pitch into the rebels in their front and serve them as their comrades had already been served by the Federals. On the other hand, when the result of the conflict was made known to the Yankees by way of the rebel line in our front, it was naturally expected that the Johnnies would pitch into us, and we governed ourselves accordingly.

Survivors of the Battle of the Wilderness will bear testimony that they never took part in a fight that was more stubbornly waged on both sides. Veterans of the Army of the Potomac who had faced death on the Peninsula, at Fredericksburg, Antietam and Gettysburg, and had become familiar with all the horrors of war, declared that the two days' hand-to-hand conflict in the Wilderness witnessed scenes of carnage the like of which had not been known in all the history of the rebellion up to that time.

The awful screeching of shot and shell, the *ping-pinging* of the missiles of death from tens of thousands of muskets, the groans of the wounded, the cheers of victory as the blue or the gray gained a temporary advantage, the yells of defiance as either line was pressed back from positions captured at the expense of hundreds of lives, the heartrending cries for water by wounded and dying—all these are recalled at the present writing.

The agonising shrieks of the helpless men who perished in the flames in that wilderness of woe, are not forgotten. They never will

In the Wilderness.

be forgotten this side of eternity. Hundreds of the wounded were burned to death, the underbrush and trees taking fire during the battle. Soldiers temporarily crippled by shot and shell, bayonet thrust and sabre-stroke—many of whom would have recovered under the ordinary circumstances of war—were swallowed up by that wave of fire that swept a portion of the battlefield and drove back the Federals where Lee's veterans had vainly sought to break the Union line. Heroic efforts were made to carry off the wounded, but the flames spread so rapidly that it was impossible to reach only those who were at a considerable distance from the point where the fire started. In some instances the clothes of men who plunged into the burning forest and attempted to save their wounded comrades were burned from their bodies, and many lost their lives while endeavouring to rescue their disabled companions. At one point on the line Union and Confederate dead and wounded were cremated together.

The wisdom of the thorough organisation of the cavalry corps, and the assignment of Phil Sheridan to its command, was fully demonstrated on the very first occasion that the Federal troopers came in contact with the enemy's cavalry. Grant was always the right man in the right place, and he possessed, most fortunately, the faculty of discovering who among his subordinates were best fitted to command at critical periods. Wade Hampton's "critter companies," as the Confederate cavalry was designated by the butternut-clad foot-soldiers, had played havoc with the flanks of the Army of the Potomac in other campaigns. And here they were, ready to cut all around Grant's flanks and put to flight any blue-coated troopers that might come in their way. But Hampton and his followers had substantial reason for changing their estimate of the cavalry of the Army of the Potomac, dating from the first skirmish in the Wilderness.

There is no question that Sheridan was the best cavalry general of modern times—of all time, for that matter. And as a commander of separate armies he was equal to every emergency, displaying superior generalship.

Gallant Little Phil is out of the Wilderness. The war is over. He has gone home. Survivors of the cavalry corps of the Army of the Potomac had waited with sad hearts for the news that all felt was sure to come from the little cottage at Nonquitt—waited as they had done through those anxious days in July, 1885, when the hero of Appomattox lay dying in a quiet cottage on the summit of Mount MacGregor.

If Phil Sheridan had never achieved glorious victories on his own hook; had he fought all his battles as a subordinate under the immediate direction of the commander-in-chief; had he never attained to high rank as a partial reward for gallant and meritorious services—the fact that Grant loved him would have been sufficient to endear the cavalry commander to the comrades who followed his lead from the Wilderness to Appomattox. But the troops loved Sheridan for himself. They fairly idolized him. They had the most implicit faith in him as a commander. His presence inspired them to deeds of daring; they were ready to go anywhere—into the jaws of death—if he but said the word.

Little Phil's last battle was fought on ground that could not be reconnoitred by his troopers. Many of them, however, preceded him down into the Wilderness of Death. They came not back to report. Others waited for the "news from the front," knowing that as long as there was a fighting chance the brave comrade would fight on. It was a struggle for life—a struggle in which the odds were too heavy. When the time came to "enter the Wilderness" Sheridan met death calmly. There was no flinching. He had never disobeyed orders. He was always ready to respond to calls from higher authority. The call came; and Sheridan was mustered out.

When the life spark was extinguished—at ten-fifteen o'clock Sunday night, Augusts, 1888—a noble soldier stood on the shores of eternity. His body has been consigned to the tomb, but his name is inscribed on the pages of his country's history beside the names of Lincoln and Grant. His name and fame will always be cherished by patriots. Old soldiers who battled under Sheridan have told the story of his grand achievements to children and grandchildren. Sheridan's ride is one of the landmarks, so to speak, of the handed-down history of the great Civil War. As the old troopers' fathers and grandfathers handed down to them the story of Bunker Hill, of Yorktown and of other revolutionary conflicts, so have the gray-haired veterans of Sheridan's cavalry corps told of Todd's Tavern, the Wilderness, Sheridan's raid. Yellow Tavern and other battles in which Little Phil led them to victory. In song and story his deeds are commemorated all over the land.

CHAPTER 18

Sheridan Ordered to Cut Loose

Saturday, May 7, Sheridan fought the rebels at Todd's Tavern again. And it was no inconsiderable affair. There was the liveliest kind of fighting for a time. Grant did not intend to go into camp in the Wilderness, even if Lee was willing to let the Union army alone pending repairs to the rebel cause. Not a bit of it. The Federal commander's determination was to go "on to Richmond," and if Lee chose to get in the way, that was the Confederate general's lookout. It was to open the road for the advance of the infantry that Sheridan was directed to feel around the enemy's right and get the lay of the land out toward Spotsylvania.

It was delicate work. The Johnnies were ugly. Although Lee had called off his forces and retired behind his breastworks in the Wilderness, the rebels gave us warning every time we dashed across the little open spaces bordering the Brock road, that their cartridge boxes had been replenished and were full. But Sheridan hustled the enemy back from Todd's Tavern. Our line was strengthened out there on the left, and when the sun went down Saturday evening it set upon the last hopes of the rebels that the Army of the Potomac would fall back across the Rapidan.

Grant visited the extreme left of his line Saturday night. Our brigade was ordered forward on the Brock road toward Spotsylvania. We exchanged shots with the rebels in the woods several times. It was dangerous business. We could not distinguish friend from foe. Grant reached Todd's Tavern soon after our advance was made, and remained there till Sunday morning, when he pushed on to Piney Grove meeting house on the Catharpin road, near the Ny River, to which point Meade's headquarters had been removed during the night. The Army of the Potomac was on the move, and pushing for Spotsylvania.

Wilson's division scouted out to Spotsylvania, and occupied the "town" for a time. There was a change in the order, we were told, so that Sheridan was not sent forward to hold Spotsylvania. At any rate, when the infantry reached the vicinity of the court house Sunday morning, they found the rebels square across their front with a substantial line of breastworks well under way. Grant ordered Sheridan, on May 8, to cut loose from the Army of the Potomac and look after Lee's communications and Stuart's cavalry.

There is no question that the raid was precipitated by an interview between Little Phil and Gen. Meade in respect of the latter's changing Sheridan's orders for the movements of the cavalry to hold Spotsylvania. Grant and Sheridan agree that if the plan of the commander of the cavalry corps had been adhered to, and Sheridan had been permitted to handle his three divisions, bringing Gregg and Merritt to Wilson's support at Spotsylvania, holding the bridge over the Po River, the battle of Spotsylvania would have been fought, if fought at all, under circumstances entirely different—the odds would have been heavy against Lee, as Grant would have been first on the ground and in time to throw up breastworks.

Sheridan's account of his interview with the commander of the Army of the Potomac is spicily told in his "Memoirs." It took place on May 8, soon after it was found that Lee's troops were in possession of Spotsylvania. Says Sheridan:

> A little before noon Gen. Meade sent for me, and when I reached his headquarters I found that his peppery temper had got the best of his good judgment, he showing a disposition to be unjust, laying blame here and there for the blunders that had been committed. He was particularly severe on the cavalry, saying, among other things, that it had impeded the march of the fifth corps by occupying the Spotsylvania road. I replied that if this was true, he himself had ordered it there without my knowledge. I also told him that he had broken up my combinations, exposed Wilson's division to disaster and kept Gregg unnecessarily idle, and further repelled his insinuations by saying that such disjointed operations as he had been requiring of the cavalry for the last four days would render the corps inefficient and useless before long. Meade was very much irritated, and I was none the less so. One word brought on another, until, finally, I told him that I could whip Stuart if he (Meade) would only

let me, but since he insisted on giving the cavalry directions without consulting or even notifying me, he could henceforth command the cavalry corps himself—that I would not give it another order. The acrimonious interview ended with this remark, and after I left him he went to Gen. Grant's headquarters and reported the conversation to him, mentioning that I had said that I could whip Stuart. At this Gen. Grant remarked, 'Did he say so? Then let him go out and do it.'

That settled it. It settled Stuart too. Sheridan kept his word. He said to his three division commanders, upon the receipt of the order to proceed against the enemy's cavalry, that he was going out to fight Stuart's troops, and that as he had told Gen. Meade he could whip Stuart he expected to accomplish nothing less than the defeat of the rebels. The division commanders were as eager as Sheridan was to cut loose. Their men had fought dismounted a good share of the time since crossing the Rapidan, and the boys were "mighty glad to get out of the Wilderness"; it was not a good place for a fair and square fight such as our commander promised to give Stuart, if the latter would face the music.

Of course, the rank and file were not informed as to Sheridan's plans, but as we were called in from picket and holding the roads in the vicinity of Piney Grove church and out toward Spotsylvania, everybody seemed to feel that a new departure was to be made. When the three divisions assembled at Aldrich's a few miles southeast of Chancellorsville, it was the first time they had been brought together since crossing the Rapidan. Three days' rations were issued to us in the evening, and each man received four quarts of oats for his horse.

"We're in for it, sure," said a battle-scarred trooper, on duty at our regimental headquarters, as orders were given to issue one hundred rounds of cartridges, extra, to each trooper.

"How so?"

"Well, it's been my experience that when three days' rations and extra ammunition are issued, especially right in sight of the wagon train, that something is going to happen."

"You fellows had better turn in and get what sleep you can tonight, for it will probably be the last chance you'll get for several days," admonished our first sergeant.

"See here. Sergeant," exclaimed Taylor, "you'll have to chloroform me if you want me to sleep. I'm anxious to know where this army is going. If we're to get into another such a squabble as we had down there in the woods, I want to sit up and write a letter home."

Somebody struck up "The Girl I Left Behind Me," and other popular war songs were hummed around the camp fires, concluding with "When This Cruel War is Over." Then the troopers not on duty went to bed with their boots on, and slept for the last time in sixteen days within hailing distance of the Army of the Potomac.

Chapter 19

Custer's Brigade at Beaver Dam

Reveille was sounded before daylight in the bivouac of Sheridan's cavalry corps at Aldrich's Monday morning.

While we were cooking coffee in our tin cups and our horses were eating their last full feed of United States Government forage for nearly three weeks, somebody started the report that we were going back toward Washington to protect Grant's communications, which, it was said, had been cut by the enemy. Before this last sensation had gone the rounds the general call was sounded and the troopers were so busy saddling their horses and getting ready for the march that further discussion of the report was indefinitely postponed.

"Stand to horse!"
"Prepare to mount!"
"Mount!"
"Form ranks!"
"By fours, march!"

We were in the saddle for one of the most daring raids on record. Now Sheridan would have a chance to demonstrate to his new command and to the country whether his faith in the ability of the cavalry corps to ride around Lee's army, whip everything that came in the way, and smash things generally, was well founded.

From Aldrich's we pushed out on the plank road in the direction of Fredericksburg. To our right and rear we heard the firing of Hancock's corps, which was on the extreme left of the Union line, and an orderly who joined us a few miles out, having been sent with a dispatch to Grant, reported that the gallant second corps had turned Lee's right flank and was doing splendid work. This was cheering news. We subsequently learned that Hancock's position was isolated from the other corps, the Po River being between them, and the advantage was not permanent. But we rode away on our raid inspired by the news that the infantry was licking the rebels out of their boots at Spotsylvania. It was the last news we had from the Army of the Potomac till the raid ended, except what we received from prisoners. The removal of the wounded from the field hospitals in the Wilderness to Fredericksburg was going on.

The plank road was crowded with ambulances and various kinds of government wagons filled with mangled and wounded soldiers. It was a sad and sorrowful procession. Six mule-team wagons that had been used to transport rations, ammunition and other ordnance stores had been made to do duty as ambulances. The train reached for miles, and now and then we were obliged to leave the road and pick our way through forest and field to make progress. The groans of the wounded could be heard, and occasionally a wagon would be halted long enough to take out the body of some poor fellow who had died on the way.

Hundreds of the wounded had lost legs and arms. In placing them in the ambulances they were sorted and arranged so that soldiers whose right legs had been cut off were put together, three in an ambulance, all lying on their left sides and "spooning it." Men with their left legs off were laid on their right sides in the ambulances. Some whose arms had been shattered and amputated were on foot, and the road was thronged with soldiers incapacitated from active service by minor wounds in their heads, arms and bodies, but who were still able to walk.

As we rode alongside the ambulances the cries of the wounded for water came to our ears. It was an appeal that could not be denied. We were making an effort to get around the enemy's flank before the rebels should discover that we had left Spotsylvania. But we had water in our canteens, and we took time to dismount and hold them to the lips of the thirsty comrades in the ambulances. And the "God bless you" uttered by the wounded, touched the hearts of the troopers till every eye was moist with tears. I saw a lieutenant-colonel—he was a regular martinet, and the boys all declared that he had a heart of stone—turn his head and wipe the tears from his eyes as a poor wounded infantryman was drinking from the officer's canteen.

"Thank you. Colonel; I would like to drink more, but I know you'll need it yourself—it's so hot—the road is so long and so rough—oh! the water is so good."

"Drink all you want, my boy," replied the officer.

"Thank you; God bless you."

"Just keep the water, canteen and all."

"But, Colonel"—

"Never mind; we'll find plenty of water on our trip."

Many of the boys followed the example of the "stony-hearted" lieutenant-colonel and left their canteens with the wounded. The surgeons, stewards and hospital attendants were doing all in their power to supply the sufferers with water; but there was great distress, and Sheridan's troopers were glad that they had an opportunity to do something for the poor fellows in the wagons. The wounded and dying prayed for water to moisten their parched lips. As fast as water could be secured it was given to them.

One of our boys handed his canteen to a wounded man in an ambulance which contained three soldiers, each of whom was minus a leg. As the canteen was raised by the first one of the three to quench his thirst, the next one moaned:

"Water, boys—for God's sake—just a drop—hurry, I'm so thirsty."

As the canteen was placed to his lips the bugle sounded "forward."

"Let the poor boy keep the canteen," exclaimed the trooper, as he sprang into the saddle.

"He don't need it now," said the driver of the ambulance.

"But he will before he gets to Fredericksburg."

"No; he'll hunger and thirst no more on this earth—he's dead."

The young hero—he was scarcely eighteen years of age—had died while the cavalryman was holding the canteen to his mouth. As we moved forward, the ambulance was pulled to the side of the road and the dead body of some mother's darling was taken out for hasty burial by the wayside.

When we reached the point at which we left the plank road leading to Fredericksburg and turned to the south, we could see the city in the distance. The long train of wagons filled with wounded was creeping at a snail's pace over the low hills toward the Rappahannock. Little Phil was now in his element, so to speak. His ten thousand troopers, as they headed toward Richmond, marching in columns of fours, were ready to go wherever their commander should direct. We were glad to get away from the ambulance train.

Our brigade was in the rear, and the advance guard was thirteen miles to the front—that being the length of the column. We did not expect that the rebels would trouble us much in the rear after we had got well around Lee's flank, but as we were crossing the Ta River, we were given to understand that although we had cut loose from the Army of the Potomac, the Johnnies were anxious to establish communication with us.

We were riding at a brisk walk, when our attention was attracted by a few shots back toward the river, and in a couple of minutes our rear guard came galloping up to the column.

"What's the matter, Sergeant?" asked a staff officer.

"The rebels are closing in on us! The advance guard of their cavalry opened on us back there in the woods. We gave them a volley and closed up to keep them from cutting us off, as they are deployed well out on both sides of the road."

Gen. Davies selected a position about a quarter of a mile up the road, and the brigade was prepared to check the enemy's advance. Our regiment was drawn up in line across the turnpike, facing to the rear. The First New Jersey or the First Pennsylvania was to our left in the woods. Our right extended well away from the road into a tangled forest, so that the ground over which the Johnnies must come was well covered. A squadron, I think of the Sixth Ohio, was thrown forward to receive the advancing Confederates, and so well was that duty performed that the rebels were held in check for fully half an hour. By that time word was received that the main column was well out of the way, and the brigade again moved forward, after exchanging a few shots with Stuart's troopers.

No sooner had the Federals returned to the road and started forward to connect with the main column, than the troopers in butternut began to seriously annoy our rear. They seemed to be familiar with the country round about, for they "cut cross lots" and came in on our flanks at different points. The exchange of leaden compliments was kept up on the march, and the enemy seemed determined to bring on a battle. It was a running skirmish, with the odds in favour of the rebels, for the reason that about the time we would get warmed up—real mad—and ready to charge the enemy, the order would be given to close up on our main column. This would inspire the Johnnies to give us fits, and they would charge down upon us with the evident determination to press us so hard upon the other brigades that the latter would make a stand in our behalf, and thus the advance of the column would be delayed.

But Sheridan was confident that Davies could take care of the rebels in our rear, so the head of the column pushed on for the North

Anna River. Stuart was making for the same point with a part of his command, hoping to reach Beaver Dam Station in time to save the supplies for Lee's army that had been sent forward to that depot. And the rebels would have stolen a march on us if Sheridan had halted his whole command to give battle to the Confederate cavalry that was fighting our brigade.

A few miles from the North Anna River the rebels pressed us so closely that Gen. Davies determined to give them to understand that we could whip them out of their boots if it were deemed necessary to stop and do so. The road wound around the foot of a hill after crossing a small creek by a wooden bridge. The fields on either side of the road were thickly wooded. Part of our regiment was formed in the woods, a little off the road, to the right, and facing the bridge. We were dismounted, our horses being led around the point of the hill out of sight. The woods on the opposite side of the road afforded cover for detachments of one or two other regiments of the brigade. Just in the bend of the road, across the bridge, a sergeant with a small detachment faced up the road in the direction from which Fitzhugh Lee's troopers were coming. The trap was set and baited for the Confederates!

On came the rebels. In the advance rode a fine-looking officer on a large gray horse. His left arm was in a sling—a reminder of Todd's Tavern, no doubt. As he came around a turn in the road and "spotted" the boys in blue on the other side of the bridge, he halted till his followers came up. Drawing his sabre and pointing it toward the Federal troopers beyond the creek, he shouted:

"Come on, boys!"

But the Johnnies "didn't come on, boys, wuff a cent," as a contraband cook for an officer in the First New Jersey expressed it. A volley from the woods west of the road attracted their attention to our boys, but before they could return our fire the dismounted troopers on the other side of the road opened on the enemy. There was nothing for the rebels to do but to get out of that hornets' nest as expeditiously as possible. They wheeled about and put spurs to their horses. They did not stop to look after their killed and wounded, but away they went pell-mell to get out of range of our carbines. The wounded officer on the gray horse frantically appealed to his men to hold on and fight, but he might as well have appealed to the wind. The officer's face was covered with blood, as he rode back after his men. He had received a pistol ball in the cheek at the first fire.

As soon as the rebels had been driven back we received orders to push on across the bridge to remount our horses. We were taking things coolly till a staff officer came galloping back from the column with the information that the rebels had cut across lots again and were flanking our brigade.

"You'll have to double-quick it to get to your horses," he said to the captain commanding the dismounted cavalrymen.

This was anything but cheering news. And it seems the rebels whom we had just repulsed understood the situation, for they again returned to the attack, and peppered us as we crowded across the bridge.

As we reached the high ground where the road turned to the south around the hill, one of the boys in the advance shouted, "The infernal jackasses have run away with our horses!"

"What's that?" chorused a score of voices.

"They've led our horses over to that hill yonder, a good three miles away."

"Then we've got to hoof it to that point?"

"Yes; we've got to hoof it, after driving back the rebs."

"What's that down there to the left crossing the field—there near that clump of trees?"

All eyes were turned in the direction in which the trooper pointed, A second look was not necessary to convince us that the rebels were getting in between us and our main column. And it was evident that they could cut us off, as we were dismounted and our horses were not at hand.

We started on a "trot" down the turnpike, feeling the necessity of reaching the hill where the horses could be seen. The rebel troopers were making for the same point.

"They'll capture our horses before we can get there," exclaimed a sergeant of Company I.

"Hurrah! hurrah! hurrah!"

"What's that cheering for?"

The cheering was by our boys who were leading in the race down the turnpike. As they turned around the bend and were taking their bearings for a cross-cut through the fields to the hill beyond, they ran right into the horses of our detachment in charge of a lieutenant.

If there ever was a time when a cavalryman appreciated his horse it was on occasions like this. As we mounted our chargers and formed ranks for a dash over the fields to drive back the rebels who were pushing for the led horses across the bottom lands, our courage rose several degrees above what it was when we started to make the race on foot. Just about the time the rebels discovered that they had made a mistake and that we were coming down on them, they received a volley from a line of dismounted cavalrymen who seemed to rise up out of the ground. The dismounted troopers—I think they were the Sixth Ohio—were the owners of the horses on the hill. The Confederates lost no time in taking to the woods, and we had the pleasure of returning the compliment the Johnnies had shown us at the bridge—we peppered them as they had peppered us.

As darkness came on we reached the North Anna River and found our division—Gregg's—and Wilson's preparing to bivouac for the night. A strong line of pickets was posted up the turnpike over which we had marched. We of the first brigade, second division, were allowed to cook our supper and unsaddle our horses.

The first division under Merritt had crossed the North Anna, and there had been rumours that our boys had met the enemy on the south bank. The reports were confirmed after dark, and we heard good news from Sheridan's troopers at the head of the column.

Custer's brigade had the advance, and after crossing the river he pushed on to Beaver Dam Station, on the Virginia Central railroad, and at that point began smashing things. Hampton had made a forced march to intercept our boys before they could reach the station, for there was a large quantity of rations and other supplies for Lee's army at Beaver Dam, including two hundred thousand pounds of bacon, and the boys in butternut were partial to meat; they wanted to save their bacon. The medical stores for the rebel army of Northern Virginia had been sent back to Beaver Dam from Lee's headquarters at Orange Court House. Custer's troops burned the station, tore up the railroad right and left, destroyed two engines and several trains of cars, with about one hundred Government wagons, and everything else that could be smashed.

The best news, however, was that about four hundred Yankee soldiers, who had been captured in the Wilderness and were en route to Richmond, where they would have been confined in Libby prison, were recaptured by Custer's men. The rebels guarding the boys in blue and a force on guard at the station were put to flight or captured by the Federals. The release of the Union prisoners was a cheering incident of the day. And how glad the boys were to be again under the stars and stripes, and to realize that the horrors of prison pens were not to be theirs, for the present at least. They stood around the camp fires of Sheridan's troopers that night and sang "Hail, Columbia," "Glory Hallelujah," "Rally Round the Flag, Boys," and other patriotic songs.

When our gallant Little Phil came to sum up the results of his first day's independent campaign he must have felt that his faith in his ability to whip Stuart and ride all around Lee's army was well founded.

CHAPTER 20

Sheridan's Raid

"Turn out, men!"
"Turn out, lively!"
"Saddle up—mount at will!" We turned out lively enough. The rebels were shelling our bivouac on the banks of the North Anna River. It was just at daylight. Our dreams of home were interrupted by the "*pinging*" of bullets, and the more distressing sounds of missiles of larger calibre.
"Look out there!"
"What's that?"
"Only a cannon ball, but it's too late to dodge now—it has gone by."
"Get into your saddles, boys—never mind your haversacks—be sure your ammunition is all right. As fast as you're saddled up, mount and ride over there where the major is forming the regiment."
The Johnnies had nearly cheated us out of our suppers Monday night, as they did not cease firing on our pickets till after ten o'clock. And now they evinced a disposition to spoil our breakfast. In this they succeeded, but some of them were severely punished. Soldiers are inclined to be ugly when attacked about meal time, and Fitzhugh Lee's cavalrymen were given a red-hot reception when they pitched into our boys before breakfast.
One of our boys got his saddle on with the pommel to the rear—he must have stood on the off side of his horse to buckle the saddle girth. After he mounted his horse he could not get his feet into the stirrups as they were "hind side afore."
"Halloo, there! what are you facing the wrong way for?"
"I'm all right; it's a new wrinkle, don't you see? I can about face in the saddle and load and fire on the Johnnies while my horse keeps

going on. I saddled up this way on purpose."

During the night Fitzhugh Lee had posted a battery so that he could make it hot for us when we came to cross the river. And very hot it was for an hour or so. The shot and shell came tearing through the bushes skirting the bank. A regiment was deployed to the rear to hold the rebels in check while the Federal troopers were crossing. The Confederates were mad—fighting mad. They understood that if Sheridan kept pushing on without halting his main column to give battle to the rebels in the rear, the Union cavalry could ride straight into Richmond. This was what caused Stuart to draw off the larger part of his command from the line of the North Anna to get in between Sheridan and the rebel capital, first making a feint on the south bank as if to attack Merritt's division in the morning. We succeeded in getting over the river without great loss, as the first division covered our crossing, and our flying artillery did splendid work in silencing the rebel battery that gave us the most trouble, and then sending cannon balls among the Johnnies who were peppering us at close range.

When we reached Beaver Dam Station—or the ruins of what had been the station the day before—we found that Custer's brigade had demonstrated the ability of the Yankee troopers to smash things.

"Golly, massa!" exclaimed a plantation hand, who had witnessed the capture and destruction of the station, "dem sojers from Massa Linkum's army dun knock de bottom out'n de las fing roun heah—shuah's yo born. Whar's yo all gwine?"

"Richmond, Uncle."

"'Pears like yo' mean it, shuah nuff, dis time. Reckon yo'll get dar if all Massa Lee's sojers am as skeery ob de Yanks as de crowd dat was heah when yo' all com' gallopin' cross de bridge las night. Whew! how dem rebels did run. Spec dey's close to Richmond by dis time, if dey not slack up some 'fore now."

The old darky was right. Custer had knocked the bottom out of everything around the station, making a total wreck. The ruins were still burning, and our boys were particular that the destruction should be complete.

The mortification of the rebel prisoners was something ludicrous. Only a few hours before they had been guarding a detachment of Yankees captured in the Wilderness. They had reached Beaver Dam Station, where they had halted for the night. The prisoners had been assured that their chances of spending a year or so in Libby prison were of the best. But while the Confederates were boasting of their ability to whip Grant's army three to one, Custer's troopers dashed down on the station, and in a few minutes the fire-eating F. F.V.'s were ready to throw up both hands and surrender. Some of the Union boys who had been released buckled on C. S. A. belts and cartridge boxes, and stood guard over the crest-fallen gray backs.

An infantry corporal of a Pennsylvania regiment, had been forced to give up all his personal effects to one of the rebel guards when leaving the Wilderness. The corporal had been "well fixed," as the boys called it when a comrade had money, a watch, etc. After the tables had been turned on the Johnnies the corporal, having taken into custody the man who had robbed him, at once singled him out, and imitating the voice of the Johnnie, said:

"That's a fine ring on your finger—think it would fit me? Hand it over."

The prisoner surrendered the ring, saying:

"You've got the drop on me this time, Yank."

"Mighty fine watch you carry—you'll have no chance to keep it in prison where you're going. I'll take charge of it for you."

The watch was handed over.

"Just go down in your pocket and see how many greenbacks you can find—you can't spend them in prison."

A pocket-book with quite a sum of money was given up.

"Let me see! They won't allow you to smoke a *meerschaum* pipe in prison; so I'll save that for you till you get out. I'll guarantee it will be well coloured."

The pipe was returned to its owner.

"Now, that half-pound plug of tobacco, please. You may bite off one more chaw, as it will probably be the last you'll get right away."

The rebel obeyed orders.

"As you will have no tramping to do after you get to the prison, and I'm liable to be on the go most of the time, we'd better swap shoes, as mine are nearly worn out."

The exchange was made.

"That canteen!"

Handed over.

"Haversack!"

Surrendered.

"Fine tooth comb!"

"I shall miss that."

"Suspenders!"

Handed over.

"Jack-knife!"

"Here it is."

"Shirt—no, never mind the shirt. I haven't got yours to return in place of it, for it was so thick with gray-backs when you took it off to put on mine, that it was run away with. I've no doubt my shirt that you've got on is in the same fix now, so keep it, Johnnie. I don't want to be too hard on a stranger. You may also keep my drawers and stockings, as I can get a supply from some of my friends in the cavalry. I see you've got a ring that you didn't take from me. Does it belong to one of our boys?"

"No, Yank; it's mine. It was my mother's. She's dead—it's all I have left that was hers. But it's yours now, as I'm your prisoner. Take it, Yank. It's hard to give it up."

"I know it is."

"Do you?"

"Yes; the ring you took from me was my mother's, Johnnie. She's dead—no, I can't take your mother's ring—keep it."

"I took yours, but you didn't tell me it was your mother's."

"No; for I didn't believe it would make any difference."

"It would have made a difference, Yank—sure's you're born, it would."

There was a grasp of hands as the tears ran down the faces of the corporal and his prisoner. A tender chord had been struck in the heart of each. They had been foes a few minutes before. They were brothers now.

Each had fought for a cause, and would go on fighting as before. They must continue to be enemies on the field of battle till the great questions at issue were settled by the sword. But all this was forgotten as they spoke of "mother."

The heart beneath the blue and the heart under the gray beat in unison. Each felt the blessed influence awakened by the utterance of that magic word "mother," which is so beautifully expressed by Fanny J. Crosby:

The light, the spell-word of the heart,
Our guiding star in weal or woe.
Our talisman—our earthly chart—
That sweetest name that earth can know.
We breathed it first with lisping tongue

When cradled in her arms we lay;
Fond memories round that name are hung
That will not, cannot pass away.

We breathed it then, we breathe it still,
More dear than sister, friend or brother,
The gentle power, the magic thrill
Awakened at the name of Mother.

"Johnnie?"
"Yes, Yank."
"Take this pipe and tobacco. You'll need them."
"Thank you."
"Here's my pocket-book."
"But you'll need the money?"
"Not so much as you will. Take it, I say."
"All right, if you insist on it."
'And this fine tooth comb—you'll need that also."
"Yes, I need it now."
"Here's my jack-knife; it'll come handy."
"It will."
"Now take my canteen and haversack—no, don't refuse; I can get more. I'll see them filled before we part."
"Thank you, Yank—God bless you!"
"God bless you, Johnnie!"
And all who stood by said, "Amen."
So mote it be.

Leaving Beaver Dam Station in ruins, Sheridan's cavalry corps pushed on toward the rebel capital early on the morning of Tuesday, May 10.

Not far from Beaver Dam we rode by a Virginia farmhouse. It was a one-storey building, with chimneys on the outside and an "entry" running through the centre. Two or three plantation hands stood near the fence, grinning and shouting:

"Bress de Lawd!"
"Hyar cum Massa Linkum's sojers—bress de Lawd! O, Glory!"
"Are you glad to see us, Uncle?"
"Yes, massa, 'deed I is."
"Where's the 'massa'?"
"He run and gune. Must be de king-dom com-in'."

The old darky had struck the keynote of one of the ditties that were immensely popular in the Union army. The boys took up the song. They made it ring as they rode along:

> Say, dar-keys, hab you seen de mas-sa,
> Wid de muff-stash on his face,
> Go long de road some time dis morn-in',
> Like he gwine to leab de place?
>
> He seen a smoke, way up de rib-ber,
> Where de Link-um gum-boats lay;
> He took his hat, an' lef berry sud-den,
> An' I 'spec he's run away!

Chorus:

> De mas-sa run? ha! ha!
> De dar-keys stay? ho! ho!
> It mus' be now de king-dom com-in',
> An' de year ob Ju-bi lo!

At another farmhouse we found a new-made grave in the dooryard. It was just inside the gate, and to the right of the walk leading up to the porch. The earth heaped over the grave was still moist, which showed that it had been filled in during the morning. A spade with the letters "C. S. A." burned in the handle, lay beside the mound. At one of the windows of the farmhouse we saw the faces of two or three young ladies. They had been weeping, but it seemed as if they were holding back their tears till the Yankees should get out of sight. We concluded that the grave in the yard was that of their brother. The eyes of many of Sheridan's raiders filled with tears as they came to understand the situation, and their minds went back to their own homes and the dear ones in the North. Mother, sister, sweetheart—in a few days they might be weeping over the news of the death of their soldier boy. Every voice was hushed. With uncovered heads the troopers rode by. Their hearts were moved with sympathy for the distressed household.

A staff officer inquired of an old negro who was drawing water for the soldiers at a well near the house:

"Whose grave is that, Uncle?"

"Young Massa Tom's, sah."

"And who was 'Massa Tom'?"

"He war missus's only son."

"And the brother of the young ladies at the window?"

"Yes; all de brudder dey had. Ole massa he war killed at Seben Pines. Den young Massa Tom cum home for a time to look after de plantation. But when de news cum dat Massa Linkum's army had cross de Rapid Ann, young massa buckle on he sode an' tell de young missuses and ole missus dat he obliged to go to de front. He only lef' home Thursday, five days ago. He war in de Wilderness and war sent wid Yankee prizners to de station which you all's sojers burn up las' night. He cum home to supper in de early ebenin, an' den went back to de station. He said dey spected to start for Richmond 'fore sun-up dis mornin'. But de Yankees sweep down on de camp, an' soon de news cum dat Massa Tom been kill. A party of Massa Lee's sojers brought young massa's body home, an' bright an' early dis mornin' we laid him away in de groun'. De sojers say: 'Better bury him 'fore de Yankees cum long,' and ole missus say: 'Yes; dey shall nebber glory ober my son's dead body.' So Massa Tom war laid away. It did seem so cruel like to jest 'rap a blanket roun' him an' put him in de groud'; but it won't make a heep ob diff'nce, I reckon, when de resurreckshun day shall cum, for de good Lawd will know his chil'ren.

"Poor Massa Tom—he's free. Ole missus say she 'spec I'll run off wid de Yankees now; but, massa, ole Ned's gwine to stay by an' help ole missus all he can, for de time'll soon cum when dis poor ole slave will be free! For whom de Lawd make free, he be free 'ndeed."

As we rode away ole Uncle Ned was singing:

Dar'll be no sor-row dar,
Dar'll be no sor-row dar,
In heb-un a-buv,
Whar all is luv—
Dar'll be no sor-row dar

The enemy did not molest us during the march Tuesday. They had received severe punishment in the early morning, and when the three divisions of the cavalry corps had secured a position on the south bank of the North Anna, Stuart concluded that it was a waste of time—to say nothing of the danger—to attack Sheridan in the vicinity of Beaver Dam. At any rate, they left us to ourselves a good part of the day.

And what a picnic we enjoyed! Foraging parties were sent out in all directions, and they returned with an abundance of corn for our horses. The corn was in the ear, and we shelled it for our chargers. Now and then a trooper who had been out on the flank would come in with a supply of eggs and butter, with a chicken or two hanging on his saddle. All such provender was classed as "forage," and was confiscated by the raiders. It was delicate business, however, and I do not believe that one out of twenty of Sheridan's troopers took anything from the plantations along the route that was not needed by the soldiers.

I would not be understood as saying that the boys did not confiscate things that were not included in the government ration. Not at all. They relished extra dishes—such as ham and eggs, butter for their flapjacks, and milk for their coffee, and wherever they found supplies of this kind they foraged them. But the Yankees showed a good deal of discrimination. When they found a dyed-in-the-wool rebel who had a goodly store of provisions, they confiscated what they needed, but in cases where the supply was scant and the farm was worked by the women and darkies, the boys admonished one another to go slow, and only a small percentage of the crop was taken into camp.

A foraging party went out to a plantation about a mile from the road on which our column was moving. We saw the planter's house on a gentle rise of ground, surrounded by magnificent shade trees. Everything about the place indicated that the proprietor belonged to the F. F.V.'s. As we rode up the broad avenue leading from the front gate to the residence, the sergeant in charge of the party said: "Boys, we've struck it rich. There must be something good to eat here."

Seated in an armchair on the broad *piazza* was the "lord of the manor," his eyes fairly snapping with the hatred he could not conceal for the visitors. He was full threescore years and ten. His long white hair hung down upon his shoulders, and served to heighten the colour in his cheeks—and the beet red of his nose. The planter arose at our approach, and demanded: "To what am I indebted for this visit?"

"Firing on the old flag at Fort Sumter, primarily," replied the sergeant, who seemed to enjoy the old Virginian's hostile attitude.

"But, sir, I did not fire on Sumter!"

"No? Then you're a Union man, I take it?"

"No, sir! I'm a Virginian, loyal to my State and to the Confederacy. If I were able to bears arms I should be in Lee's army today, fighting the vandal horde that has invaded the sacred soil. Sir, we are enemies!"

"I am sorry to hear you say that. If you were a Union man you could get pay for the forage we were sent to secure. But as you are a sworn enemy of the United States of America we will be obliged to confiscate some of your corn and other supplies."

"I knew you were a band of robbers when you rode through my

gate. The Northern mudsills make war on private citizens and rob them by force of arms."

"It's the fortunes of war."

"You may call it war. We of the South call it the unholy attempt to subjugate freemen—to destroy the sovereignty of the States. But Abe Lincoln with all his vandal horde will never conquer the South!"

"Well, stick to your State's rights, old man; but in the meantime we must have corn for our horses to brace them up so's we can ride into Richmond and hang old Jeff Davis"—

"Jeff Davis! He's a saint, sir, when compared with your negro-loving railsplitter in the White House!"

"All right; I don't propose to quarrel with you. Please show us where the corn can be found."

"Never, sir! If you will plunder my plantation I am powerless to defend myself; but I'll not help you to anything."

"Then we'll prospect on our own hook. Perhaps we can find what we want."

"I protest in the name of the sovereign rights of a Virginian."

"Uncle Sam's a bigger man than 'ole Virginny,'" replied the sergeant.

We had no difficulty in finding the corn crib and the old Virginian's commissary department. A young darky "*let the cat out of the bag*" on his master, and we soon had our horses loaded with forage. We had struck it rich, indeed, for the plantation yielded "corn, wine and oil" in abundance. There was food for man and beast. A large number of hams, cured on the plantation, sides and sides of bacon, and a goodly store of "groceries" were among the "forage" we confiscated. But we did not strip the planter of all his provisions; enough was left to run him for several months.

"I'll give you a receipt for this forage," said the sergeant, as we were about to leave.

"What would the receipt of a robber be good for?" exclaimed the old planter.

"You can present it to the government when the war's over and get pay for the forage."

"Do you want to add further insult to the injury you have done me? I scorn you and your government. You can never whip the South, sir, never, and under no consideration would I disgrace myself by taking pay for stores used by the enemies of the Confederacy. Leave my plantation. Go back to your general and tell him that my prayer is that he and his followers will get their just deserts—that they will all be hanged."

The enraged planter walked back and forth on the *piazza*, and shot defiant glances at us as we rode away with our plunder. I have no doubt that he would have "bushwhacked" us if there had been an opportunity.

A couple of miles south of the big plantation we came to a farmhouse on a cross road. We stopped at the well to fill our canteens, and one of the boys explored the premises to see what he could find. He came back with the report that the house was occupied by a widow with a large family of children.

"There don't seem to be anything to eat on this farm," the trooper remarked.

"I'll see about it," said the sergeant, as he rode up to the porch. "Halloo, inside there!"

A middle-aged woman came out into the entry and advanced timidly toward the Yankee.

"We're out after forage," the sergeant said. "Have you any corn around here?"

"We have nothing but the crap that's gro'in'. We had some provisions until a few clays ago a lot of soldiers came along and took all our corn and bacon. We've got a mighty little meal and a trifle of bacon left."

"I didn't know that any of our men had been through here lately."

"They were not Yankees; they were our own soldiers. They said they were hungry, and when they begun to eat it seemed like they would never quit. They fairly ate us most out of house and home. It's mighty sorry times with us. I don't know what we'll do to get along till harvest."

"Where's your husband?"

"Done killed in the wah."

"Have you no sons?"

"Yes, sir; two fighting under General Lee."

"And you're short of provisions?"

"Very short indeed."

"Boys, leave a couple of hams, a bag of meal and some bacon with this lady."

The boys gladly complied with the instructions, and they also went down in their haversacks and contributed quite a number of rations of coffee and sugar.

"Oh! that's real coffee," exclaimed the oldest of the children, a girl of about twelve years.

"I expected you would take what little we had to eat," said the head of the family, as the tears rolled down her face. "I never thought the Yankees would be so kind to the widow of a Confederate. The Richmond papers said if you all came this way you would destroy everything; they said heaps of black things about you."

"Do you all have hams on your saddles and sacks of corn to carry along all the time?" ventured the young miss who had listened to all that had been said.

"No, no; we confiscated these back at the big plantation yonder."

"Where 'bouts?" inquired the widow.

"At that fine house a couple of miles north."

"Was there an old gentleman there?"

"Yes; he gave us his benediction when we left, by expressing the wish that we would all come to the gallows."

"And these hams and other things came from his plantation?"

"Yes."

"I declare, '*vengeance is mine, saith the Lord.*' Yesterday I called there and asked the colonel—they all call him colonel—-to help me along by letting me have a little meal and bacon. I promised to pay him back when we gather our crop, by and by."

"He assisted you, of course?"

"No, indeed. He said he could not afford to distribute his provisions among other people who had no claims on him. He refused to let me have a pound of meat, or a quart of meal."

"He knows your husband was killed fighting for the Confederacy—and that you have two sons in Lee's army?"

"To be sure he does; he urged them to go into the army, to hurl back the invaders; but he now says I must look to the government at Richmond for help. I'm thankful for what you all have done for us. It's a right smart help. But I believe the colonel would come down here and take the provisions away from us, if he knew you all had left them here."

"Let's go back and take what's left at his plantation and burn him out," exclaimed one of the troopers.

"No; not this time," said the sergeant. "But we shall probably come this way again, and then we can pay our compliments to the old skinflint."

"Do you think the wah's coming to an end soon?" the woman asked as we were about to move forward.

"I hope so," replied the sergeant. "I think this campaign will wind it up."

"Who's going to whip?"

"We are."

"You'll be obliged to do some powerful hard fighting, I reckon, for our side won't give up so long's there's anything to eat in the Confederacy. But if we're to be overcome, sure enough, I hope it will be soon—before my sons are killed. Our boys'll die game, sure's you're born."

"I hope your sons will be spared."

"I trust they will. They believe they are fighting for a just cause. They are Virginians, and they have great faith in General Lee. They will follow him to the end. But it's a cruel wah. Somebody must be wrong; both sides cannot be right. I don't understand it thoroughly, but I feel that somebody has made a terrible mistake."

"Ma, the Yankees hasn't got horns, has they, ma?" exclaimed one of the children, a girl about five years old, and who was gnawing at a hard-tack one of the troopers had given her.

"No, my darling."

And the Confederate soldiers widow joined in the laugh that followed this juvenile outbreak. Goodbyes were said, and the foraging party hastened to rejoin the column.

CHAPTER 21

A Christian Father's Sacrifice

In camp Tuesday night, at Ground Squirrel Bridge, on the bank of the South Anna, eighteen miles from Beaver Dam: At two o'clock Wednesday morning. May 11, Gen. Davies's brigade saddled up and struck out for Ashland Station, on the Richmond and Fredericksburg railroad. We came down on the rebels early in the morning. At the station we encountered Colonel Thomas T. Munford's cavalry—the Second Virginia and detachments of other regiments—with whom we had a lively fight, Davies lost thirty men, and the enemy about the same number.

Our regimental loss included Lieutenant Edward P. Hopkins, who was killed at the head of his company while gallantly leading a charge on the Virginia troops. There was no time to bury the dead. Stuart with the aid of re-enforcements from the breastworks around Richmond was setting a trap for the Union cavalry general. Lieutenant Hopkins, and the other troopers killed at Ashland, were buried by coloured men after the cavalry had pushed on to Yellow Tavern.

The death of Lieutenant Hopkins was greatly regretted by all his comrades. I was deeply grieved at the sad event. He had enlisted me and two other runaways from Berlin at Williamstown. He was one of the bravest and best officers in the regiment. He was a true friend, and one who could be counted on to stand up for the right at all times and under the most trying circumstances.

Edward Payson Hopkins was born at Williamstown, July 22, 1844. He was the only child of the late Professor Albert Hopkins. His mother's maiden name was Louisa Payson, daughter of Rev. Edward Payson, D. D., of Portland, Me., and to whom Professor Hopkins was married August 25, 1841. He was at Williams College studying for the ministry when he entered the army. His father had desired that Edward should consecrate his life to the ministry or to the missionary service. Lieutenant Hopkins continued on recruiting service till January 6, 1864, when he was mustered into the service as first lieutenant in the First Massachusetts Cavalry, joining the regiment at once.

It was the spirit of patriotism and devotion to the cause of the Union that is breathed forth in the following letter that enabled loyal fathers and mothers to give up their sons that the Union might be preserved. The letter was written from Williamstown to Dr. Calhoun, by Professor Hopkins:

November 18, 1864.

Dear Friend and Brother:—At the time of your writing you had not heard and may not since have heard, of the death of my son Edward Payson. He fell at Ashland, Va., on the 11th May last, a few days after what is known as the Battle of the Wilderness, which he passed through uninjured. He was first lieutenant in the cavalry under Sheridan, and went with him between the rebel army and Richmond, and fell in a charge on the place above mentioned. He was athletic, brave, and yet cool, so I am told by his captain, and also by others who were in the ranks. He left his class (the junior) at New Year's, so that his course was short. I had hoped he might be spared to me, but we are living, my brother, at a time in this country when the very foundations of morality, religion and government are imperilled.

No sacrifice less costly than the best blood of me nation can meet the demands of these evil times. It was an absolute necessity that this battle should be fought, and, however near it may come to some of us, however vitally it may touch what is to us most precious, we yield it freely. I know that many escape whose lives seem worthless, but this is according to God's inscrutable mode of dealing at such times. I hope you who are looking on at a distance will not despair of the republic, as I know you do not of the kingdom. We shall, with God's help, fight it out till the principles are revindicated for which we are fighting.

Our nation will stand on far higher ground when the conflict is ended, as an instrument for the spread of light and truth in the earth. Entertaining these views, I feel that the sacrifice of my son in this cause is as acceptable to God as though he had laid down his life in a foreign field. He was a child of many prayers, and I trust a true Christian. I cannot, therefore, repine, though by this providence I am left *'without a soul in Israel.'* . . . I think I am more and more impressed with the preciousness and almighty power of the gospel. The greatest obstacles will yield if we can only bring the power of sovereign grace fairly to bear upon them. Yours, with unabated friendship and Christian love,

A. Hopkins.

In June, 1865, Professor Hopkins went to Virginia in the hope that he could recover the body of his son.

The spot where Lieutenant Hopkins and five other Union soldiers were buried in two trenches by the slaves was identified, but the bodies were so much decomposed that recognition was impossible. The father was almost heartbroken. During the fall of 1865 he learned that there were means of identification other than those which he had found were of no avail—means which could not fail of certain knowledge. He accordingly, in the month of December, again visited Ashland, this time with authority from the government, and attended by soldiers, a surgeon and government officials. He found that not only could the body be fully identified, but the swampy character of the burial place had so arrested decay and disintegration that almost the entire body was recovered.

Professor Hopkins returned to Williamstown with the remains of his son. Funeral services were held Sunday, December 31, 1865, Rev. Henry Hopkins, a cousin of the deceased, officiating.

It seems fitting to close this reference to Lieutenant Hopkins with the following extract from the diary of his father, the late Professor Hopkins:

Sabbath, 31st Dec, 1865.

A week ago last Tuesday left for Richmond. Spent last Sabbath there; a stormy day. Next day, Christmas, spent in Ashland, disinterring. Day beautiful. Much water on the slacks where the dead were buried. Returned next day to Washington. Found much peace and comfort, especially in contemplating Christ as treading the path of suffering. It seemed strange, but consoling, that he should have trod that path. Have seldom had greater peace.

Today have committed to the earth the remains of my dear son in a peaceful, solemn hour. Day mild, calm and beautiful, in harmony with the scene. This is one of many instances which have occurred during the journey which appear like special acts of love and favour.... Feel more comforted than I expected in the fact that he has been placed at last by his mother's side. Lord sanctify this last experience to me.

Chapter 22

Sheridan at the Front

The brigade of Gen. Davies, after disposing of Munford's men at Ashland, destroyed the railroad for six miles, tearing up the track, burning ties and trestle bridges, and demolishing culverts. The railroad station and a warehouse were burned, with a train of cars and a locomotive. Then we pushed on to rejoin the cavalry corps at Glen Allen Station. It was understood that the rebel cavalry commander was in our immediate vicinity, and would pass through Ashland on the way to Yellow Tavern, where he made another stand to oppose Sheridan's further advance toward the rebel capital.

When our brigade rejoined Gregg's division, the first division under Merritt was pushing for Yellow Tavern, with Devin's brigade in the lead.

Yellow Tavern proved a Waterloo for the Confederate cavalry. Gen. Stuart was mortally wounded. He died in Richmond, May 12, the day after the battle. General James B. Gordon was among the killed, and the rebel cavalry corps was routed all along the line. Splendid fighting was done by Sheridan's men, and after preliminary skirmishing a general advance was ordered, and everything in Sheridan's front had to give way. Fitzhugh Lee succeeded to the command of the Confederate cavalry upon the fall of Stuart, and, with the demoralized troopers in butternut, he fled toward Mechanicsville, leaving Sheridan in his rear, and between Richmond and Fitzhugh Lee's command.

A detachment of the First Massachusetts cavalry got into a tight place at Yellow Tavern, during the early part of the fight. Gregg's division was covering the rear, and the detachment was sent to explore a road on the right flank of the column.

We were "all broke up" for the want of sleep. Even the "Johnny come latelys," as the recruits were called, had become so used to the saddle that they could snatch quite a nap on the march.

There was fighting by the advance guard, the rear guard and the flankers nearly all the time. I was sound asleep, with my chin bobbing on my breast, and my cap gone. I was braced in the saddle by my overcoat, blankets and other personal effects, strapped to the pommel and the cantle. I was disturbed and about half-awakened by what I thought were bumblebees buzzing by my ears.

"Look out, there!"

Then there were more bees.

"Fire to the right, boys; into that clump of trees near the fence."

I opened my eyes to find myself on the skirmish line, and under a hot fire from rebels only one hundred yards to our front. We had been deployed and sent to dislodge the "handful" of Confederates in the woods. Our first effort was not a success. As I remember it, the services of "all hands" were necessary to rout the enemy, for we had struck Stuart's main line at Yellow Tavern. It was a desperate fight; the rebels contested every inch of ground. But Sheridan was in no humour to be trifled with.

Our flankers were driven in, and there was a dreadful racket back where the rear guard was skirmishing with the enemy.

"If they whip us, which way'll we run?" said one of the boys in our platoon, as we were forced back around a bend in the road by a withering fire from the rebels.

"Run? We can't run; there isn't any rear; the Johnnies are all around us."

"But if we're whipped we'll be obliged to go somewhere."

"If we're whipped they'll take us into Richmond, sure's you're born. We can't get out of this."

"Hold on; here comes Sheridan!"

Little Phil dashed up to the place where our boys had rallied, after falling back from the "bumblebees" nest."

"What's the matter here?" he inquired.

"Too many rebels over there in the woods," was the answer.

"Cavalry or infantry?"

"Cavalry."

"Get ready to go in again, boys; we're going through on this road. There isn't cavalry enough in the Southern Confederacy to stop us."

Sheridan made a hasty survey of the enemy's position. Then he gave orders to his division commanders, and pretty soon Stuart's defeated troopers were looking around for the rear. They were routed all along the line, and their commander—who had been a "thorn in the flesh "to the Army of the Potomac in several campaigns—was killed. The rebels taxed the going qualities of their horses to the utmost in leaving Yellow Tavern behind them. It seemed as if each Confederate trooper that survived the fight had constituted himself a committee of one to carry the news to Jeff Davis in Richmond, only six miles away. It was one of the most exciting skedaddles of the war. Little wonder is it that the news from Yellow Tavern created a panic in the rebel capital, when the defeated cavalrymen dashed in with the information that "the entire vandal horde" was at their heels.

If Sheridan had had a good-sized division of infantry at hand, Richmond would have been taken, for this would have given more force to the report that the whole of Grant's army was at the "gates of the city," inside the outer line of breastworks.

We followed the rebels to within two miles or less of Richmond, up to the trenches of the main line of works. We could have gone in, but we might have been compelled to stay, as the works were soon filled with Confederates, who rallied from every direction to the defence of the capital. We could hear the ringing of bells and the blowing of steam whistles in the city.

While the fight at Yellow Tavern was opening, Grant was hammering away at Spotsylvania, and about the time Sheridan declared that, "We're going through on this road," Grant wrote that famous dispatch—Wednesday, May 11, 1864—that contained the announcement:

> I propose to fight it out on this line if it takes all summer.

For a time during the fight at Yellow Tavern our brigade was drawn up in line in an open field to the left of the road leading toward Richmond. Every now and then a Federal trooper would tumble out of his saddle, shot by a rebel sharpshooter in the woods at our front. After three or four of our boys had been killed or wounded, the location of the Confederate was discovered. The sharpshooter wore white pantaloons and a white shirt. He was in a tree immediately in our front, and not more than twenty yards in the rear of the rebel skirmish line. We could see him load and fire. There would be a little puff of smoke, and about the same instant the bullet would *"ping"* about our ears. Then the report of the rifle, sounding like a small firecracker, would be heard.

It was not pleasant to sit there as a target for that white-clad gray-

A Rebel sharpshooter.

back. An officer of a New York regiment—I think it was the Tenth—was organising a party to make a *coup de main*, to dash out and capture or kill the Confederate with the long-range rifle, when a "mule whacker," who drove an ambulance, came up with a doughboy's musket that he had picked up in the Wilderness, and had carried on his wagon.

"Maybe there's a gunner here who can operate this long-barrelled weapon," he said. "I never fired a gun in my life."

"Have you got cartridges for it?" asked the officer who had called for volunteers to go over and "stop that fellow's shooting."

"Only three rounds."

"Let me have the musket and the cartridges."

The driver handed the gun to the officer, who carefully loaded it, and then rode to our skirmish line, which was a little out of carbine range from the sharpshooter. He dismounted and gave his horse in charge of a vidette. Then he advanced cautiously to a rail fence between the two lines. The sharpshooter discovered the officer, and sent a ball whizzing close to his head.

The Yankee returned the compliment, resting his musket over the fence.

"He hit him!"

"A line shot!"

"That Johnnie won't shoot any more!" were some of the remarks made by our boys, who were watching the long-range duel.

The rebel clapped his hand on his hip at the Yankee's first shot. But he was not disabled. He could discount the Federal cavalryman in getting his muzzle loader ready for another shot, and almost before the officer had bit off the end of his second cartridge, the Confederate was ready to fire again.

But our long-range man was not to be caught napping. As the Johnny brought his rifle to his shoulder to again draw a bead on the bold boy in blue, the latter dropped down behind the fence and rammed home his cartridge.

It was an interesting situation. The rebel's rifle was pointed at the spot where the Yankee had stood when he fired his first shot. But the Federal officer crept along behind the fence until he was several rods to the left of his first position. There he found a good place to poke his gun through the fence and draw a bead on the sharpshooter, who no doubt supposed he still had the Yankee under cover. The officer fired, and there was one less rebel in arms against the Union.

The Confederate fell from the tree into the bushes below, where his body was found after the rebels were driven back.

Stuart took desperate chances in fighting Sheridan, and made an effort to demoralise the Federal cavalry by attacking them in front, on the flank and in the rear at the same time. But he found Sheridan could not be shaken off. Little Phil cut loose from the Army of the Potomac to whip Stuart and smash things in the rear of Lee's army. He fulfilled his mission to the letter.

CHAPTER 23

Jeff Davis rides out to see the Yankees Whipped

In speaking of the alarm in Richmond during his operations in that neighbourhood, Sheridan in his *Memoirs* says:

The Confederate authorities in Richmond were impressed, and indeed convinced, that my designs contemplated the capture of that city. Some Confederate writers have continued to hold this theory and conviction since the war. In this view they were and are in error. When Stuart was defeated, the main purpose of my instructions had been carried out, and my thoughts then turned to joining Gen. Butler to get supplies.

As soon as the Confederates became satisfied that Sheridan was not going to assault the interior fortifications, they lost no time in rallying to the "defence of their capital." A "contraband" who came into our camp after we had reached the James River, said:

Dar was mighty skeery times in Richmon', boss, when yo all cum down de rode from Yellow Tabern. I hyar'n one ob de gen'rals say, "f dem Yankees march right down to de bressworks, we mus' get way from hyar right smart.' But when de Yankees cross de Chick'hominy, and de sojers in Richmon' see yo all gwine way to de James Ribber, den de gen'ral say, "f dem Yankees had dun cum near nuff, we'd kill de las' one ob dem. De Yankees no good to fight, no how.'

The night after the Battle of Yellow Tavern was filled with experiences calculated to dishearten the Federal troopers. There was a good deal of moving about in the dark, marching nearly all night without gaining much ground. We could hear the whistles of locomotives that were drawing trains loaded with Confederates into Richmond, from Petersburg and other places. Now and then we got glimpses of the lights in the city. While Sheridan knew what he was about, the contrary was true of the rank and file. Major-generals were not given to publishing their plans among the enlisted men, nor was it necessary. We had the utmost confidence in our commander, and knew that he would take us safely through. Still it was discouraging to be hustled about in the dark, with the rain pouring down nearly all the time. We marched by "fits and jerks," as Taylor expressed it.

"Corporal Swift," said Taylor, "can you tell us where we are going?"

"No, I can't; and I don't believe anybody else can," was the reply.

"Don't Sheridan know.?"

"I suppose so."

"And don't he tell his corporals?"

"I should say not."

"Then if I's you I'd resign."

"Shut up, Taylor, or I'll put you in the guard house."

"Say, Corporal, if you'll put me in somewhere out of the rain, I'll give you an order on the sutler for ten dollars."

"Silence in the ranks!" thundered the corporal.

A good deal of the time we sat in our saddles, waiting for the order to move forward. We would march on for half a mile or more, and then come to a standstill. We could not dismount and lie down, for we had no data on which to base calculations as to how long we would stay in any one place. Cavalry horses had a way of keeping closed up on their own hook, and if perchance a worn-out trooper took advantage of a long halt to dismount and throw himself on the ground, bridle-rein in hand, and the horse in the next set of fours to the front moved up a few steps, the horse of the dismounted soldier would follow suit, and the sleep-seeking warrior was obliged to let go or be dragged along.

At daybreak on the morning of May 12 we were still in the saddle, feeling our way along. There were rebs to the right of us, rebs to the left of us, rebs to the rear of us, and rebs in our front. But they had learned from dear-bought experience to keep a little beyond the range of our carbines. We knew that the Confederates were receiving re-enforcements all the time, and while we were confident that we could "cut our way through" the enemy, we also knew that that sort of work was always attended with great risk.

Wilson felt the enemy on the Mechanicsville road—and the Confederates felt the Union troopers in return. The breastworks and batteries manned by the rebels under Gen. Bragg blocked the way in that direction. Gregg's division was looking after the rear—toward Richmond, now. Word came back that we must take care of the enemy, to give Merritt's division an opportunity to rebuild Meadow bridge, which had been destroyed by the enemy. Wilson's division was held in readiness to "work both ways"—assist Gregg in repelling the enemy from the Richmond defences, or push toward the Chickahominy, should Merritt find the rebels north of the river too strong for him.

General Wesley Merritt was equal to the emergency. He had succeeded to the command of the First Division in the Wilderness, Gen. Torbert being forced by serious illness to retire from the field. Merritt had been at the head of the reserve brigade of the First Division, being an officer in whom Little Phil had the utmost confidence.

Merritt's orders were to rebuild the bridge, and that "the crossing must be made at all hazards." Fences and buildings in the country round about were levied on by Merritt's troopers. An old Virginian who was watching the movements of Sheridan's cavalrymen from the veranda of his house, saw a Yankee trooper gallop up to his barn. After prying around with a fence stake for a few minutes, the soldier succeeded in getting off a clapboard, which he put on his shoulder and rode away to the Chickahominy.

The planter saw an officer riding at the head of a detachment of Union cavalry, and he sang out:

"Captain, one of your men has just left here with a board which he stole from my barn. I wish you would arrest him and have him punished."

"Show me where he got the board," said the officer.

"There, on the side of the barn next the road."

"How did he get it off?"

"He pried it off with a fence stake."

"Boys, do you hear? He pried off the board with a fence stake!"

In less than five minutes every board on that barn, as high up as the troopers could reach from the backs of their horses, had been pried off, and every man in the detachment was galloping to the river with a board or piece of timber on his shoulder, while the proprietor of the place anathematized the "vandal horde" and the Federal Government.

It did not take long for Merritt's men to secure enough timber to rebuild the bridge. While the work was going on, the rebel cavalry on the north side of the Chickahominy kept up a brisk fire on the builders. A battery posted on a knoll only a few rods from the river swept the bridge. The butternut-clad braves had thrown up a line of breastworks, and had determined to prevent Sheridan from crossing the river. The Confederate theory was that Fitzhugh Lee could keep the Federal cavalry south of the Chickahominy till the rebels in Richmond could muster a sufficient force to come out and jump on Sheridan and annihilate his command. But in this they made another mistake. Merritt soon had the bridge ready for the crossing of the troops, but Little Phil had concluded to give the rebels another round before going on to the James River. And he carried out his plan to the letter.

As soon as the bridge was completed Merritt's division, dismounted, was thrown across the river, and the boys made quick work of the rebels on the north bank, carrying the breastworks on a run, and sending the panic-stricken Confederates pell-mell toward Gaines's Mills. The way was now open for crossing the Chickahominy, but in the meantime a red-hot engagement had been brought on by the attempt of the rebel troops from Richmond to drive us into the river.

Wilson and Gregg's divisions were still facing the rebel capital, the former being a little farther to the west and closer to the entrenchments. Jeff Davis rode out toward Meadow bridge to see how the battle was going, and when the troops in gray filed out of the breastworks and moved forward with their long toms at a right shoulder, they were inspired by the presence of their president, and admonished by their officers to "strike till the last armed foe expires," and all that sort of thing. As the column of Confederate infantry came sweeping up the road, and deployed to the right and left for a general advance, we felt that a crisis was at hand.

None of us knew at the time that Jeff Davis was one of a group of mounted men that we could see near a clump of trees by the roadside, but some of our boys remarked that the officer in command of the rebels was probably reviewing the troops as they pressed forward into battle, for there seemed to be a good deal of cheering and waving of flags as the Confederates marched by the group near the trees. If we had known at the time that Jeff Davis was out there, almost within rifle-range of our line of battle, the Confederate president would have been given an opportunity to test the running qualities of his horse when the tide of battle was turned against his followers. And come to think of it, there is good reason to believe that Davis did use whip and spur to take his precious person back inside of the fortifications, that day, for when the Yankee troopers swept over the ground—a short time after the Confederate advance—Jeff was not there.

On came the rebels. In their front were Wilson's men, mounted. The skirmish firing soon became lively. The Confederates would halt long enough to take aim and fire, and then rush forward, loading as they advanced. But there was a surprise in store for the Johnnies, a surprise that was fatal to their hopes of being able to crush Sheridan. Little Phil tells the story of that last desperate effort of the enemy as follows:

> Wilson's troops were driven back in some confusion at first; but Gregg, in anticipation of attack, had hidden a heavy line of dismounted men in a bushy ravine on his front, and when the enemy marched upon it, with much display and under the eye of the president of the Confederacy, this concealed line opened a destructive fire with repeating carbines; and at the same time the batteries of horse artillery, under Capt. Robinson, joining in the contest, belched forth shot and shell with fatal effect. The galling fire caused the enemy to falter, and while still wavering Wilson rallied his men, and turning some of them against the right flank of the Confederates, broke their line, and compelled them to withdraw for security behind the heavy works thrown up for the defence of the city in 1862.

This ended the battle, and we were permitted to cook and eat our dinners without further molestation from the Johnnies.

"Richmond *Examiner*. Full account of de defeat of de Yankees."

"Here's de Richmond papers! De latest from Sheridan!"

There was a rush to secure the papers, which were brought into our bivouac by two little lads who wore soldier caps and gray jackets. As I recall it, one of the papers stated that Lee had whipped "Grant, the butcher," at Spotsylvania, and the Union army had retreated toward Washington, or was pushing for Fortress Monroe to get under cover of the gunboats. Sheridan, the papers announced, was completely hemmed in—had ridden directly into the trap set for him by the Confederates! If the papers had delayed going to press an hour or so, they could have published under the subhead of "Later from the Front," the information that when the trap was sprung it failed to hold the Federal troopers, and the secessionists were sent flying back behind their breastworks.

Sheridan's cavalry bivouacked at night on the north bank of the Chickahominy, on ground that had been moistened with the blood of Union and Confederate soldiers in the hard-fought battle of Gaines's Mills. Gen. Merritt had crossed the river as soon as Meadow bridge had been rebuilt, and with his division he had pushed on through Mechanicsville, putting to flight Fitzhugh Lee's cavalry, which had made an effort to check the advance of the Federals in that direction. The rebel troopers had been so severely punished at Yellow Tavern the day before that Merritt had little trouble in opening the road to Gaines's Mills.

When the Johnnies discovered that the Yankees would insist on going through, they put spurs to their horses and galloped away in search of another rallying place. Merritt had sent word to Sheridan that he had struck the enemy again, but the rebels had skedaddled before we came up with the First Division. I was glad of it. Several troopers in my platoon declared that they were still thirsting for rebel gore—this was after we received word that the Confederates had fled—but I was well-nigh played out, and felt that a cup of coffee and an opportunity to stretch myself on the ground would more than make up for the escape of what was left of Jeb Stuart's boys in butternut.

We had been in the saddle night and day, almost constantly, since we broke camp at Warrentown, May 4, and started for the Wilderness. I recall but one night out of the nine in which we had what the boys called "all night in." We secured cat-naps now and then in our saddles while riding along, and occasionally we had part of a night's rest, but we slept with our boots on and "one eye open" when we did sleep. After we cut loose from the Army of the Potomac it might be said that we slept with both eyes open. The excitement of battle and the presence of the enemy had served to keep us from breaking down. Eternal vigilance was necessary to frustrate the plans of the enemy to destroy us. We were isolated from Grant's army and too far away from any Union force to expect assistance should the Confederates get us in a tight place. If there was any heart to the Southern Confederacy we were in it, for we fought the rebels at the very gates of their capital.

Our regiment bivouacked in the edge of a strip of woods a little off the road. As we were drawn up in line before dismounting we were informed that we could "make down" for the night, and we expected to enjoy a good night's rest. Just as I settled down to sleep the first sergeant shouted:

"Sergeant Regan, Corporal Goddard, Privates Adams, Allen, Atwood, Belcher, Boyd, Clark, turn out! Saddle up and report to the adjutant at once. Be lively!"

It was a rude and cruel awakening. The voice of the first sergeant brought me back from the pleasant realms of dreamland to the stern realities of war.

It was on occasions like this that I discovered that there was a good deal in a name, after all, as was demonstrated in my case. Our orderly sergeant—as was the rule with nearly all the companies—had his roll-call memorised. On the march or in bivouac when an order came for a detail from Company I he would sing out as above, taking the privates in alphabetical order and going on down the list of names till the required number was secured. This was strictly in accordance with military red tape, to be sure, but as it could not be expected that the sergeant could remember where he left off—during the excitement of active campaigning—when the next order came it would be the same; "Privates Adams, Allen," would again step to the front.

Waterman nearly always escaped these details. And it was the same when we went into camp for a few days. Then the first sergeant would unpack his books, and in order that there might be no mistake in keeping the roster he began at the top, and "Privates Adams, Allen," would be the first for duty. We seldom staid in camp—except in winter—till the details would get down to the boys whose names began with W.

Little wonder, then, that when we were hustled out of bed at Gaines's Mills and ordered to report for duty to the adjutant that one of the boys entered a protest.

"Sergeant, couldn't you call the roll backwards once, so that Waterman and Warren and Vining and Vose and the other fellows at the other end of the roll might get a chance to distinguish themselves? I'm getting tired of this."

"Give that man an extra detail for talking back to his superior," said the company commander who had been awakened by the loud talking.

"If you'll explain how he can do it, I'll be satisfied," said the "kicker."

The officer subsequently made inquiry and found that the soldier's complaint was entitled to consideration. He gave the first sergeant orders to comply with the suggestion to begin at the bottom of the roll once in a while in making details, and also to begin in the middle and detail both ways occasionally, to give all the boys a chance at extra duty.

We saddled up, buckled on our equipments and reported to the adjutant.

"We're going on a scout on the Bottom's Bridge road," said the officer who took charge of the party. "If we find the road clear we'll be back in a couple of hours. See that your carbines and pistols are in good shape, ready for instant use. We may run into the rebels."

We pushed out through the picket line of the First Division and explored the road for several miles down the north bank of the Chickahominy. Once we halted and prepared to fight, as the trooper in advance reported that mounted men were coming up the road.

"Break to the right and left and keep well in among the trees," whispered the officer.

The night was dark, and although we could hear the approach of the enemy we could not see them till they came within a few feet of us. We felt somewhat relieved when we discovered that there were but two men for us to combat. Still they might be the advance guard of a large body of the enemy.

"Who comes there?" challenged our sergeant.

"Lawdy, massa, don't shoot—it's only ole Julius an' Pomp."

"Where are you going?"

"See hyar; is yo all sojers of which army?"

"Gen. Lee's."

"Pomp an' I jes gwine to de nex plantation—dat's all, sah."

"What takes you to the plantation at this hour of the night?"

"Pomp gwine to see he gal, an' I jes ride long to keep de Yanks from runnin' off wid Pomp."

The darkies were mounted on mules and we were satisfied that they were searching for the camp of Sheridan's raiders. The lieutenant in command struck a match and held it up so that he could get a good look at the "contrabands." Julius and Pomp's eyes seemed to be bulging out of their heads; but one glance at the troopers gathered around them appeared to convince the "runaways" that they were in the hands of friends.

"Golly, massa, yo all been foolin' us."

"How so?"

"'Cos yo all's Massa Linkum's sojers, shuah's yo born."

The lieutenant acknowledged the identity of his detachment, and Julius and Pomp admitted that they were on the way to cast in their lot with the Yankees. They said they had been at work in the trenches around Richmond. They had heard of "freedom," and when Sheridan's troopers came so near they determined to make their way into the Union lines. So they had confiscated two C. S. A. Government mules and started out to find our camp. They assured us that the road to Bottom's Bridge was clear, and we returned to the bivouac, and again unsaddled and turned in, catching a couple of hours' sleep before reveille.

We marched to Bottom's Bridge, May 13, and the next day we recrossed the Chickahominy to the south bank, and continued on to the James River at Haxall's Landing, by way of Malvern Hill. The last day's march was hard on men and horses; a number of troopers hoofed it nearly all the way, because their horses were practically played out. We had put in a full week.

At Haxall's Landing we found an abundance of supplies provided from Butler's army of the James, which had been operating against Richmond on the south bank of the river. And how comforting it was to lie down at night under the protection of the gunboats Of course we had come to understand that Sheridan's cavalry corps was well able to protect itself, but the troopers were worn and weary. They needed rest and a chance to inventory themselves. And they needed washing, too. Though hungry and tired, a large majority of the troopers in our regiment enjoyed a swim in the river before they cooked their supper. Plenty of soap was issued to the men, and there was a general scrubbing. Everybody shouted, "Bully for Butler!" when it was announced that the Bay State General had given orders to the officers of his commissary department to give Sheridan's men all they could eat, and of the best to be had.

We were told that we could take things easy for three or four days, a privilege that we appreciated. Sheridan's wounded were put in charge of Butler's surgeons, and our prisoners were turned over to the provost marshal of the army of the James. Then the Federal troopers pulled off their boots and turned in for the night.

CHAPTER 24

Butler's Advance on the South Side

Sheridan's weary troopers appreciated the three-days' rest given them at Haxall's Landing. An opportunity was afforded the recruits who had never been on a raid before to doctor their saddle boils, and rub horse liniment on the contusions they had sustained while being banged around on the march from the Wilderness to the James.

While we were recuperating in camp, the army of the James was operating against Richmond. A courier came in from General Kautz's cavalry, then smashing things out beyond Petersburg, bringing encouraging news. Butler had sailed up the river with a fleet of mixed vessels—that may not be a strictly nautical phrase, but it expresses the character of the flotilla. Nearly every class of vessel, from the latest improved ironclad down to the slow-going canal boat, ascended the James to Bermuda Hundred, from which base Butler moved his troops in his attack on the rebel fortifications at Drewry's Bluff.

We did not know, at the time, what Butler was trying to accomplish, except the general statement that Grant had ordered him to co-operate with the Army of the Potomac in the advance on Richmond. The intricate details of the plan were altogether too perplexing for worn-out troopers to puzzle their brains with. An outline of what had taken place on the south bank of the river was given out, and as I remember it, the day that we started on our return to Grant's army, it was generally understood that Butler had Been driven back from Drewry's Bluff into his breastworks at Bermuda Hundred, although we did not hear that he had been "bottled up" till several weeks later.

I did not know at that time that Butler had been declared an outlaw by Jeff Davis, but I suppose the commanding general of the army of the James was aware of the fact. Whether the same had any influence on Butler's retreat down the river when worsted by Beauregard,

I am not prepared to assert. It would be a serious breach of discipline for one of the few surviving privates of the great rebellion to intimate that the Bay State's favourite major-general turned his back on Richmond, and sought the security of breastworks, with gunboat supports, to escape falling into the hands of the Confederates. And yet I have since discovered that had Butler been captured, he would have been hanged by the neck until he was dead, dead, dead.

Butler, as is well known, had given the Confederacy no end of trouble at New Orleans, when in command down there. He had caused the rebels to understand that the assassination of Union soldiers must be atoned for by the punishment of the assassins.

In *The Rise and Fall of the Confederate Government*, by Jeff Davis, an account is published of what the rebel president declared to have been the "murder" of William B. Mumford, a "non-combative" citizen of New Orleans, by Butler's order. General Lee had written to General Halleck about it, as instructed by Davis, and Halleck refused to receive the letters, because, as he expressed it, they were of an insulting character. Davis continues:

> It appeared that the silence of the Government of the United States, and its maintenance of Butler in high office under its authority, afforded evidence too conclusive that it sanctioned his conduct, and was determined that he should remain unpunished for these crimes. I therefore pronounced and declared the said Butler a felon, deserving capital punishment, and ordered that he be no longer considered and treated as a public enemy of the Confederate States, but as an outlaw and common enemy of mankind; and that, in the event of his capture, the officer in command should cause him to be immediately executed by hanging.

According to General G. T. Beauregard, who commanded the rebels at Drewry's Bluff, General Butler's salvation from summary execution was due to the failure of the Confederate General Whiting, to carry out the instructions given him by Beauregard, for the latter, in an article in *Battles and Leaders of the Civil War*, says:

> Nothing would have prevented Whiting from capturing the entire force of General Butler, had he followed my instructions. ...We could and should have captured Butler's entire army.

I do not know but Beauregard's expectations included the capture of Sheridan's cavalry at Haxall's, and, possibly, Grant's army, too; but the modest Confederate is silent on this point.

I beg pardon for going outside the lines a little in speaking of Butler's operations. Whatever may have been that general's failings—if he had any failings—as a military commander, one thing the survivors of Sheridan's cavalry corps will never forget: he fed them when they were hungry, and filled their haversacks for the march to rejoin the Army of the Potomac.

We started on the return trip Tuesday evening, May 17. I would have volunteered to be transferred to the navy, had there been a chance to do so. My saddle boils were all ripe, and a few hours' riding brought matters to a crisis. But I became hardened to it later on, and never again suffered affliction of that character.

Scouting parties were pushed to the front to feel the way, the exact location of Grant's army being unknown to us. Our horses had recovered from the effects of the fatiguing march, and the troopers were in good spirits. The "new hands" began to feel confidence in themselves, and as they had not shown the white feather thus far, the old veterans were considerate enough to admit that the four new companies had the "makings of a good battalion."

We crossed the Chickahominy at Jones's Bridge, and camped in the vicinity of Baltimore crossroads Thursday night. From this place our division and Wilson's were sent to explore the roads around Cold Harbor. Our movements were not opposed by the Confederates, and we rested our horses on what proved to be, a few days later, one of the bloodiest battlefields of the campaign.

At the old tavern at Cold Harbor we filled our canteens with water, the tavern being dry so far as liquor was concerned. We were only twelve miles from Richmond, yet the rebels were willing to give us full swing so long as we would keep away from their capital.

While the second and third divisions were scouting around Cold Harbor, Custer took his brigade to Hanover, destroyed Confederate stores at that station, and burned several bridges.

In the meantime, Merritt's men had repaired the railroad bridge over the Pamunkey, and upon our return from Cold Harbor, everything was in readiness for continuing the march to rejoin the Army of the Potomac. Custer's men reported that Lee's army was entrenched along the North Anna, and that meant that Grant's troops were on the opposite side, facing Lee.

Tuesday, May 24, just a week from the day we left the James, we joined the Army of the Potomac near Chesterfield. We had been absent sixteen days. Grant and Meade highly commended Little Phil upon the success of his daring raid, and the doughboys admitted that the cavalry, with Sheridan in command, was able to take care of itself, and could make a march in the enemy's country without a column of infantry to keep off the rebels. The cavalry corps lost six hundred and twenty-five men and half as many horses on the raid.

The first and second divisions of Sheridan's cavalry corps led the advance from the line of the North Anna, when the Army of the Potomac executed another left-flank movement, crossing to the south bank of the river the day after our return from the raid around Richmond. The third division, commanded by Wilson, was detached from the corps, and sent to look after the right flank of Grant's army. Sheridan accompanied the advance, and he was instructed to put out and feel the enemy.

Gregg's division engaged in a lively brush with the rebels at a place called Hawes's Shop, May 27. The enemy had us at a great disadvantage, being posted behind breastworks. An infantry brigade with long toms kept the minie balls pinging around our ears, while the sharp reports of carbines, the cheers of our boys as they pushed forward, the rebel yell and the booming of field pieces gave warning to the troops in our rear that the cavalry was at it again.

We ran into the rebels rather unexpectedly, although we knew that they were close at hand. Our advance guard was fired on as the detachment approached a belt of timber skirting the road. In a few minutes our whole division was under fire, and the Johnnies stubbornly contested every inch of ground which they occupied.

While we were closing in on the rebel entrenchments, a young trooper on my right asked me if I had any water. I reached him my canteen. Just as he raised it to his lips a bullet from a rebel musket struck it, knocking it out of the trooper's hand.

"That's blasted mean!" he exclaimed.

"Pick up the canteen, maybe the water hasn't all run out," I shouted.

"It's all gone," he said. The ball had passed through, tearing; a big hole in the tin.

"Take a drink from my canteen," said another trooper, who had witnessed the incident.

"Thank you." And holding the canteen up above his head, the thirsty soldier shouted: "Now, you miserable gray backs, shoot away;

spoil this canteen, will you?"

Whiz! thug! And the second canteen was struck by a musket-ball and ruined.

"I guess I'm not as thirsty as I thought I was," remarked the young cavalryman, as he declined the offer of another canteen.

A sergeant of a Pennsylvania regiment in the second brigade, was severely wounded in the leg. Two comrades attempted to assist him back behind a tree to the left of the road. The wounded non-commissioned officer was carried on a piece of board, which the troopers held between them, and supported himself by holding on to their shoulders.

Just as they were passing our position in line, a shell struck the board, and stove it into splinters. The sergeant was thrown on one side of the road, and his two comrades on the other. I thought they were dead, but in a few seconds the sergeant raised up on his elbow and called out:

"Jackson, are you killed?"

"No, sir; but I'm unconscious."

"Where's Corbet?"

"Here, sir; but I'm unconscious, too. There's no breath left in me body."

Then the two troopers lifted their heads and looked cautiously around. They had escaped serious injury, but the sergeant's other leg was badly shattered. They picked him up and bore him to the rear.

General Gregg fought his division well, and the survivors of the engagement at Hawes's Shop will bear testimony that the rebels held their ground bravely.

We pressed forward to the breastworks, but were unable to carry the line. The Confederates poured volley after volley into our ranks. Still the troopers, with averted faces, worked their way to the front, securing a position and holding it within pistol range of the enemy. Boys in blue and boys in butternut went down.

The regiment on our right made a sudden dash, and swept back the Confederate line. But our boys were unable to hold the advance position. The Johnnies fired upon them from both flanks, and back they came, slowly and with their faces to the foe, loading and firing as they retreated. They brought in a score or more of prisoners.

"Halloo, Reb! What are you fellows blocking our road for?" shouted a blue-clad trooper to a Confederate sergeant, as the prisoners were hustled to the rear.

"Who's a-blocking the road, Yank? I'm done. You all gobbled me in a squar' fight."

"Where do you hail from?"

"Ole South Carliney, and if you'll give me my parole, I'll go down thar and stay till the wah's over."

We were having a lively exchange of leaden compliments, when the boys in charge of our horses—we were fighting on foot—began to cheer, and we knew that help was at hand. In a few minutes we saw General Custer, at the head of his Michigan brigade, coming up the road.

Sheridan had sent Custer to Gregg's assistance at the request of the latter, who had informed Sheridan that he could drive the rebels from their breastworks with the help of a few more men. Of the closing up of the battle General Gregg says:

"Soon Custer reported with his brigade. This he dismounted and formed on a road leading to the front and through the centre of my line. In column of platoons, with band playing, he advanced. As arranged, when the head of his column reached my line, all went forward with a tremendous yell, and the contest was of short duration. We went right over the rebels, who resisted with courage and desperation unsurpassed. Our success cost the Second Division two hundred and fifty-six men and officers, killed and wounded. This fight has always been regarded by the Second Division as one of its severest."

The Confederates left us in possession of the field and the dead and wounded. Inside the earthworks, a little to the left of the road, a young rebel lay dying. A bullet had struck him in the breast, and his life's blood was flowing from the wound and from his mouth. He was not more than seventeen years old. The dead and dying were thick around the boy, showing that he had fallen where the fight was the hottest.

"I can't do anything for you, my son," said a gray-haired Federal surgeon, who had examined his wound.

"Am I dying, Doctor?"

"Yes, my son; the wound is fatal."

"Can my head be raised?"

"Certainly. Here, boys! bring an overcoat or a blanket."

The old doctor's voice was tremulous and his eyes were moist with tears. A dozen blue overcoats were offered, but only one was needed. This the surgeon folded so as to make a pillow for the wounded Confederate. Tenderly the doctor raised the boy's head and placed it

The Federal surgeon aids a dying Confederate

on the overcoat. As he did so the blood flowed afresh from the wound in the breast.

"Doctor—picture—mother—pocket—let me see it."

"Yes, my son."

The surgeon took from the boy's butternut jacket a picture of a sweet-faced woman, and held it before the dying soldier's eyes.

"Closer, Doctor."

The boy had attempted to take the picture in his hand, but his strength was gone—he could not use his arms. The doctor held the picture against the lips of the youth. It was stained with blood when taken away, but there was a smile on the face of the boy.

"Doctor," he said faintly, "tell mother I died like a soldier—will you write to her?"

"Yes."

The old doctor's tears were flowing freely now. And so were the tears of fifteen or twenty Union troopers who had gathered around the dying boy.

"Yes, I'll write—what's the address, my son?"

"Mother's name is"—

The voice sank to a whisper, and the Federal surgeon placed his ear close to the lad's mouth.

"Is what?"

"Mother—O, Doctor!—meet—heaven—goodbye!"

He was dead.

"He was so much like my boy who was killed at Antietam," said the surgeon, as he folded the dead Confederate's hands over the mother's picture.

Search was made for a letter or writing that would identify the boy or reveal his mother's address. Only one letter was found in his pocket. There was no envelope; no postmark. It began, "My darling soldier boy." and breathed the mother's anxiety for the welfare of her son, and the prayer that he would be spared to return and make glad that mother's heart. And the signature—"Your fond and affectionate mother." Nothing more. There was no time for ceremony; barely time to bury the dead. The boy's body was wrapped in a U. S. blanket and put in a trench hastily dug and hastily filled.

The advance on Cold Harbor was led by the First and Second Divisions of the cavalry corps under Sheridan. The Third Division under Wilson had been sent out on the right flank to tear up the Virginia Central railroad. That duty was performed, and at the same time Wilson's division engaged the Georgia cavalry under General P. B. M. Young, at Hanover Court House. The Confederates were driven out. In the meantime we were having our hands full at Cold Harbor, toward which place we marched all night, after the fight at Hawes's Shop. Sheridan had pushed forward Torbert's division, and a severe fight was had with the enemy, resulting in the occupancy of Cold Harbor and the important cross-roads by the First Division. While Torbert's men were fighting at Cold Harbor, our division guarded the road near Old Church. An order came from Sheridan for Gregg to send re-enforcements, to Torbert, and Davies's brigade was ordered to the front. We arrived too late to help the First Division drive out the rebels, but we were in time to assist in holding Cold Harbor the next day till the infantry came to our relief.

Sheridan had concluded that he could not hold Cold Harbor without infantry support, and the doughboys were eight or ten miles away. Orders were given to fall back to Old Church during the night of May 31. The withdrawal was made in good order, and we were congratulating ourselves on escaping from the trap the rebel infantry was preparing to spring upon us at daybreak, when we received orders to face about and hold Cold Harbor "at all hazards." Back we went, and preparations were made for resisting the attack of the enemy, which we felt sure would be made at daylight. If the rebels had discovered that we had moved out of the breastworks in their front, and had advanced and occupied the line, they could have held Cold Harbor against our four brigades, as the Confederate cavalry was supported by Hoke's and Kershaw's infantry.

Our position at Cold Harbor was anything but satisfactory, as we "turned doughboys" and began to dig for our lives, the necessity of entrenching our line being well understood, as we were to fight on foot. Sheridan says in his *Memoirs*, speaking of the return to Cold Harbor:

> We now found that the temporary breastworks of rails and logs which the Confederates had built were of incalculable benefit to us in furnishing material with which to establish a line of defence, they being made available by simply reversing them at some points, or at others wholly reconstructing them to suit the circumstances of the ground. The troops, without reserves, were then placed behind our cover, dismounted, boxes of ammunition distributed along the line, and the order passed along that

the place must be held. All this was done in the darkness, and while we were working away at our cover, the enemy could be distinctly heard from our skirmish line giving commands and making preparations to attack.

Thursday morning, June 1, the rebels attacked Sheridan at Cold Harbor. The troopers were not directed to withhold their fire till they could "see the whites of the eyes" of the foe, but they permitted the Johnnies to come within short range before opening on them. The Confederate infantry charged the breastworks, the rebel yell being heard above the terrible din of battle. Sheridan's men demonstrated to their commander and to the world that they could fight afoot or on horseback. The rebels did not get near enough to stick any of our boys with their bayonets, which had been fixed for that sort of butchery. Before they came within bayonet distance they were so badly demoralized by the raking fire of the Federal cavalrymen armed with breach-loading carbines, that they took to their heels and skedaddled back to the woods from which they had started on their charge. Their flight was accelerated by the terrible fire poured into their ranks by our flying artillery, which had opened on the rebels as they came forward to the attack.

Again the Johnnies came, after they had recovered somewhat from their first repulse. But the Yankees gave the enemy another red-hot reception, and the rebels were forced to take to the woods. Before the second charge our regiment was mounted and sent out on the flank to support a battery that had been ordered to shell the Confederates out of a piece of woods.

It was a very trying situation. The artillerymen ran their guns out to the skirmish line, unlimbered and opened on the woods. The rebels replied with artillery and infantry, and the enemy's gunners got our range in a short time. The shells were bursting all around and over us for fifteen or twenty minutes. We sat on our horses ready to charge the rebels should they dash out of the woods and attempt to capture our artillery. It was far more trying on the nerves to sit bolt upright in the saddle as a target for rebel cannoneers and infantry, than it would have been to charge the enemy's lines and engage in hand-to-hand conflict.

A solid shot cut Corporal Goddard's haversack from his saddle without injuring the corporal or his horse. Corporal Jack Hazelet was on the left of the squadron. The corporal was given to stammering, and so was the captain and brevet major in command of the next squadron on our left. As a shell went shrieking through the air just over our heads, the boys naturally began to dodge. Then the captain shouted:

"Wha-wha-what you, you, you dod-dod-dod-dodging at, Cor-cor-corporal?"

"You-you're dod-dod-dodging, Cor-cor-corporal!"

A shell burst in front of the captain, and he was seen to duck his head as a piece of the shell went whizzing close to his ear.

"Wha-wha-what you, you, you dod-dod-dodging at, Ma-ma-major?"

"Who-who-who's a dod-dod-dod-dodging, Cor-corcorporal?"

"You -you-you're dod-dod-dod-dodging. Ma-mamajor!"

Of course everybody dodged—it was natural that they should under such circumstances.

I was detailed with another trooper to go down in a ravine to the right of our position, to fill the canteens of the company. I jumped at the chance, as I thought it would take me out of the direct range of the rebel artillery for a little while. We kept well to the rear of the regiment till we reached a row of trees and underbrush skirting the ravine. Then we faced to the front and followed a fence about half a mile. We found water and dismounted to fill our canteens. Pieces of shell began to drop all around us and into the water. We sprang up to ascertain the cause of this new departure, and discovered that the rebel artillery was shelling the woods. It was subsequently learned from a rebel prisoner that the Johnnies thought a column of Federal infantry was advancing upon their position under cover of the trees.

"We can't stay here," exclaimed my companion.

"I should say not."

"Let's go back to the company."

"All right; go ahead."

We sprang into our saddles and hastened to get out of the woods.

As we came into the open field near where we had left our company, we saw a column of infantry moving into position. The doughboys were rushing forward at a dog trot, with their long toms at right shoulder. It was a division of the Sixth corps, and was commanded, I think, by General David A. Russell, who was wounded that day or the next while gallantly leading his division against the enemy's lines. He was subsequently killed at the Battle of Opequan, while serving under Sheridan in the valley. The cavalrymen were rejoiced at the arrival of the infantry, and at once mounted and pushed out toward the Chickahominy to cover the left flank of Grant's army.

Our regiment and the battery had been withdrawn as soon as the infantry had arrived, and had moved to the left with the rest of Davies's brigade. When the two water-carriers, who had been shelled out of the woods, reached the position where we had left our company, the regiment was nowhere to be seen.

"Which way did the cavalry go?" I asked an infantry colonel.

"They pushed on to the front," he replied.

"Into the woods?"

"Yes."

We put spurs to our horses and dashed down the road in that direction.

We reached the edge of the woods and pushed on, jumping our horses over temporary rifle pits and rail barricades which had been occupied by the Confederates, and from which they had been ousted by the fire of our battery. We saw dead rebels in the rifle pits and in the road. We galloped on, and as we were beginning to wonder what had become of our regiment, we came against a column of rebel infantry marching toward the rifle pits we had passed a few minutes before.

"Whew!"

"Where's our cavalry?" I stammered, scarcely knowing what I was doing.

"What cavalry?" asked a rebel sergeant, who was in charge of the advance guard of the column.

"Hampton's?"

"Off to the right."

"We must get there at once—important dispatches."

Our advent was so sudden that the meeting was as much of a surprise to the rebels as it was to us, and as it was not uncommon for rebel cavalrymen to don blue jackets when they could get them by stripping prisoners, the Confederates did not seem to grasp the situation till we had turned about and were galloping back over the road toward the Federal lines.

"Halt!"

"Halt, you infernal Yankees!"

The order was backed up by a volley from the rebel advance guard. The bullets whistled about our ears, but we bent low in our saddles and never looked behind us until we had placed the Sixth corps between us and the Confederates. Then we drew rein and took an inventory. Several canteens were missing, but otherwise we were "all present or accounted for," and we rode out to the left and rejoined our company.

Chapter 25

The Rebels Routed

After the Battle of Cold Harbor, Sheridan's cavalry corps remained in camp around Bottom's Bridge and New Castle ferry until preparations were completed by Grant to make another change of base. This time it was announced that the Army of the Potomac was to be concentrated on the south bank of the James, and that Richmond would be attacked from the new line. We expected to be pushed to the front to open the way for the infantry, but when orders came for Sheridan to march we found that only Wilson's division was to accompany Grant's army, Sheridan being directed to cut loose again with Torbert and Gregg's divisions, and slash around north of the rebel capital while the Federal troops were crossing the James.

Sheridan's instructions for this raid included the following:

"With two divisions of your corps you will move on the morning of the 7th inst. to Charlottesville, and destroy the railroad bridge over the Rivanna River near that town; you will then thoroughly destroy the railroad (the Virginia Central) from that point to Gordonsville, and from Gordonsville to Hanover Junction, and to the latter point, if practicable."

Upon the completion of this duty, Sheridan was directed to rejoin the Army of the Potomac. A canvas pontoon train of eight boats and tools and implements for tearing up the railroad were supplied from the engineer and quartermaster departments. Grant also informed Sheridan that Gen. Hunter, who was operating in West Virginia, was moving toward Charlottesville and might be expected to co-operate with our two divisions. We were to begin at Charlottesville and work west along the Virginia Central, and Hunter, beginning at or near Lynchburg, was to move eastward, tearing up the road. The canal near the James River was also to be destroyed where possible.

Supplies were issued at New Castle Ferry—three days' rations, to last five days we were told. Extra ammunition was carried in the wagons. Forage—two days' rations of oats—was issued to each trooper for his horse, and was carried on the saddle.

Our march from New Castle Ferry to the vicinity of Trevilian Station was made interesting by occasional skirmishes with rebel scouting parties. One object of our expedition was to draw Wade Hampton and his cavalry away from Lee's army. This part of the programme was successful. Hampton and Fitzhugh Lee were detached from Lee's army, and infantry under a general named Breckenridge, *en route* to the valley, was instructed to move so as to support the troopers in butternut. The rebel cavalry had wisely decided that it was poor generalship to attack Sheridan without having a good-sized body of foot troops and artillery close at hand to rally behind when hard-pressed.

We struck Trevilian Station early in the morning, June 11, 1864. Our advance began skirmishing with the Johnnies at daylight. Soon Torbert's division went in with a cheer, and the fight became general all along the front. Our brigade was deployed near the forks of the turnpike at Buck Child's. The wagon train was drawn up west of the road and we were charged with its protection and at the same time cautioned to keep our eyes open for any flank movement of the enemy. The second brigade of our division, commanded by Colonel J. Irving Gregg, was formed down toward the railroad, east of the station, and on the left of Merritt's brigade of Torbert's division. Custer, with his Michigan troopers, was sent around below the railroad to attack the enemy's right flank. He crossed midway between Louisa Court House and Trevilian Station, and headed for the Gordonsville turnpike.

From our isolated position we could hear the firing away to the southwest, where we understood Custer was at work on Hampton's flank. More directly in our front Torbert's men were pushing their way toward the station, and we knew by the sound of battle that the enemy was falling back. A sergeant and five or six men of the second brigade came over to the train with a squad of rebel prisoners. The latter had been captured near the railroad, and had come from the direction of Louisa Court House. The prisoners were questioned by a staff officer:

"What brigade do you belong to?"

"Lomax's brigade of Fitzhugh Lee's division."

"Where is Lee's division?"

"Don't know."

"When did you leave it?"

"'Bout sun-up."

"Where was it then?"

"On the Gordonsville road, near Louisa Court House, just south of the railroad."

"Which way was Lee going.?"

"He was headed this way. We were sent ahead to feel the Yankees, and your men gobbled us down there by the railroad."

"Was Hampton with Lee?"

"No; we heard say that Hampton was at Trevilian Station."

A courier was started off on a gallop from Gen. Davies's headquarters. It was stated that things were getting mixed on our left. From what meagre information the rank and file could get hold of, it was evident that while Custer was swooping down on Hampton's flank and rear, Fitzhugh Lee was closing in on Custer's rear. Several other couriers were sent forward to give warning of the approach of Fitzhugh Lee's division. We expected our old enemies would give us a call at any moment, and we made preparations to tender them a red-hot reception. But the Johnnies did not reach our position, their attention being drawn to Custer's headquarter wagons, that had been left south of the railroad.

In speaking of the movements of the Michigan brigade at Trevilian, Sheridan in his *Memoirs* says:

"Custer, the moment he found himself in Hampton's rear, charged the led horses, wagons and caissons found there, getting hold of a vast number of each, and also of the station itself. The stampede and havoc wrought by Custer in Hampton's rear compelled him to turn Rosser's brigade in that direction, and while it attacked Custer on one side, Fitzhugh Lee's division, which had followed Custer toward Trevilian, attacked him on the other. There then ensued a desperate struggle for the possession of the captured property, resulting finally by its being retaken by the enemy. Indeed, the great number of horses and vehicles could not be kept on the limited space within Custer's line, which now formed almost a complete circle; and while he was endeavouring to remove them to a secure place, they, together with Custer's headquarters wagon and four of his caissons, fell into the hands of their original owners."

In the meantime Torbert's other brigades—Devin and Merritt's—had swept everything before them, and Hampton was driven west from Trevilian Station toward Gordonsville. Gregg's division was called upon to resist the advance of Fitzhugh Lee, and the latter was forced back toward Louisa Court House, all his efforts to break through our line and rejoin Hampton, west of the station, having been frustrated.

Sheridan camped at Trevilian the night of June 11, and bright and early the next morning Gregg's division demonstrated its ability to spoil a rebel railroad. The track was torn up for five or six miles, the ties and timbers were burned and the rails twisted out of shape by heating them and bending them around trees or telegraph poles. The rebels did not molest us. They were throwing up breastworks at Molloy's Crossroads, two miles or so west of Trevilian Station, where Torbert found them in the afternoon while reconnoitring to clear a road for Sheridan's march toward Spotsylvania, our commander having concluded to return to the Army of the Potomac by that roundabout way to keep Hampton's cavalry from rejoining Lee. The return was decided upon because it had been ascertained that Gen, Hunter was moving west toward Lynchburg, instead of toward Gordonsville, and it would be a waste of time for Sheridan to attempt to form a junction with him.

The gallant First Division only waited for the order to "dismount and go in, boys." Hampton's men had improved the time and a strong line of breastworks had been thrown up. Butler's rebel troopers were armed with "long toms," which they used with deadly effect, being able to drop our boys before the latter could get within carbine-range of the Confederates. In this fight the rebels had great advantages over the Federals. One brigade armed with Enfield rifles and posted behind breastworks ought to be a match at any time for more than an entire division of dismounted cavalry, Hampton's division included Butler's brigade, made up of the Fourth, Fifth and Sixth South Carolina; Rosser's brigade of Virginians; Young's brigade, including Cobb's legion, Phillips legion, Jeff Davis legion, the Seventh Georgia and Milieu's Georgia battalion. These organisations held the breastworks with three batteries of artillery. This left Fitzhugh Lee's division, mounted, to attack the flanks of the assaulting column. Several unsuccessful charges were made on the breastworks, and when night set in the rebels still held the line.

Soon after dark Torbert's division was called in, and with Gregg's division took up the march for Carpenter's ford, on the North Anna, which was crossed at daylight. During the two days' fighting at Trevilian, Sheridan lost about eighty-five men killed, and four hundred and ninety wounded. The rebel loss was greater. The rebels were so badly used up that they did not venture outside of their breastworks when Sheridan withdrew toward the North Anna. Sheridan reached the river with three hundred and seventy prisoners. The Union wounded, who were unable to be transported in ambulances, and the Confederate wounded were left at the station and cared for by a Federal surgeon and several enlisted men who were selected to remain for that purpose.

CHAPTER 26

Ghastly Sights in the Trenches

June 15, 1864, Sheridan's cavalry arrived at Spotsylvania Court House *en route* from Trevilian Station, to rejoin the Army of the Potomac. After crossing the North Anna we had marched in a northeasterly direction on the Catharpen road, passing a few miles south of the battlefield of the Wilderness, where the third battalion of the First Massachusetts had received its baptism of fire a few weeks before.

The terrible destruction wrought by bullet and shell at Spottsylvania, was attested by the appearance of the timber that skirted the fields. In many places large trees had been cut down by minie balls, and others were completely honeycombed by the missiles of death.

That both the armies of Grant and Lee had suffered severely, was proved by the long rows of trenches, in which the boys in blue and the boys in gray, who fell on that bloody field, were buried.

The graves had been hastily covered, and the heavy rains that had fallen after the battle had washed off the earth here and there, and cut large holes into the resting-places of the dead. Arms from which the flesh had nearly rotted away, and feet and legs badly decomposed or fleshless, protruded from the ground, and a glance into the trenches would cause men with iron nerves to stagger back with horror at the ghastly sight of skulls and human skeletons which had been partly uncovered by the rain.

Quite a number of wounded Union soldiers were gathered into our ambulance train at Spotsylvania and the immediate vicinity. They had been left behind when Grant's army moved by the left flank to the North Anna.

At a farmhouse a mile or so from Spotsylvania, our ambulance squad found a wounded soldier of a Pennsylvania regiment, belonging to the Sixth army corps. He had been shot in the breast and shoulder,

Calling for water

and left for dead on the field. A plantation darky had found the Yankee "out dar in de woods." The soldier had revived, and was calling for water.

"Dick toted the poor boy to the house, and we've done our best for him," explained the mistress of the plantation.

She was the widow of a Confederate who lost his life at Gettysburg, we were told. With the help of a few coloured men and women who had not run away with "Massa Linkum's sojers," she had managed to grow a small crop, but the frequent visits of scouting parties, Federal and Confederate, had drawn heavily on her commissary department.

The "poor boy," as the widow called her patient, must have been about thirty-five years old, and several years the senior of his darkeyed nurse. He was evidently well along the road to convalescence, and seated in an easy chair, with a *pickaninny* on either side to fan him and look after his personal comfort, the soldier from the Keystone State seemed to be tolerably well fixed.

"Are you able to travel?" he was asked. "Oh! travel—why, it would kill me to be moved."

"Couldn't you ride in an ambulance.?"

"No; the jolting would surely kill me."

"The doctor who came over here from the Court House to see after him, said nothing but perfect rest would keep him alive," interposed the widow.

"Well, we will leave you here if you're willing to stay," said the non-commissioned officer in charge of the squad.

"A word in your ear, sergeant," exclaimed the wounded man, as the soldiers were leaving the house. "I'm getting along nicely, and in a few days I shall be able to travel. My shoulder is permanently disabled, and I shall never be fit for active service with my regiment again. I shall go over to Fredericksburg and get a sick furlough, and after a short visit to my mother in Pennsylvania, I'm coming back here. The lady of the house wants an overseer. She's from my State originally, and she's for the Union. Her husband's dead, and we've laid out a programme that will include the calling in of a clergyman. If you come this way next summer, be sure and call."

"Yes, come and see us," added the widow, who had heard the remark about calling in a clergyman.

Whether the programme was carried out as arranged by the wounded Federal and his fair benefactress, I never had an opportunity to ascertain. But the boys all expressed the hope that nothing would interfere with the plans of the interesting couple at the Virginia farmhouse.

From nearly every plantation along the line of march, our column was reinforced by negroes. Gray-headed old "uncles" and "aunties," broad-shouldered farmhands, male and female; mothers with from two to a dozen children, and promiscuous troops of *pickaninnies*, who knew not what had become of their parents, joined the contraband contingent that kept pace with the troops during the day. They swarmed through our camps at night, and amused the soldiers with their plantation songs and droll dialect.

"Where are you going?" a soldier asked an old darky, whose hair was as white as wool, and who joined the column at a cross-roads, followed by six or eight children, and something like a score of grandchildren of both sexes.

"Boun' for the Promis' Lan', massa," was the reply.

"Where is the Promised Land, Uncle?"

"Don't know 'zactly, massa; but its up dar vvhar Massa Linkum's sojers come from, I reckon."

"Why don't you stay at home?"

"Home, massa? I'se got no home. My ole wife been sold 'way to nudder county. My chil'ren and gran'chil'ren all scattered frevv slavery."

"You seem to have quite a number left."

"Dese ain't half, massa. We'se gwyne to de lan' ob freedom and maybe de ress will meet us dar."

"Then you have heard of emancipation?"

"Don't know what dat is, massa."

"Freedom; President Lincoln's proclamation setting the slaves free?"

"Yes, sah; we dun heard ob dat. Bress de Lawd!"

Sheridan did not know the whereabouts of the Army of the Potomac, and he decided to push for West Point, at the junction of the Mattapony and Pamunkey Rivers, which form the York River at that place. We crossed to the north bank of the Mattapony near Bowling Green and not far from the junctions of the Mat, the Ta, the Po and the Ny branches, which unite their waters and their names a few miles southeast of Spotsylvania. We were handicapped by five hundred rebel prisoners and nearly the same number of wounded, transported in ambulances, plantation wagons and various kinds of vehicles appropriated in the enemy's country. Scouting parties were kept well out in the front and on the flanks to give warning of any approach of the rebels. Hampton s cavalry was reported to be several miles south of our column and marching parallel with it. Three days marching brought us to King and Queen Court House, near which we camped the night of June 1 8.

When the camp fires were lighted in Sheridan's bivouac that night the picture was a wonder to behold. Everybody was tired, hungry and sleepy. Yet it was long after taps before the groups around the camp fires began to disperse. I made a tour of the camp with a corporal of Company K.

The ambulance train, what there was of it, was parked in a field not far from headquarters. The surgeons and attendants were busy caring for the wounded. Troopers and darkies volunteered to render such assistance as they could. The poor fellows in the wagons were made as comfortable as possible for the night.

"Do we march again tomorrow?" a wounded trooper inquired of the surgeon who was dressing his leg, which had been shattered by a shell at Trevilian.

"I understand so," the doctor replied.

"When will we get to a hospital?"

"In a day or two, I think."

"Well, doctor, I don't want to complain, but I'm afraid that two days more of this sort of thing will bring my final statements."

"No, no, my man; you've got too much backbone to be talking about final statements. You'll pull through all right and be ready for another charge on the rebels in a few months."

The trooper did pull through, but his leg was amputated at West Point, and he never returned to his regiment.

"Yo, Liza Jane—stop dat crying, chile. Don't you know dat we'se boun' for de lan' ob freedum? Dar'll be plenty ob hoe cake dar, chile. Hush yo fuss!" The above admonition, was given by an old negro woman to one of her descendants as we approached the field where the coloured contingent was picnicking under the trees.

And such a picnic! The darkies were filled with enthusiasm— which was fortunate for them—as all hands were on short rations.

Under a large tree a white-headed old patriarch had gathered his family for worship. The aged pilgrim's prayer was about as follows:

"O, Lawd, we thanks thee. Thou hast brot thy chilren up out ob de Ian' of de 'Gyptians, an' we'se gwyne to foller on after de piller ob cloud by day and de piller ob fire by night. We'se rejoiced, O, Lawd, dat Massa Linkum's sojers hab cum to lead us out and to destroy de hosts of Pharaoh Davis if dey try to bring de chilren back into bondage. Guide us frew de wilderness and de desert. Gib Massa Linkum's sojers wisdom to keep in de right road and bring us safe to de Promis' Lan'."

The "amens" were frequent and fervent. The prayer circle was enlarged, other families coming over to join with Uncle Reuben in lifting their voices in praise and thanksgiving for their wonderful deliverance. Their faith in God and "Massa Linkum" was unshaken, although they were footsore, hungry and homeless. The fitful glare of the campfires made the scene all the more weird and solemn.

While still on their knees the worshipers broke out in song:

O Cana-an, bright Cana-an,
We'se boun' for de lan' ob Cana-an!
O Cana-an is our happy home—
We'se boun' for de lan' ob Cana-an.
Hallelujah!

If you get dar befo' I do—
I'se boun' for de lan' of Cana-an.
Look out for me, I'se coming, too—
I'se boun' for de lan' ob Canaan!
Hallelujah!
Glory!

Farther down the road in the edge of the woods we found a score or more of the younger negroes celebrating the "year of jubilee" by a walk around to the tune of "Ole Virginny Nebber Tire." A darky called Zeb furnished the instrumental music, plying the bow vigorously on the strings of a cracked violin. He improvised vocal outbreaks something after this sort:

Gib dat darky room;
He's gwyne to walk aroiin'.
Dance by de light ob de moon.
Put de heel an' toe on de groun'.
Break-er-down—Jimbo, Jim.
Breaker-down—Jimbo—
Break-er-down—Jimbo—
Breaker-down—Jimbo, Jim.
Hy, dar, Jimbo, Jim!

The children were having "juber dats" here and there. A majority of them had but one garment, and the antics of the *pickaninnies* were not the least interesting feature of the exhibition. As we passed back through the bivouac to the camp of our regiment little woolly heads bobbed up all along the line to look at "de Yankees." It was a memorable event in the history of the black people, old and young. They were, indeed, coming up from the land of bondage to be free men and free women. It was a new and novel existence for them, and while they did not at that time fully take in the importance of the change, they did believe and manifest their faith that God had raised up President Lincoln to break the shackles of slavery and bid them stand forth free from the bondage that had so long enslaved their race and disgraced the government founded on the principle that "*all men are created equal.*"

Chapter 27

The Rebels Fall Back

From King and Queen Court House Sheridan with Torbert and Gregg's divisions of cavalry intended to march to West Point, at the head of York River, but the evening we arrived at the Court House, it was ascertained that the Union troops still held White House on the Pamunkey, which had been Grant's base of supplies before crossing to the south bank of the James. Our line of march was changed, therefore, and only the wounded, the prisoners taken at Trevilian and the two thousand or more negroes who had refugeed and followed our column were sent under escort to West Point.

We reached White House, on the Pamunkey River, about sundown Monday, June 20. We were told by a contraband that Wade Hampton's cavalry was scouting around between the Pamunkey and the Chickahominy and preparing to gobble up everything north of the James. We heard the booming of cannon during our march Monday afternoon, and the general impression among the rank and file was that Grant and Lee might still be hammering away at each other in the vicinity of Cold Harbor.

As we reached the brow of a hill north of the river we saw the stars and stripes flying from a flag-pole at the landing. The bank was lined with tents, and an enormous wagon train was parked near the camp.

"Here's Grant's army!" exclaimed a trooper.

"I thought the Army of the Potomac had moved south of the James," said a corporal.

"Maybe the army was driven back."

There was more speculation of the same character, but after we went into bivouac near the river we were informed by visitors from the infantry camp at the landing that Gen. Abercrombie was in command of the troops guarding White House, and that Grant's army had crossed the James below Richmond.

There was a standing order against horse-trading in the cavalry corps; but officers who owned their chargers—and a good many who appropriated government horses to their own use—traded whenever they had opportunity and could find anybody who desired to swap, always, of course, to get rid of an undesirable animal. When once a soldier secured a good mount he would hold on to his horse to the last. On one occasion it was discovered that there had been a large number of trades between troopers of the First Massachusetts and other regiments in Davies's brigade. Major Lucius M. Sargent, who was in command of our regiment at the time, had the companies formed in line, and he then promulgated the following:

> I don't propose that this regiment shall be dismounted by horse-trading, to benefit the First Pennsylvania, the First New Jersey or any other command! The next soldier of the First Massachusetts cavalry who trades horses—without getting the best of the man he trades with—shall be tied up by the thumbs and sent to the dismounted camp. Dismiss the companies.

A detachment of mounted infantry, detailed as orderlies and couriers, was at White House. These doughboys were a part of the miscellaneous command under Gen. Abercrombie. Before we had fairly dismounted several of them were at our bivouac, stumping our boys to trade horses. My steed was on his last legs, so to speak. Another day's march would surely have placed me *hors de combat* as a cavalryman. I had favoured him in every possible way on the raid, but he was homesick—a disease that killed scores of horses and soldiers as well—from the hour a curb-bit was first put in his mouth, and he had grown worse day by day. "What kind of a horse have you got?" I asked of one of our visitors who had come over to trade.

"A splendid bay—he's just the horse for a cavalryman, but I'm not used to riding, and I'm afraid he'll throw me."

"How do you like my horse there?"

"First-rate. He seems to be gentle and kind; I don't like a high-spirited horse."

"Well, I'll go over and look at your animal."

The doughboy had told the truth. He had a fine horse, one of an invoice of fifty or more that had just been received by the quartermaster. The animal was a recruit, as was attested by the fact that the wound was still fresh where the letters U. S. had been branded on his shoulder.

"Is he used to the saddle?" I inquired.

"Yes, I'm told so; but I haven't tried him yet. To tell you the truth, I'm no horseman, and I'd rather be shot on my feet than to have my neck broken by a runaway horse."

"How much boot will you give me?"

"I'll trade even."

"No! It's worth a good deal to have a gentle horse that you can depend on."

"I'll give you five dollars."

"Why, that horse of yours will kill a whole platoon of doughboys before he will allow you to saddle him, let alone getting on his back."

"Do you really think he's vicious?"

"I know it; look at his eye."

"I'll give you ten dollars."

"It's a trade."

We arranged our plans to make the exchange after retreat. I was to ride over to the camp of the headquarter detachment and meet my victim at the place where he kept his horse. He had exacted from me a promise that I would attend to the "harnessing of the horses" as he called it.

I was at the rendezvous on time, and so was the doughboy, who fairly danced around with delight when I handed him the halter strap of my broken-down steed after taking off the saddle.

"There's your horse," said I.

"And there's yours, tied to that wagon wheel."

The new horse did not take kindly to the saddle. He pranced around considerably, and tried to walk on me when I reached under him to get hold of the girth. But in course of time I managed to get the saddle strapped on and the bridle in its proper place.

Then I prepared to mount.

And the curtain rose on one of the most exciting incidents that I ever had anything to do with.

I got into the saddle, but the horse reared and plunged so that I could not get my feet into the stirrups. Then I discovered that I had not untied the halter, and the animal was still fast to the wagon wheel.

"Cast off the shore lines!" shouted one of the headquarter detail who came out to see his bunkey's new horse. He had been a sailor before he enlisted in the army.

"Cut the halter shank!" I yelled.

But the doughboys kept a most respectful distance away from the plunging charger. And I went up and down at the pleasure of my new horse.

Years afterward while serving in the Fifth United States cavalry on the frontier I had to do with bucking broncos of the worst kind, but I never straddled a bronco that could beat the record made by that American horse at White House. If it was not the genuine bronco buck that he treated me to, it was first cousin to it.

Finally the halter shank broke.

"Clear away!" shouted the nautical spectator, as he crawled under the wagon.

In his struggle to throw his rider the horse had broken the bridle reins, pieces of which were now hanging from the curb. I did not observe that the reins were broken until my charger started on a run across the low strip of ground near the landing. As I was now firmly seated in the saddle I felt that I could master the fiery untamed steed, but when I reached for the reins I was startled to find myself "*at sea in a heavy gale and without a rudder*," as the old sailor would have described it.

On we went. The horse ran through the camp of the headquarters detail, knocking down shelter tents, upsetting camp kettles, wrecking things generally and almost causing a panic.

After dashing around among wagon trains and infantry camps my steed started for the cavalry bivouac. Two or three sentinels had fired at me as I was carried outside the picket line and back again above the landing. As we neared the camp of Sheridan's troopers I felt my saddle slipping back, but I clung to the horse's mane and thus kept from dropping off behind.

"Don't shoot—it's a runaway horse!" I shouted, as the animal dashed by brigade headquarters and in among the horses of the troopers.

The horse was pretty well "winded" by this time. The stable guard came to my assistance, and I dismounted all in a heap, as the saddle turned with me when I let go of the mane. I had been severely shaken up, but I found I was "all there."

My new horse proved to be an excellent campaigner. He was high-spirited, but he was not vicious. I never knew him to "buck" after that night. I rode him on several raids below Petersburg, and up to the time

I was carried to the hospital at City Point in July. I do not think Major Sargent's order about being tied up by the thumbs could have been applied in my case.

Two days later we passed a mounted infantry detachment on the road to Charles City Court House, and I saw the doughboy with whom I traded horses at White House walking in rear of the column and trying to drag along by the bridle the broken-down horse I had ridden in the Trevilian raid. I made up my mind to give him back the ten dollars boot-money.

"How do you like your horse?" I asked.

"Say, he's perfectly safe, but he's dreadful slow. I'm afraid, though, that he won't live to reach the James. But whether he dies or lives I shall always be under obligations to you for saving my life. That horse you're riding would have killed me. I felt sure when he started with you at White House that I was responsible for your death."

"It was a close call," I remarked.

As the weary foot soldier accepted the situation so philosophically, and really seemed to think I had done him a good turn by taking the new horse off his hands, I concluded to keep the boot money.

The morning after our arrival at White House our division was ordered to cross the Pamunkey and march, dismounted, to dislodge Wade Hampton, who had taken up a position along the west bank of a small stream that crossed the turnpike on the road to Tunstall's Station. The first division, mounted, under Torbert, also crossed the river. The first brigade of Torbert's division, headed by Custer, took the road toward Cumberland, south of White House, and the second brigade (Devin's) pushed out toward Baltimore Cross Roads. Merritt's brigade of the first division supported Gregg in the movement against Hampton.

I do not know how many troops the rebel cavalry commander had concentrated near White House. He had been throwing shells into the Federal camp the day before, and his troopers had scouted all around Gen. Abercrombie, threatening to attack and capture the force holding the landing. Gregg's men were marched briskly forward, and they expected a lively battle with the boys in butternut. This time, however, the Johnnies decided to get out of the way, and they fell back on the road to Richmond, across the Chickahominy.

We returned to our camp on the Pamunkey. Bright and early the next morning a sergeant from corps headquarters came over to our camp fire with the news that we were to move at once.

"We're in for it this time," he said.

"How so?"

"Gen. Sheridan has been ordered to move all these trains to the James River. It's too bad!"

"What's too bad?"

"Why, that the infantry should be taken across the river and their supply trains left for us to guard. We're left all alone on this side of Richmond. The Army of the Potomac is all on the south side below Petersburg. We have no supports."

"But we've got plenty of rations in the wagons?"

"Yes, and Hampton's men are hungry."

"Well, if Lee doesn't send anybody but Hampton to capture the trains the Johnnies won't get fat on Yankee rations this summer. Sheridan can whip Hampton any day, before breakfast."

The corporal had expressed the sentiment of a majority of Sheridan's troopers. But the knowledge that Grant was on the other side of the rebel capital and that Lee could send infantry supports to his cavalry commander at short notice grave rise to the thought that we might find ourselves in a tight place before we could bring all the trains under cover of the gunboats on the James. Still there was comfort in the assurance that Little Phil was equal to the emergency. The trains would be a great temptation to the Confederates, and we naturally expected they would make extraordinary effort to capture the wagons between White House and Deep Bottom, the point on the James River to which we were ordered to escort the trains.

Chapter 28

Holding on to Save the Wagons

Friday, June 24, 1864, was a red-hot day in the history of the second division of Sheridan's cavalry corps, commanded by Gen. D. McM. Gregg. Wade Hampton, with his Confederate troopers, pitched into Gregg at St. Mary's Church, on the road between Jones's bridge and Charles City Court House. The rebels expected to put our division to flight, as they outnumbered Gregg's command and were perfectly familiar with the lay of the land. When they opened on us they came with a yell that was intended to convince us that they meant business. But Gregg's troopers had heard that yell before and had come to understand that the Johnnies sometimes made the most noise when they had the least fight in them.

Gregg's division was marching on the right flank of the enormous wagon-train that Sheridan had been ordered to escort to the pontoon bridge over the James at Deep Bottom. The crossing of the Chickahominy had been effected at Jones's bridge without serious trouble, and the line of march was almost due south from that point to Charles City Court House. Torbert's division was in the advance, and when the attack was made on Gregg the latter saw that he would be compelled to check Hampton and hold him back for several hours or the wagon-train would fall into the hands of the Confederates.

The gallant commander of the second division was always ready to fight, and when his scouts and flankers reported that the rebel cavalry was closing in on our right flank Gregg gave orders to his brigade commanders to form a line of battle facing to the west and to build such barricades as could be thrown up before the arrival of the enemy. The light batteries commanded by Capt. A. M. Randol and Lieut. W. Neil Dennison, of the regulars, were posted so that they could sweep nearly the whole front of Gregg's two brigades.

"Uncle Danl" gives the boys in blue a timely hint

While Gregg was making preparations to fight Hampton at St. Mary's Church a courier arrived with instructions from Sheridan to our division commander to "hold fast near the church without fail till all the transportation had passed Charles City Court House." The trooper that brought the order stated that Torbert had been fighting Lomax's brigade south of Charles City Court House and the rebels had been driven back. Sheridan had decided to park the train at Wilcox's Landing until the road to Deep Bottom could be cleared, or other arrangements made for crossing the James.

Gregg was unable to use more than seventy-five *per cent*, of his aggregate force. The troopers were dismounted, numbers one, two and three of each set of fours going in on foot, while number four took charge of the four horses. Our brigade was posted on the right, and Col. J. Irving Gregg's brigade had the left. There were but ten regiments in the two brigades.

Against Gregg's comparatively small force Hampton brought nearly his entire corps—Lomax's brigade, which had confronted Torbert below Charles City Court House, being the only force detached from Hampton's command at the time of the battle at St. Mary's Church. Gregg was facing a force that outnumbered his command three to one; but he was equal to the emergency.

We could see the rebels preparing for the attack. They seemed confident of their ability to sweep all before them when they should get the command to charge.

"I wish I had enlisted in the infantry," said Taylor, who was a few feet to my right.

"Why so?"

"Because the doughboys don't have to stay up all night doctoring sick horses, and then fight on foot, and have their horses led off so far that if they get whipped they can't use them to run away with. Here's the whole Southern Confederacy coming down on our one little division, and the general has had our horses taken so far to the rear that we never can reach them if we are obliged to get out of this. This is going to be a worse place than the Wilderness."

"Well, they can't kill us but once."

"But I'd rather be killed in an open field, on horseback, than to be sabred to death behind a fence."

About four o'clock in the afternoon Hampton's men moved forward to the attack. Before they got in range of our carbines Randol's and Dennison's batteries opened fire. The Yankee cannoneers worked their guns lively, and the rebel troopers needed but one volley at close range to convince them that they had a bigger job on hand than they had bargained for. The first assault was repulsed all along our front, and the attack on our left flank by the brigades of Chambers and Geary of W. H. F. Lee's division did not succeed in breaking Gregg's line. The Federal troopers cheered as the rebels withdrew to prepare for a renewal of the onslaught.

In speaking of Hampton's attack on Gregg at St. Mary's Church, Sheridan in his *Memoirs*, after referring to the first assault, says:

> For two hours he (Hampton) continued to attack, but made little impression on Gregg—gain at one point being counterbalanced by failure at another. Because of the evident strength of Hampton, Gregg had placed all his troops in line of battle from the first, and on discovery of the enemy's superior numbers sent message after message to me concerning the situation, but the messengers never arrived, being either killed or captured, and I remained in total ignorance till dark of the strait his division was in.
>
> Toward night it became clear to Gregg that he could maintain the unequal contest no longer, and he then decided to retreat, but not until convinced that the time won had enabled all the trains to reach Charles City Court House in safety. When he had got all his led horses fairly on the way, and such of the wounded as could be transported, he retired by his right flank—in some confusion, it is true, but stubbornly resisting—to Hopewell Church, where Hampton ceased to press him. Gregg's losses were heavy, and he was forced to abandon his dead and most seriously wounded, but the creditable stand made ensured the safety of the train, the last wagon of which was now parked at Wilcox's Landing.

When Gregg's division reached the train near Wilcox's Landing it had been decided by Sheridan that it would be useless to attempt to reach the pontoon bridge at Deep Bottom. Hampton's cavalry already covered the road to Malvern Hill. After considerable manoeuvring to determine the position of the enemy we were directed to hold on where we were until the arrival of ferry boats to take the wagons to the south side of the James. The wagons were all ferried over the river, and the cavalry was then taken across on the boats sent by Gen. Meade for that purpose.

CHAPTER 29

Operations South of the James

Our horses were about used up, but before their backs had fairly cooled after being unsaddled on the south bank of the James a courier came dashing into camp with the news that Wilson, who had been operating out on the left of Grant's army, had been cut off at Ream's Station, and Sheridan was ordered to go to the rescue of his third division.

In a few minutes the weary troopers were again in the saddle and *en route* to Prince George Court House. It was hard on the men; it was harder on the horses. We made what was called a forced march, and our poor chargers needed to be forced all the way.

We reached Prince George Court House some time in the night, and pushed on to Ream's station, where we found the sixth corps. The Federal scouts stated that Wilson, finding the enemy had interposed between his column and the Union army, had turned about and crossed the Nottoway River. He rejoined the cavalry corps at Light House Point, July 2, after an exciting trip made through the enemy's country.

He had been on the "go" ten days, and found himself about one thousand men short, and minus his trains and artillery. But he damaged the enemy's communications to such an extent that the Confederates were seriously crippled in supplying Lee's army with rations for several months.

Returning from Ream's Station we remained in camp at Light House Point during the long hot days in July. The rest was appreciated by the troopers, and their horses began to "pick up right smart." We had a little drill now and then and a dress parade occasionally. The boys polished up their brasses, blacked their boots and began to adopt the regulation step again.

During a cavalry "excursion" out on the left a planter named Lee, expressed a desire for protection, and Taylor and myself were directed to remain and see that he was not molested by our troops.

Neither of us had ever been detailed for safeguard before. We had no clearly-defined ideas about such duty. A brigade staff officer said to us as we rode into the yard in front of Mr. Lee's house:

"You will remain here till relieved. Don't let our men trouble this gentleman or his family. Prevent all wanton destruction of property. You'll be all right should the enemy come, for it's against the law to molest a safeguard."

Mr. Lee was a white-haired gentleman of the old school—an F. F.V. His wife and one daughter constituted the family at home, though it was said there were other members in Petersburg. We were hospitably entertained, and the ham and eggs and "soft bread" with vegetables proved a most acceptable substitute for hard tack and salt pork. And the Lees seemed to enjoy our government coffee as heartily as we did their "square meals."

There were a dozen or more negroes on the plantation. There had been more earlier in the war. But many "refugee" to "Massa Linkum's sojers' camp" when the Union Army pitched its tents south of the James. Still there were some who remained with their masters to the end—some are with their old masters yet. Those about the Lee plantation were kept so busy discussing the exciting events near at hand that their master could get little if any work out of them. Yet they managed to be on hand when their rations were given out. Mr. Lee fed them from his store of flour and meat, and even after the plantation had been stripped by the soldiers of nearly everything they could find in the shape of forage, old man Lee divided what little flour and meal he had left with the "hands." He said to me:

"These slaves have stood by me till now. They helped me work a crop, and we'll share our last pound of meat and meal with them."

But this was the day the safeguard was called in. When we were first stationed at Lee's there seemed to be a daily supply of provisions, fresh every morning. About the second day a scouting party of a New Jersey regiment visited us. It was difficult to make them understand that it was against the law to molest a safeguard.

"We don't propose to molest you," said one of the officers; "but our horses need corn, and we must help ourselves!"

The men belonged to the third New Jersey cavalry. There was a sprinkling of all nations in the regiment, and the "butterfly "troopers pretended that they could not understand our protest. Lee's corn disappeared that day.

The next morning I saw a detachment of Federal cavalry interviewing one of the darkies. Said the officer in charge:

"Uncle, is there any applejack about here?"

"Spec dere is, sah; but 'twould broke Massa Lee's heart to see de Yanks a drinkin' it—'deed it would, sah!"

"Where did Lee hide it?"

"See heah, sah; I'se done promise not to tell. But if you's right smart a-fishin' down 'n de mill pon', I reckon you 'ns might get a bite."

Then the boys in blue went fishing. Hooks and lines were brought forth from some of their saddle bags, and "Uncle Dan'l" showed them where poles could be secured.

"Fish near de bank," was the old slave's parting admonition, as the troopers prepared to try their luck.

The fishing-party was in plain sight from the *piazza* of the Lee house.

"Have the soldiers got any bait?" the proprietor asked.

"Dey done say dey don't need any bait—dat fish always bite Yankee hooks jes' as dey am," said "Uncle Dan'l."

It was soon demonstrated that bare hooks were sufficient to catch the fish the Yanks were after. Pretty soon one of them landed, not a fish, but a three-gallon jug of applejack. With the end of his pole he had poked along in the water near the shore till he found a stout cord attached to a root or stone under the bushes. And this led to further investigation. A strong pull on the cord brought up a jug filled with applejack, which had been anchored on the bottom, and attached to the cord. In a short time other soldiers had "bites," and it was interesting to watch the changes in expression on Mr. Lee's face as jug after jug of applejack made on the premises was fished out of the mill pond.

"Dan'l."

"Yes, sah."

"You're a scoundrel!"

"Yes, sah."

"Dan'l."

"Yes, sah."

"You love the Yankees?"

"Yes, sah."

"Goodbye, Dan'l; this plantation's too small for both or us.

"Sorry, sah, but I can't go 'n leave ole massa now. I'll stay frough de wah."

And he did.

The Yankees fished that pond dry of applejack inside of twenty-four hours. After the first squad had reported what big luck they had, several other detachments of cavalry, with now and then a corporal's guard of infantry, went on fishing expeditions to the mill. The protests of the safeguard were met with the declaration that applejack was a contraband article, and not entitled to exemption from confiscation by Uncle Sam's army. We could not get around this logical conclusion, and the applejack was taken into camp.

About the same time another darky informed a scouting party that there were "some queer kind o' trees down in de woods near de mill." And the darky was right. The soldiers were not slow to "scent forage from afar off."

"Dese trees lie on de groun', and look all swell up," the coloured man continued.

The boys were soon sounding the fallen trees. Once in a while a blow with a sabre would shatter the bark, and inside would be found barrels or sacks of flour, which had been carefully concealed upon the approach of the army. The flour would not have been discovered had the darkies who assisted in hiding it kept "mum." But that they generally failed to do when told by the blue-coats that the Union Army was fighting for their freedom.

"Golly! I done forgot dat; yas, I'll p'int de way to de corn an' de bacon," was the response.

Yet the safeguard did what they could to protect Mr. Lee's property. Nothing in the house was disturbed by the raiders. And such provisions as had been left in the buildings contiguous to the residence was saved to the family,

Mr. Lee stated to me the day the safeguard was called in, that he had a few hams buried under a smokehouse, and also about fifty pounds of flour in the pantry. This would last but a few days among the family and the darkies.

Chapter 30

Sent to the Hospital

I had stood the fatigues of the campaign thus far without once answering sick call, but in the latter part of July I began to feel "*de misery in de bowels*," as the contrabands described the disease that attacked the soldiers when in camp, and sent so many of them to the cemeteries. I fought against it as long as I could, but I was finally compelled to give in, and allow the first sergeant to put my name on the sick book. I was very weak, and Taylor assisted me over to the surgeon's tent. The doctor marked me "sick in quarters" the first day, and I swallowed medicine every two hours all night. The next morning I was unable to get out of the dog tent Taylor had arranged for me.

Along in the middle of the day I fell asleep. Taylor had insisted that I should "take a nap between drinks," as he called it.

"I'll wake you up in time for your toddy," he said.

I was awakened by the sounding of "boots and saddles" all through the camps.

"What's up?" I asked Taylor.

"Got to move right away; guess the Johnnies have broke in on us somewhere. But I'll ask the major to let me stay and take care of you."

And my faithful nurse ran over to the commanding officer's tent and made the request.

"We ran away and enlisted together, Major, and the doctor says the chances are against him unless he's tended with great care. I don't want to shirk duty, but I'd like to stay and see my towny through."

"I'll speak to the doctor about it," replied the officer. "Tell the doctor to come here."

When the surgeon appeared, he stated that the sick were to be sent to the hospital, and so it was decided that Taylor could not be spared to remain with me, as the movement was to be a reconnaissance in force on the north bank of the James, and every man would be needed. Taylor had to hustle to pack his traps and saddle up. After he had "buckled on his harness," as he called it, he came back to me, and assisted the hospital steward and the driver in lifting me into an ambulance. I had just strength enough to raise my head and thank my comrade, who stood with a canteen of fresh water he had brought for me, beside a trooper who had been wounded in the arm while on picket, and who was to go with me in the ambulance.

"Thank you, Giles. Write and tell my folks about me the first chance you get."

"I'm sorry to leave you, but I'll come over to City Point and see you in a few days. Keep up your courage; you'll pull through all right. But the company's leading out. I must go. Goodbye."

"Goodbye, Giles."

I did not have strength enough to sit up in the ambulance and see the boys as they rode by, but Taylor had told them I was in the vehicle, and I could hear them say, "Goodbye, Allen," as they passed along.

Then I was "all shook up" as the ambulance driver cracked his whip and shouted to his mules to "git out o' hyar!" I do not remember how long we were on the road. I did not know then, for I was unconscious part of the time. Now and then we struck a long stretch of corduroy road. Oh! how it tortured me. Only old soldiers who "have been there" have any idea of the agony experienced in a ride over a corduroy road in an ambulance, particularly when the passenger is so weak that he cannot help himself at all.

"Drive around to the third tent there!"

"Yes, sir."

"How many men have you?"

"One wounded, and one sick or dead boy, I don't know which. He's been fainting like, all the afternoon." The above is what I heard upon regaining consciousness. We had arrived at the cavalry corps hospital on the bank of the Appomattox, just above City Point. I was taken from the ambulance and placed on a cot in one of the tents. Then I became unconscious again, but restoratives were given me, and I was able, when the attendants came around with supper, to swallow one spoonful of tea, after which I was given an anodyne which put me to sleep.

The cavalry corps hospital was separate from the general hospital of the Army of the Potomac at City Point, and was used exclusively for sick and wounded troopers. The best possible care was taken of the patients, and delicacies in the shape of corn starch, farina, beef tea, canned fruit, jellies and other articles not included in the regular rations were supplied. It was several days after my arrival before I was considered to have one chance in twenty of pulling through, but I had a strong constitution, and nature and the surgeon's prescriptions won after a hard struggle.

What a luxury I found the cot with its mattress, clean sheets and a pillow—just think of it!

After I had passed the critical point, hovering between life and death for several days, and began to mend, I took as deep an interest in my surroundings as was possible under the circumstances. Part of the time I was in a sort of semi-unconscious state, the quinine and other drugs causing my brain to be fired up so that the incidents from the campaign of the Wilderness to the crossing of the James were all jumbled together with recollections of home and the events of my boyhood.

My cot was near the open fly of the tent, and one day, early in August, I was bolstered up so that I could get a view of the grounds sloping away toward the Appomattox. The tents were on a little knoll, and the ground fell away toward the river for a short distance, and then there was quite a stretch of open land sloping upward to a ridge, on the other side of which was the Appomattox.

The intervening space, beginning at the foot of the slope and extending nearly to the rising ground toward the river, had been converted into a cemetery. Here were buried the troopers of Sheridan's command, whose bodies had been brought from the battlefields, and also those who had died in hospital. I soon tired of looking at the rows of headboards, and asked to be laid back on my cot. Just as the attendant was removing the bolster which had supported me in a sitting posture, I fancied I saw the name "Taylor" on one of the slabs out there in the field.

As the nurse laid me back on my cot I was so fatigued that I could not collect my thoughts for some time. Then I began to think about the regiment. Why had not Taylor been to the hospital to see me? Was the cavalry on the north bank of the James? Had there been another raid? Was Giles sick? I went to sleep, and my dreams were of the kind that causes one to wake with his mind more confused than when he goes to sleep. The real and the unreal were so linked together that it was difficult to separate them.

The next day I was permitted to sit up in bed again. Then I began to search for that head-board that had made such an impression on me the day before.

After a time I located the one which had "Taylor" on it. But I was so weak that my eyes gave out before I could make out the rest of the inscription.

"Taylor?" said I to myself, "Taylor? Why, there are hundreds of Taylors in the army. This Taylor could be nothing to me.

"But where is my Taylor? Why hasn't he been to see me? Of course if anything had happened to Giles the boys would have sent me word."

The ward master came along, and as he seemed to be a good-natured fellow, I said to him:

"Will you do me a favour?"

"Certainly, my boy, if I can. What is it?"

"Tell me what the inscription is on that headboard out there—the one with 'Taylor' on it?"

"Taylor is all I can make out from here, as the board is a little obliqued from this point; but if it'll be any accommodation to you, I'll go down there and see what it is."

"I would be so thankful if you would."

The ward master went down the slope and to the grave in which I had come to be so deeply interested. I was confident, or thought I was, that nothing could have happened to Giles, but at the same time I could not rest until I found out the full name of the trooper who slumbered in that particular grave. In a few minutes the ward master returned.

"It's Taylor," he said.

"Yes; but what's the other name?"

"Giles Taylor."

"What regiment?"

"First Massachusetts cavalry."

"What company?"

"Company I."

"What else?"

"Killed, July 28, 1864."

"Where?"

"Near Malvern Hill."

"Lay me down, please."

"All right, my boy; did you know the trooper buried out there?"

"Yes; we ran away together to enlist. He nursed me in camp when I was stricken, and helped put me in the ambulance when I was sent to the hospital; he was my bunkey, and the best friend I had in the company."

"It's too bad; but war is a terrible thing."

The day that I started for the hospital Sheridan crossed to the north bank of the James, to support a movement intended to cause Lee to withdraw the bulk of his army from the works in front of Petersburg. There was some lively fighting out near Malvern Hill, and during one of the attacks of the enemy Taylor was shot. The bullet entered his groin, severing the main arteries.

Daniel Booth, a bugler who was near Taylor when the latter was struck, assisted in getting the wounded man back out of range. Booth told me that Giles did not flinch—he was in the front rank when he was shot. He did not fall from his horse, but fired one or two shots after he was struck. Then he said to Booth:

"I'm hit—the blood's running into my boot; guess I'm hurt bad."

Booth hastened to Taylor's assistance. The latter was growing weak from loss of blood. Just then General Davies's headquarters ambulance came along, and the general who was near at hand and had seen Booth and another soldier supporting Taylor in the saddle, directed them to put him in the ambulance.

"No; don't let them put me in the ambulance—it'll kill me if they lay me down. Let me stay in the saddle, boys."

Booth remained with Taylor till they reached the landing where the wounded men were being loaded on boats to be taken to City Point. A surgeon examined Taylor's wound.

"It's fatal," the doctor whispered to Booth. "But he can't stay here; help him on board the boat."

The boy bugler and others raised the dying trooper and bore him tenderly on board the steamer. They laid him down on a blanket among other wounded soldiers. Then the whistle blew, and the command was given, "All ashore that's going!" Taylor was sinking fast, but he pressed Booth's hand and said:

"Goodbye, Booth; I'm dying. Send word to my folks at home—tell them I faced the music, and was shot with my harness on. Remember me to the boys."

"Goodbye, Giles."

Booth jumped ashore as the gang plank was being pulled on board, and hastened back to the regiment. Poor Taylor was a corpse before the boat reached City Point. His body was taken to the cavalry corps hospital, and buried in the grave the headboard of which attracted my attention.

Chapter 31

On the Picket Line

If ever I felt homesick it was the day I walked down between the rows of headboards and stopped at the grave of my comrade. He had left a wife to whom he had been married but a few days, to go with Waterman and myself to enlist at Williamstown. Of the quartet who rode from that village to North Adams in Professor Hopkins's lumber wagon two were now dead; Lieutenant Edward Payson Hopkins, killed at Ashland, and Giles Taylor, mortally wounded at Malvern Hill. The last I had heard from Waterman he was in the dismounted camp at Light House Point, or thereabouts. I sat down by Taylor's grave and wept for half an hour, being then so weak that I had to call one of the nurses to assist me back to the hospital. That night I had a relapse, and for several days it was "nip and tuck" between the disease and myself—that was what the hospital steward told me when I began to mend again.

When I was reported convalescent and had regained my strength pretty well, I secured a pass to go over to City Point. As I recall it the hospital of the Army of the Potomac was about a mile from the cavalry corps hospital—possibly two miles. It was between our hospital and the point. Passing down through a ravine, the road wound its way over the brow of a hill and then down into the camps and hospitals.

Viewed from the top of the hill City Point presented an interesting picture. Everything in sight bore testimony to the fact that war was waging close at hand. A fleet of miscellaneous vessels dotted the James and Appomattox Rivers, and crowded the landings. Several ironclads anchored with their guns trained up the James formed a picket line above the junction of the two rivers. *Boom! boom! boom!* The artillery over in Butler's territory was banging away, and an occasional shot on the Appomattox line indicated that siege operations were going on.

Off to the right a column of infantry was marching over the dusty road *en route* to the front. It was one of Grant's veteran divisions changing position. It had been on an expedition north of the James and was now going back to its camp in front of Petersburg. The uniforms of the men were so covered with dust that they could easily have been taken for Confederates but for the regimental and national colours and the division and brigade standards.' They carried their long toms at will and marched at rout step. A light battery of four guns was moving on a crossroad, and there was an endless line of supply wagons pushing out from the base. Here and there could be seen staff and general officers with cavalry escorts going and coming. Earthworks were on all sides, and nearly every foot of soil in sight had been dug up for breastworks or graveyards.

Ascending a heavy grade a mile or so away was a mixed train on Grant's military railroad, with the locomotive puffing and blowing as it tugged at its load. On top of the freight cars were soldiers going to the front. The engine reached the top of the hill and the engineer blew his whistle—rejoicing that he had made the climb. But just then the train parted near the middle, and while the locomotive and the first half went on down the grade on the other side, the rear section backed rapidly down the hill toward the station. Another train was starting out from City Point, and but for the presence of mind of the soldiers on the freight cars, who promptly put on the brakes and brought the cars to a standstill, a collision would have resulted.

On the hill at the point was a tall flagpole from the top of which floated the stars and stripes. There were a few wooden buildings surrounded by tents shaded by brush arbours. This was Grant's headquarters. On the docks were storehouses filled with supplies, and from steamers and barges an army of men was at work unloading quartermaster, commissary and ordnance stores.

A large steamer at the dock was used as headquarters of the sanitary and Christian commissions, and soldiers from the front were assured a hearty welcome and a good square meal on board if they could show a pass or authority for being away from their commands. These commissions did valiant service in relieving the wants of the soldiers, and spiritual food was dealt out in allopathic doses between meals. Testaments, pens, ink and paper and other articles were supplied the troops by the agents of the commission, free of charge. Three cheers and a tiger for the mothers and sisters and sweethearts who knit and sewed and put together the housewives and other things so useful and handy to soldiers in the field!

From the brow of the hill I had a fine view of the hospital of the Army of the Potomac at City Point. Its streets were laid out with mathematical regularity, and it was a vast city of canvas. Brush arbours shaded the tents more or less, but the difficulty of obtaining green boughs to replace those wilted by the sun was great. There was no confusion in the arrangement of the tents and wards at the hospital. No matter how much the wounded might get mixed on the battlefield and in the smaller hospitals at the front, they were "sorted out "when they reached the main hospital at City Point, and the army, corps, division brigade and regimental lines were observed as far as practicable in placing the patients in wards. A few hundred yards in rear of the hospital was the cemetery, and details could be seen removing bodies from the dead houses skirting the hospital to the graves already prepared.

After calling on a friend of the One hundred and twenty-fifth New York who was in the hospital, I walked on to the landing and enjoyed a cup of good tea on the sanitary commission boat. Then I returned to the cavalry corps hospital, and the next morning I made application to be sent back to my regiment, which was granted. I rejoined my company after a delay of a week at the dismounted camp waiting for a squad to be made up to march out to the cavalry camp.

A short time after my return to the regiment the survivors of Company I were distributed among other companies. I was one of the number transferred to Company C, then doing escort duty with Company D at the headquarters of the Army of the Potomac in front of Petersburg. The squad was sent to report to Capt. E. A. Flint, commanding the squadron of the First Massachusetts cavalry at Meade's headquarters. We regretted very much that our company was to be broken up, but we accepted the situation as best we could.

We found a welcome with the boys of Company C, and Charles Legg, the first sergeant, did all possible to make us feel at home. The cavalry escorts' camp was only a few rods from headquarters. The men were quartered in log houses with canvas roofs. Details were made each day to report to the adjutant-general to carry dispatches and for escort duty. We were kept pretty busy in these directions, but it was better than sitting on a horse all night way out on a picket line, with the rain pouring down and drenching the poor videttes to the skin. Except when on stable guard we had every night in bed.

Major-General George Gordon Meade, commanding the Army of

the Potomac, was a splendid soldier. He had won the battle of Gettysburg the year before. He was tall and slim, with gray hair and beard. He wore spectacles, and was seldom seen about headquarters with a blouse on, wearing his dress coat and top boots nearly all the time. He was called to the command of the Army of the Potomac only a few days before the great battle of Gettysburg, in which he displayed generalship of a high order.

Gen. Meade's staff included three volunteer aids who were as jovial a trio as could be found in the army. Young, ambitious, brave and chivalrous, they made friends all along the line. They were Major George Meade, son of the general; Major Campbell D. Emory (son of Gen. W. H. Emory, I think), and Major Jay, whose Christian name I have forgotten. The "old man," as Gen. Meade was called by some of the younger officers about headquarters—though not in his hearing—sometimes found it necessary to scold the boys, who were given to practical joking to such an extent that even the general commanding the Army of the Potomac was their victim now and then. When called up to be disciplined the three aids would wear solemn faces assuming an air of injured innocence. They meekly accepted the chiding of the "old man," standing at attention, and saluting with the precision of a regular drill sergeant as they retired from the general's presence when admonished to "go and sin no more."

On these occasions Gen. Meade gave utterance to his feelings with a vehemence that would have frightened a stranger out of his boots. But the boys were faithful and efficient officers. When duty called they were ready to go into the thickest of the fight, and they were devoted to their commander, although sometimes, when in camp, they allowed the reins of military discipline to slacken and played their pranks about headquarters.

Major Meade and Major Emory I think remained with General Meade until his death, several years after the war. Major Emory was a captain in the Ninth regular infantry, and died at San Antonio, Texas, March 11, 1878. I never heard of Major Jay after the war, and the last I knew of Major Meade he was serving as a captain in a regular infantry regiment on the frontier. I think he left the service fifteen years ago. The three aids were popular with Meade's escort and the provost guard at headquarters. If any of the escort needed a canteen of commissary whiskey—for medical purposes, of course—it was not difficult to secure the autograph of one of the aids to an order for the liquor.

One day I secured a pass and rode over to Fort Sedgwick, known in army circles as Fort Hell. I was acquainted with some of the boys on duty in the fort. They lived in bomb-proofs—go-for-holes, the boys called them. The fort was one of a chain of works that extended from the Appomattox River on the right to Hatcher's Run on the left. Nearly in front of Fort Sedgwick the Federal and Confederate breastworks were so close together that our pickets could converse with the rebels in an ordinary tone of voice. A soldier invited me to accompany him to the picket line. He was going out with a message to the officer in command of the brigade picket in front of the fort. I accepted, and went out to the advance rifle-pits.

The entire space between the lines—the main breastworks—at this point was dug up and occupied as rifle-pits for the pickets. At one place the rebels were so near our boys that they could almost reach them with their muskets, A mutual understanding was had to not fire upon each other without warning. The truce was pretty generally observed. Some of the Federal and rebel pickets became well acquainted, and the merits of the controversy were frequently the subject of animated discussion.

A sergeant of a Georgia regiment and a corporal from Vermont "had the floor" when we reached the front. They were pretty well warmed up with the subject.

"You all had no right to invade our country," exclaimed the Georgian.

"It's our country as much as yours—one country, one flag," replied the Yankee.

"But we had a right to withdraw from the Confederation."

"You fired on our flag."

"Because you all set out to free the slaves."

"No, we didn't; there was nothing done toward freeing the slaves till two years after you fellows begun the war."

"Well, Yank, you all can't whip us."

"We'll keep coming till we do, then. We're bound to win in the end, and the old flag will wave from Maine to Texas."

"Say, Yank, have you got any coffee to spare?"

"I guess so. Got any tobacco?"

"Reckon I have."

"Toss 'er over."

"Here she comes!"

"That's the genuine article."

"And your coffee is first-class; I'll cook a cup as soon as I can get back to the reserve. Say, Yank?"

"Hello!"

"I don't mind saying that the coffee smells like befo' de wah, and, and—well, it makes me wish de wah was over. Come to think about it, there's something about your old flag that causes us to consider the fact that our grandfathers stood shoulder to shoulder to free this nation from the oppression of a cruel monarch."

"Yes, Johnny, that's so; and don't you forget that this is a Nation with a big N."

"Here comes the officer of the day; look out."

"All right."

I had been told that I would have an opportunity to get a Richmond daily if I would take with me a paper to trade for it. I could not find a newspaper at camp that morning, but Sergeant Legg had a Sunday-school paper that had been brought in by one of the boys from a scouting expedition. It was printed sometime in the forties, I think. After the Confederate officer of the picket had moved on I asked the rebels in the rifle-pits just in front of us if they wanted to trade papers.

"Yes; I'll trade, for I want to see how much longer your people think this war's going to last," said a butternut-clad picket.

"Toss over your paper."

"Here it comes!"

And the Confederate sent over a copy of the Richmond *Dispatch*. It was rolled up and tied to a small stone. I rolled up the Sunday-school paper and tossed it over to the rebel. He untied the string and opened the paper.

"Yank?"

"What?"

"I can whip you."

"What for.?"

"For cheating me in this trade. I expected to get a New York daily with all the news, and you give me a religious paper published before I was born."

"Well, read it; it'll do you good."

"Will you come half-way, without arms, and fight me?"

"No; thank you. You're mad, and you might hurt me."

"You deserve to be hurt. If I ever get you near enough I'll make you sorry for this."

Retreat was sounding in the Union and Confederate camps as we started to return from the picket line to Fort Sedgwick. We could hear the fifes and drums and bugles in the rebel lines as distinctly as we could hear those in the Union camps. We were walking leisurely along through the rifle-pits and trenches when we heard a rebel picket yell:

"Lay down, Yanks; we're gwine to fire!"

"Follow me," exclaimed my companion, as he jumped down into a deep trench through which the relief picket marched to the outposts when hostilities were going on.

Ping! ping! ping! came the bullets from the rebel rifle-pits.

It was not necessary to repeat the invitation. I got down into the ditch and ducked my head so that it was below the surface.

The picket firing became general in a few minutes, and in the early twilight we could see the flashes of the rifles as the Blue and the Gray exchanged leaden compliments. As the darkness came on guns of heavier calibre took up the quarrel, and the *boom-m-m-m* of the great siege cannons was heard.

"Somebody's brought on an all-night row," said my friend as we crawled along in the trench toward Fort Sedgwick.

On the way in we met a regiment from one of the camps near the fort marching to the outposts to re-enforce the pickets, for it might be that the firing would precede an attempt to break through the Federal lines. The long roll was sounded in the camp. The men formed ranks, counted off and stood to arms until the wire edge of the excitement had been worn off. The signal corps was sending messages back and forth all along the line, and word came that there had been discovered no indication that the Johnnies intended to venture outside of the breastworks. Then the men were allowed to break ranks and return to their dugouts and log cabins, after being cautioned to be ready to fall in at a moment's notice.

It was one o'clock in the morning before I mounted my horse at Fort Sedgwick and started on my return to Meade's headquarters. It was a cloudy night, making the glare of the bombardment all the more striking. The flashes from the muskets outlined the course of the works away toward the Appomattox, and off to the left where the second corps signal tower could be seen above the cloud of smoke that overhung the chain of forts. The course of the bombs thrown by the mortars and large guns could be followed by the eye as they left a trail of fire from the burning fuses behind. The display was grand—awful, when one came to understand that it was not a Fourth of July pyrotechnic exhibition, but war, stern, cruel, terrible. The firing continued all night. Such outbreaks were common during the siege of Petersburg, and for a time the rebels would begin to fire at sunset and keep it up till sunrise. They said they did it to prevent deserters from their works running into our lines, but in spite of their vigilance and picket firing a good many scantily-clad and poorly fed gray-backs crawled into the Union breastworks that winter.

Chapter 32
A Furlough for Twenty Days

After Grant had settled down to the siege of Petersburg several attempts were made to reach out on the left and gobble the South Side railroad. The Weldon road was captured by the Fifth corps under Gen. Warren, August 18, 1864, and the Union lines were extended. Then Grant seemed to have an increased hankering after the South Side road, which crossed the Richmond and Danville railroad at Burkeville and entered Petersburg from the west. It was all the railroad the Confederates had left to supply Petersburg, except from the rebel capital, and its destruction or capture would sadly cripple the enemy. In the fore part of December Warren pushed out, down the Weldon railroad, crossing Stony Creek and destroying the depot of that name.

On went the gallant commander of the Fifth corps, crossing the Nottaway River, breaking up Jarrett's Station and tearing up the railroad to Hicksford, near the border line of North Carolina' The rebels never found time to repair the damage. The day after Warren started on this expedition I was sent to overtake him with a dispatch from Gen. Meade. I reached the column soon after dark. It was raining hard and the troops were doing their best to get a little sleep in their bivouac.

I found Gen. Warren standing in front of an A tent, which was his headquarters, giving directions to officers who were to go out and look after the pickets for the night. The dispatch from Meade was in a large official envelope. I dismounted and handed the document to Gen. Warren.

"Is it from Gen. Grant?" he asked, as he tore open the envelope.

"No, sir; it's from Gen. Meade." Gen. Warren read the dispatch by the light of the camp fire in front of his tent.

"We are expected to destroy the railroad as far south as we can go without being cut off and captured," he said to the officers around the fire.

Gen. Warren turned to me and said: "I see by the date of the dispatch that you have made good time in reaching us. It's a hard ride and you must be hungry."

"Yes, sir; I have had no dinner or supper."

"Orderly!"

"Here, sir," responded the general's attendant.

"Take this courier to my cook and give him the best he's got to eat and a cup of hot coffee. After supper I will have my answer ready, as I see by a memorandum on the dispatch you are to return at once."

"Thank you, General." The civilian will not see anything but what might have been expected in Gen. Warren's hospitality; but old soldiers will remember that such kindness and solicitation for a humble private were not always manifested by superior officers.

It was during Warren's expedition referred to above that Major Lucius M. Sargent, our regimental commander, was killed. December 9, while engaged with a strong line of the enemy, Major Sargent rode to the front and charged the rebels with his regiment. He was struck by a piece of shell and instantly killed. He sat bolt upright on his horse after being struck. Two soldiers, one on either side, supported his body in the saddle, and as they passed to the rear with it there were but few who knew that the major was dead—the general impression being that he was not dangerously wounded. He was a gallant officer, and daring even to rashness.

It was very dark when I started from the bivouac of Warren's troops on my return to Meade's headquarters in front of Petersburg. I trusted entirely to my horse to keep the right road. After riding a few miles I heard the sound of a horse at full gallop behind me. My first thought was of rebels, and I examined my revolver to see that it was in working order. I reined my horse to one side of the road and waited for developments. The horse slackened his speed as he approached and stopped alongside my charger. The horse was saddled and bridled and the saddle was packed with a cavalryman's outfit. His rider had probably been shot on the picket line, or the horse had broken away from the bivouac. I had no time to take the animal back to Warren's line, and I concluded to lead him to our camp at Meade's headquarters.

"Who comes there?"

I was startled by the challenge which came to me out of the darkness ahead. I heard the "click" as the challenger drew back the hammer of his musket.

"A friend."

"Dismount, advance and give the countersign!"

"I can't dismount very well, as I have an extra horse."

"Well, are you Yank or rebel?"

"I'm a Yank."

I knew that a Confederate picket would not be apt to use the word "rebel."

"Then it's all right. Where are you going?"

"To Meade's headquarters."

"I'm going back to our camp near Globe Tavern, and I'm glad to have company."

"All right. Jump on to the extra horse and I'll take you along."

The doughboy—for the stranger proved to be an infantry soldier—had no little trouble in climbing into the saddle. He was in heavy marching order with his knapsack and full outfit. Finally he got on and we continued the journey.

Rattle-te-bang-bang! went the doughboy's canteen, tin cup and frying-pan as they jostled against the saddle equipments. The horse was not used to such a racket, and began to prance around, much to the terror of his rider.

"Whoa, horsey! whoa!" shouted the infantryman.

"We'll take up the gallop—that'll quiet him, "I said. "Come on!"

My horse responded to a touch of the spur and the other animal kept close alongside. The doughboy was riding his horse all over, I should say, for he was first out on the pommel of the saddle on the horse's neck, and then back behind the saddle. And the way he shouted "Whoa!" and "Murder!" and all that, did much to relieve the monotony of the ride. Finally he yelled in despair, as he bobbed up and down and back and forth:

"Sh-oo-oo-oot me, or stop the hor-or-or-orse!"

"Keep your feet in the stirrups, but let your weight rest evenly in the saddle."

"Murder! Oh! stop him! stop him! I'll go back to my company. I'd rather be shot by rebels than to be murdered this way!"

I reined in my horse and we came to a halt.

"So you're a runaway, are you?"

"I was tired out and had lost the command. There was nothing for me to do but to go back to camp."

The doughboy "climbed down" off the horse and crawled into

the bushes by the roadside. He declined my invitation to ride on to Globe Tavern.

"You're outside the lines, and if you don't turn around and go out and join your regiment before daylight, you will be gobbled up by the bushwhackers in the morning."

"I'd rather be shot than to ride that horse another rod. Take the horse with you, I don't want him."

"Well, goodbye."

"Goodbye."

While we were in front of Petersburg I received a letter from home requesting me to go to the general hospital at City Point, and see Eleazer Reynolds of Company B, One hundred and twenty-fifth New York Volunteers, one of the Berlin boys. The letter stated that Leaze was reported to be on his last legs, and it would please his parents, Mr. and Mrs. Amos Reynolds, to have me call and converse with him so that I could write just what their boy had to say. I rode down to the hospital the same day that I received the letter, which had been delayed several days on the road. I was fearful that I would be too late.

Soldiers from the same towns, and sometimes brothers serving in different regiments, were now and then camped within a few miles of each other at the front, and yet without special effort were made they might not run across each other during their entire term of service. This was particularly true of the infantry. Cavalrymen had better opportunities for visiting around when not on the march. A letter sent home from a soldier out on the left in front of Petersburg would often contain a request to "be remembered to John when you write; tell him I am able to eat my full rations—when I can get them." And John would be a brother serving in a regiment over on the right of the Petersburg line, or, perhaps, on the other side of the James in front of Richmond.

I had no difficulty in finding the ward to which Reynolds had been assigned. I glanced at the rows of cots in the ward, but I could see nothing of Leaze, and I began to fear that he was already dead.

"Did you have a patient here named Reynolds?" I asked the ward master.

"Yes."

"Is he dead?

"Not quite."

"Where can I find him?"

"Come with me."

I followed the ward master out to the cook tent in rear of the ward. A man with his back toward us was stirring the soup in a camp kettle. Pointing at the cook, the ward master said:

"Does he look like a corpse?"

It was Leaze. And he would have tipped the scales at something like two hundred pounds. He told me he had been sent to the hospital when dangerously ill, and that for some time his life hung on a slender thread.

"You see," said Reynolds, "I was so low for several days that the doctors said I might pass in my checks, and one of the boys in the ward wrote home that I was as good as gone. But I pulled through, and when I got convalescent they detailed me to work in the kitchen. I'm getting along and shall go back to my regiment the first chance I get."

I enjoyed the visit with Reynolds, and also the dinner he provided. While at the hospital I wrote a letter home, in which I stated that Leaze was considered "out of danger." Like hundreds of other soldiers, Reynolds had been neglectful in writing to his parents, and as the last letter they had received—from a comrade in the same ward—had stated that he was near death's door, they were seriously alarmed. But he survived the hardships of the campaigns, came out alive, and now resides at Berlin.

During the winter of 1864-65, and while the Army of the Potomac was in front of Petersburg, furloughs were given to a few men in each company, whose records were the best.

Our first sergeant, Charles Legg, sent in my name. Capt. Flint approved the application, and a furlough for twenty days was granted "by command of Major-Gen. G. G. Meade," and signed by the assistant adjutant general. The next morning I turned in all my equipments to the quartermaster sergeant, and one of the boys rode down to City Point with me to take my horse back to camp.

I boarded a steamer at City Point, bound for Washington, stopping at Fortress Monroe, and then sailing up the Potomac. The steamer was crowded with soldiers, rebel prisoners and civilians and refugees from the Confederacy, white and black. One old gray-haired man on crutches told of terrible persecutions he had suffered at the hands of the rebels.

"I'm a Union man," he said, "and because I wouldn't take an oath to stand by the stars and bars, they burned my house, caused the death of my wife, destroyed my property, conscripted my two sons and threatened my life. Thank God, I'm beneath the glorious stars and stripes again. If I could stand up under a musket, I'd go into the ranks of the Union army today. My prayer is that I'll live to see Jeff Davis and his followers wiped from the face of the earth. I don't know what fate my sons have met with, but I'm trusting that God will bring them through."

"Father?"

"Whose voice is that? Is it Harry—can it be my son."

"Yes, father; here am I."

And a lad of about eighteen years stepped forward from a squad of rebel prisoners on the main deck of the steamer, and clasped the old man to his heart.

"Thank God, thank God!" exclaimed the father. The tears were streaming down the faces of both, and there were moist eyes among the spectators.

"And Willie?"

The old man's voice faltered as he made the inquiry.

"Dead."

"Willie dead! My youngest boy dead! Oh! don't tell me that."

"Yes, father. He was killed on the Weldon railroad. He fell at my side as we made a charge. I couldn't stop to see how badly he was hurt, for the line pressed on at the double quick. Then we were driven back, and as we retreated I found his body. A minie ball had pierced his heart, and he must have died instantly. The fatal bullet cut through mother's picture that he always carried in a breast pocket, over his heart. Here is the picture. I had scarcely time to secure it when the Union troops came upon us again, and we were driven from the field. That night we were recalled from the right of the line, and transferred to the Richmond defences."

"And how came you here, Harry?"

"I was taken prisoner on the picket line about a week ago, and I understand they are taking us to Annapolis. How did you leave mother?"

"Your poor mother died three weeks ago. She was failing fast at the time our house was burned by the guerrillas. After that we camped out, and her death was hastened by the exposure. My wife murdered, my home laid waste, Willie killed and you a prisoner—oh! my son, my cup of bitterness is full."

"Poor mother," groaned the boy in gray, as he tried to console his aged father, whose grief was heartrending.

An agent of the Christian commission, who became interested in the old man and his soldier boy, suggested that the latter's release might be secured if the facts in the case could be brought to the attention of President Lincoln when the steamer reached Washington.

"I'll go with you to see Mr. Lincoln as soon as we land," said the agent.

"Thank you," replied the venerable refugee. "I have been told that the president has a tender heart and I have no doubt he will give heed to my prayer, for my poor boys were forced into the rebel army against my vigorous protest. They did not want to go, as they have been taught loyalty to the flag of the Union."

I never ascertained what success attended the visit of the old man to the White House, whither he hastened in a cab when the steamer touched the wharf. But I have no doubt that Father Abraham helped the visitor out of his trouble in some way. Many such instances have been recorded, and it is altogether probable that the loyal heart of the old patriarch was made glad by an order for his surviving son's release.

Chapter 33

Home on Furlough

Home on furlough! How the memories of that eventful period of my war history come back as I write. It seemed that the train would never leave Washington, and when it did pull out from the station, I fancied I could walk and keep ahead of the locomotive, so impatient was I. But I reached home in due time.

I had a splendid time on furlough. And how the soldier boy was feasted and lionised. To be sure, soldiers were not such curiosities at that time as they had been at the beginning of the war, but when "our boy" came home, the entire family and all the community turned out to give him a hearty welcome. The girls, as was natural, took a shine to the boy in blue, and the village lads good-naturedly accepted the situation, and smiled when jilted by their sweethearts, knowing very well that in a few days the soldier would return to his regiment, and the maidens to their first love.

Boys, do you remember the make-up of the girl of the period during the war? Short-waisted dresses with enormous hoop-skirts, anywhere from ten to thirty feet in circumference, according to the taste of the fair damsels, whose heads, arms and shoulders protruded from this balloon-looking arrangement. A lady in full dress—the larger the hoops, the fuller the dress—could not go through the door of any ordinary building without seizing her hoops in her hands, and "skewing" them up to one side.

I have before me as I write pictures from the illustrated papers, showing costumes of the ladies who attended the inauguration ball in honour of President Lincoln at Washington, March 4, 1861. Special pictures are given of Miss Carrie Bean, Miss White of Washington, Miss Rose Cowan, Mrs. Col. Yates, Mrs. Drake Mills and others.

Some of the dresses had from five to ten flounces. The charming

The girl in the war period

ladies represented were dressed to perfection in those days. And such hoops!

The ladies all wore their hair combed down over their ears, and caught in a net or roll behind. Another full-page picture of Miss Harriet Lane, presiding lady of the White House in 1860, gives a fair representation of the prevailing style of dress at that time.

But I only call up the subject to jog the memories of the boys, who will join me in a hearty laugh, I know, as they recall their awkward attempts to get near enough to their sweethearts to salute them in regulation style without walking on their crinoline.

How nice it was to have three—more if desired—square meals a day of home grub. The delicious bread and knickknacks—mother made them herself—and the buckwheat cakes and maple syrup "supplied a long-felt want."

Then when the furloughed volunteer retired for the night, and was settling down to dream of the distant battlefield, or the "gay young girl with her hair in curl," who had kissed him for his mother as he said goodnight, there would be heard the soft step of mother as she ascended the stairs to the room of her soldier boy, to tuck up the bed-clothes to keep him from taking cold. Then with a mother's kiss and a whispered, "God bless my boy," she would walk backward out of the room, holding the light above her head so that it would shine on the face of her son, pausing for a minute in the doorway to take yet another look. There were tears on mother's cheeks and her lip trembled. From her heart went up praises to God for sparing her boy, and prayers for his safety when he should—too soon—be again at the front, that place so terrible to mother hearts. And mother thought the boy was asleep.

Then in the morning the children must go about the house on tiptoe for fear of disturbing the slumbers of the soldier.

But the furlough soon expired. Then came the hour of departure. Home never before seemed so dear. All the neighbours had come to say goodbye. It was worse than charging the enemy's picket line.

"You'll be killed this time, sure," sobbed one.

"Of course he will," chorused half a dozen neighbours.

"My boy, my boy!" cried mother.

"These horses won't stand another minute!" exclaimed father, who was at the door with a team to drive the soldier to the city.

Father was beginning to "break," too, and he did not want to "show off" before the neighbours. Finally we got away, and I was again *en route* to Dixie. Father drove me to Troy, and I took a train for New York, and thence proceeded to Washington.

The steamer down the Potomac was crowded with soldiers returning to their regiments, and new recruits for Grant's army. I was homesick all the way, but when City Point was reached, and I met three or four of the boys from Meade's headquarters who had come down on escort duty, I became somewhat reconciled to the situation. I received a hearty welcome at the camp of Company C in front of Petersburg. My basket of homemade bread, pies and cakes had held out all the way, and there was enough left to give my bunkey a reminder that the folks at the North did not live on pork and hard-tack.

I remember that I returned to Meade's headquarters Friday, because it was hangman's day. Near Hancock Station, on the way out to headquarters of the Army of the Potomac, we could see a large number of troops drawn up in a hollow square over on our left. In the centre of the square we could distinguish the gallows, on which three or four poor wretches were paying the penalty of their crimes. Some of them had deserted from the Union Army, and were subsequently captured while serving under the Confederate flag. Another was a rebel spy captured inside the Federal lines.

The field in which the execution took place, was but a short distance in rear of the fortifications, and the rebel gunners now and then sent a solid shot unpleasantly close to the troopers paraded to witness the hangings, which occurred every week or so.

Chapter 34
President Lincoln's Visit to the Front

Deserters from the Confederate Army at Petersburg came into the Federal lines with doleful tales of hunger and hardships. The "bull pen "near Meade's headquarters was filled with Johnnies who had run away from Lee's army. They had seen the handwriting on the wall, and were convinced that they had been fighting for a lost cause; the hopelessness of the struggle had struck home to their hearts—and stomachs. In March, 1865, before Grant began the movement on the left of Petersburg, a number of rebels came through the lines and surrendered.

"We can't stand another campaign," said a rebel deserter at the bull pen. "We can't march and fight on quarter rations of meal and only a smell of meat."

"Do you think the Confederacy is gone up?"

"Shuah's yo born, but Bobby Lee's game. He'll fight till the last ounce of powder is used up."

"What's the use?"

"No use, except to show his fidelity to the cause."

"He has shown that already."

"So he has, and he's in a mighty bad way."

In the latter part of March the signs began to indicate that a general break-up was at hand. Dispatch bearers were seen on all sides, dashing away with messages from army headquarters to corps commanders in the lines in front of Petersburg. Horses were being shod, army wagons overhauled—the thousand and one things betokening a move were noticed in the camps.

At Meade's headquarters it was understood that Grant intended to begin hammering again on or about the first of April, and the boys were satisfied that there would be no April fool business about it.

President Lincoln visited Grant's headquarters, and was present when the Federal army moved "on to Richmond" for the last time. The president arrived about March 22, and he did not return to Washington till after the fall of Richmond, which city he entered the day after Jeff Davis fled. Lincoln was at City Point when Sheridan arrived after he had whipped Early out of the Valley. And here, too, came Sherman, the hero of the March to the Sea.

Tuesday, March 28, General Meade rode down to the point and conferred with the general-in-chief. It was the day before that fixed for the movement. An informal council was held between Lincoln, Grant, Sheridan, Sherman and Meade. It was the first and last time that these five great men were ever together. In Richardson's *Personal History of Grant*, the following pen-picture of the group is given:

> Lincoln, tall, round-shouldered, loose-jointed, large-featured, deep-eyed, with a smile upon his face, is dressed in black, and wears a fashionable silk hat. Grant is at Lincoln's right, shorter, stouter, more compact; wears a military hat with a stiff broad brim, has his hands in his pantaloons pockets, and is puffing away at a cigar while listening to Sherman. Sherman, tall, with high, commanding forehead, is almost as loosely built as Lincoln; has sandy whiskers, closely-cropped, and sharp, twinkling eyes, slouched hat, his pantaloons tucked into his boots. He is talking hurriedly, gesticulating to Lincoln, now to Grant, his eyes wandering everywhere. Meade, also tall, with thin, sharp features, a gray beard and spectacles, is a little stooping in his gait. Sheridan, the shortest of all, quick and energetic in all his movements, with a face bronzed by sun and wind, is courteous, affable and a thorough soldier.

Lincoln visited Meade also. I was one of the detachment sent to the railroad station to receive the president and escort him to headquarters. Orders had been issued for a grand review in honour of the chief magistrate, but before Lincoln had reached the station the troops were more seriously engaged. General Lee had discovered that his situation was becoming more critical each hour that he remained in Richmond, and he determined to make a break for the Union works near the Appomattox, on the Petersburg line. If he could capture and hold Fort Steadman and the ridge in rear of it, he could seriously cripple Grant's army and perhaps seize City Point.

General John B. Gordon was the commander selected by Lee to

undertake the capture of the works. The assault was successful so far as getting into and taking possession of Fort Steadman was concerned, but the Federals rallied and recaptured the fort, the guns of which had been turned on our works to the right and left. The rebels had plunged into the Union lines in the darkness. The pickets were scarcely one hundred and fifty feet apart in front of Fort Steadman, and the main earthworks were separated by about as many yards. It is said that Gordon had the utmost confidence in the success of the expedition. He had been assured that the assault would be supported by troops from A. P. Hill and Longstreet's corps. It was a bold attack, but the gallant boys in blue, though driven from the fort and some of the works in the immediate vicinity at the outset, returned to the front, and the rebel general found that he had no time to spare in getting back behind the Confederate breastworks. The Johnnies were routed with great loss, and nearly two thousand prisoners were captured by the Federals.

The attack on Fort Steadman woke up the whole army. Meade concluded to give the Johnnies all the fighting they wanted, and he ordered the Second and Sixth corps—occupying the line to the left of the Ninth corps in the front of which the rebel assault was made—to push out and see what was going on in their front.

The boys went forward with a cheer, and the Confederate pickets were driven back into the main fortifications, the rifle pits and the strongly entrenched picket line being taken by the assaulting forces. Nearly nine hundred Johnnies were captured.

Several counter charges were made by the rebels to drive our boys out of the works, but they satisfied themselves that the Yankees had come to stay. It was a cold day for the Confederates all along the line.

President Lincoln witnessed the battle in front of the Second and Sixth corps. He was on a ridge near the signal tower of the Second corps. Several ladies—I think Mrs. Grant, and I don't know but Mrs. Lincoln was in the party—were there. They had been driven out from the railroad in an ambulance to see the review, but the president came to the front mounted. As a horseman Lincoln was not a success. As I remember it, he rode Grant's best horse. Several staff officers were at the station with a detachment of cavalry to look after the President. The latter's clothes seemed to fit him when he got into the saddle, but before he dismounted at the signal tower he presented a sorry spectacle indeed. The cavalry escort reached the station a few minutes before the train from the Point came puffing along.

The president stood on the platform of the only passenger coach. The escort presented sabres and Lincoln acknowledged the salute by raising his hat. Then he came down from the cab and shook hands with the staff officers, who seemed to feel highly complimented to be recognized by the commander-in-chief. But when the president extended his hand to a high private of the rear rank who stood holding the horse His Excellency was to ride, and insisted on shaking hands with each soldier of the escort, the wearers of shoulder straps appeared to be dazed at such familiarity. The honoured head of the greatest nation on earth recognizing in the wearer of the plain blue blouse of a humble private a fellow citizen! Military red tape could not comprehend it, but it made no difference with "Father Abraham"; he had a way of doing just as he pleased on such occasions. As the president advanced to mount, the orderly in charge of the horse, with a sly glance at Lincoln's legs, said:

"You ride a longer stirrup than the general, sir. I'll fix them in a jiffy."

"No, no, my man; never mind. The stirrups are all right. I don't like to stand on my toes in the saddle."

Then the president threw his right leg over the horse's back and smiled at the orderly's surprise at such an unmilitary exhibition as Lincoln made of himself in getting into the saddle.

"Thank you," said the great emancipator, as the orderly relinquished his hold of the bridle, and the horse with his distinguished rider began to dance around ready for the word "Forward."

The staff officers sprang into their saddles, the escort broke into columns of fours, and the party started for the front. The president had jammed his hat well down over the back of his head to keep it from falling off. He leaned forward in the saddle so that his chin almost touched the horse's mane. His coat was unbuttoned and soon worked itself up around his arms and flapped out behind. His vest seceded from his pantaloons and went up toward his neck, so that his white shirt showed between the vest and trousers like a sash. And it did not take long for the pantaloons to creep up the long legs of the distinguished visitor. Up to the knees they went—and higher. The president discovered that he was not cutting a very fine figure, but he had no time to fix things. His horse required all his attention, and more, too. The animal knew he was entitled to the head of the column, and he kept there.

Some of the staff officers, fearing perhaps that the horse would run away with the president, essayed to ride alongside and seize the bridle. The attempt proved a dismal failure. On went the fiery steed, bearing his honoured rider out the road toward the breastworks. Lincoln held on. Now his feet were in the stirrups with his knees bobbing up nearly to his chin; *anon* his feet were out of the stirrups and his long legs dangled down almost to the ground. As we approached the line of battle of the Second corps, it was understood that the horse had "taken the bit in his mouth." Would he stop when he reached the group of officers up on the knoll, or would he go on and carry the president into the battle over there between the forts? Whatever apprehensions may have been felt by the chief magistrate or any of those in the escort on this score, were quieted as we drew near to the signal tower. The horse slackened his speed and gave the president an opportunity to shake himself a little, so that his coat and pantaloons were to some extent brought back where they belonged.

The president seemed to regain his wonted good nature at once upon halting, and when some of the general officers who came to greet him asked him how he had enjoyed his ride, he exclaimed, with a merry twinkle in his eye: "It was splendid. I don't know but I rode a little too fast for the gentlemen who followed, but I was anxious to get here—or somewhere—where I could have a good view of the fight and get off and pull down my pants."

And Father Abraham laughed heartily as he joined the group near the signal tower. Did the president relate an anecdote or two called up by the incidents of the trip? No; for the booming of the cannon, the roaring of the musketry and the cheers of the troops as they marched by and took up the double quick to join in the assault on the enemy's outer works in front of Petersburg, called the attention of all to the serious events transpiring so close at hand.

How the soldiers cheered when informed of Lincoln's presence! They waved their caps and held their muskets over their heads as they pushed on, many of them to die in a few minutes in that desperate struggle for the rebel pits and breastworks.

Meade succeeded in capturing and holding several important points in front of Petersburg, and the poor Johnnies were more discouraged than ever before. The president and his party returned to City Point that night, and he remained at Grant's headquarters till after the lieutenant-general moved out to the left and until the fall of Richmond.

Chapter 35

How Jeff Davis faced the Yankees

And now came the orders for what Grant intended should be the last grand campaign of the gallant Army of the Potomac. Sheridan, as usual, was to lead off and push out around the right flank of the rebel forces cooped up in Petersburg and Richmond. The bulk of the army was to follow, and it was evident that unless the Southern Confederacy got out of the way "right smart," somebody would get hurt. Everybody was on the move, or ready to move, even the troops who were to remain in the fortifications having their knapsacks packed. The feeling was general among the rank and file that a decisive battle was to be fought, and all felt that the Union cause would triumph. There were no spread-eagle proclamations promulgated through general orders. Grant was never given to that. His instructions to his lieutenants gave them to understand just what they were expected to do—they were to move against the rebels and go in to win.

Little Phil opened the ball at Five Forks on the last day of March. The army had moved March 29, but the infantry had been unable to make much progress, being stuck in the mud, for the rain set in during the evening of the twenty-ninth and continued all night and the next day and night. The rebels pressed Sheridan hard. Yet the hero of Winchester held on like grim death. The next day with the aid of the infantry sent to his support, he pitched in and routed the rebels, capturing more than five thousand prisoners and putting to flight fifteen thousand or more, who skedaddled in such a hurry that they left behind all their cannon and supply wagons. The battle was anything but an April-fool joke.

Meade, Ord and Parke made a general assault on the works in front of Petersburg, April 2. It was Sunday morning. The roar of battle could be heard from away over on the Appomattox above City Point, all along the line. It was a magnificent sight to see the infantry going in. As the charge was being made, General Meade sent Major Emory of his staff with a dispatch to General Wright commanding the Sixth corps. I was directed to accompany the major. General Wright was said to be hotly engaged in capturing entrenchments off to the left of Petersburg, and to reach him it would be necessary to make a wide circuit to the left and rear, or ride directly across the field where the battle was raging. Major Emory decided upon the latter course, and away we went.

The Johnnies, realizing that their time had come, were making a desperate defence of the works, and the shot and shell screeched over and under and around us on all sides as we rode the line of battle. One shell exploded directly under the major's horse, throwing up a cloud of dirt and smoke, and for a moment I felt sure General Meade had lost one of his aids. Then I heard the major shout:

"Come on. I'm all right."

It was dangerous work. The infantry soldiers were falling on all sides. But we came out alive and reached General Wright, who had broken through the outer lines and was pushing toward Petersburg.

The fall of Richmond! All Sunday night the rebels were getting out of Richmond and Petersburg. The backbone of the Confederacy was broken indeed. The news seemed too good to be true. We rode into Petersburg Monday morning, bright and early, and without dismounting, we kept on and immediately took up the line of march in pursuit of Lee's army, which was now retreating up the Appomattox.

It was a hot chase—a sort of go-as-you-please. Of course when Richmond was evacuated, the boys in blue felt that the end was at hand. When the Confederate commander telegraphed to Jeff Davis that the "enemy" had broken the line in front of Petersburg, it was a cold day for C. S. A.

It is recorded that Jeff Davis was attending church when he received Lee's dispatch, and that he quietly stole away without waiting for the doxology or the benediction. It was a clear case of "every man for himself." The "president" didn't whisper even to the brother in the next pew that it was time to flee from the wrath to come. No. Perhaps he had heard the echo of that familiar Yankee hymn:

We'll hang Jeff Davis to a sour apple-tree,
As we go marching on.

The "president" made better time in getting away from the seat of government than was made by the braves in butternut. He did not draw a long breath till he had distanced the retreating Confederates and reached Danville. To stimulate his soldiers to deeds of daring—and to induce them to beat back the Union army if possible till he could make good his escape—Davis declared in a proclamation, issued on the wing at Danville, April 5, 1865, that:

> Virginia, with the help of the people, and by the blessings of Providence, shall be held and defended.
>
> Let us, meet the foe with fresh defiance, and with unconquered and unconquerable hearts.

Before his signature to the document was dry, Jeff was making a bee-line for Georgia. He was willing to meet the foe face to face on paper. "You hold Grant in check till I can get far enough South to establish a rallying-point," was the burden of his messages to the rebel general when read between the lines. At all events, the president of the Southern Confederacy took to the woods, and was next heard of at Irwinsville, Georgia, May 11, 1S65. Wilson's troopers took the fugitive into camp on that day.

The circumstances of the capture of Jeff Davis have been the subject of heated controversy—in magazine articles and newspaper publications. Whatever may be the fact in respect of his wearing apparel at the time the Yankee cavalrymen overhauled the rebel president—whether he had on his wife's petticoats or was clad in masculine attire—certain it is that in abandoning the "lost cause," and leaving Lee and his followers to "meet the foe with fresh defiance," while he skedaddled, the "rebel hero"—still idolised and worshiped by the solid South—made a sorry exhibition of himself.

On the chase up the Appomattox our boys were kept busy—in the saddle night and clay—carrying dispatches to and from Meade's headquarters. It was a very interesting period. Sheridan was neck-and-neck with Lee, while the grand old Army of the Potomac was hot on the rebel commander's trail.

General Meade was seriously ill for several days preceding the negotiations that led to the surrender. But he kept in the saddle most of the time, in spite of the request of the headquarters' medical men, that he should "avoid all excitement!" It was strange advice to give under such circumstances. The hero of Gettysburg realized that the boys were knocking the bottom out of the Southern Confederacy, and he was determined to be in at the death.

Whenever there was heavy firing at the front, Meade would get out of the ambulance, in which he rode when compelled to leave the saddle, and call for his favourite horse "Baldy." Then he would ask his son George, one of his aids, or Major Jay or Major Emory, to assist him into the saddle. Once mounted, the general seemed to have a way of shaking off his sickness. He would press on to the head of the column and make a personal reconnaissance. As soon as the rear guard of the rebels—left to check the Union advance while the Confederate wagon trains and artillery were hurried to the west—was brushed out of the way, and the line of march resumed, the general would return to his ambulance, at times completely exhausted.

April 4, 1865, was one of the hardest days of the chase. It was a forced march with only an occasional breathing spell when the advance was feeling its way along the roads leading toward Appomattox. That night we unsaddled with what we considered fair prospects of rest. But before we had settled down for sleep, a trooper dashed up to Meade's headquarters. The general was so ill that he could scarcely hold up his head, but when told that Sheridan had intercepted the Confederates, and predicted the capture of Lee's army if the Army of the Potomac would push to the front near Jettersville, Meade got out of bed and gave orders for the march to be resumed at two o'clock in the morning.

The boys were waiting for the wagons to come up with the hard tack and coffee, and the prospect of pushing on without grub was anything but transporting. Still when the time came to "fall in," the men obeyed with a cheerfulness characteristic of the veterans of the gallant army that for four years had fought Lee's soldiers with varied success.

The next morning Sheridan's men—a scouting party under General Davies, our brigade commander—played havoc with a Confederate wagon train that was "sifting west." Nearly two hundred wagons were destroyed. It was hard for the Johnnies to witness the destruction of their supply train. Poor fellows, they needed all the grub they could get, and more, too. They fought desperately, but the battle was against them. The Federal column moved on, and the surrounding of Lee's army was pushed on all sides. The boys in blue were hungry, but they kept in good spirits. "We can stand it if the rebs can," was remarked now and then as the boys were ordered to move on just before the supply train would get up.

On the battlefield of Sailor's Creek I picked up General Lee's order book. The last order copied into the book was dated Saturday, April 1, 1865, and, as I remember it, the order referred to the sending of re-enforcements from the works in front of Petersburg to oppose Sheridan's advance on the Union left. The ground was strewn with the debris of the rebel headquarters' train. Army wagons with spokes cut out of the wheels were overturned on both sides of the road. "In the last ditch;" "The C. S. A. is gone up;" "We all can't whip you all without something to eat," and other humorous inscriptions appeared on the canvas covers of the wagons. I wish I had held on to Lee's order book. It would have been valuable today. But it was heavy, and I threw it aside.

April 9, 1865, while Sheridan was square across the road preventing Lee's further advance without cutting his way through, and the Army of the Potomac was on the flank and rear, came the news that white flags were displayed along the rebel lines and that Grant and Lee were negotiating for the surrender of the Confederate army of Northern Virginia. Meade's headquarters contingent was bivouacked just off the road leading to Appomattox Court House from Farmville.

Lee's going to surrender!

The boys could scarcely credit the report that the Confederate commander had asked terms, for, somehow or other, after a week's hard chase the Yankees had begun to fear that Lee would effect a junction with Johnston in North Carolina. But when an orderly from Grant's headquarters dashed up and handed Meade a letter from the lieutenant-general confirming the report that Lee had accepted Grant's terms, there was the greatest joy at headquarters.

The news spread like wildfire, and in a few minutes the tired soldiers were dancing with joy. I was broiling a confiscated chicken in the angle of a rail fence when the orderly rode up. When I was told of the tidings he had brought I threw the chicken as high as I could, kicked the fire in every direction, and shouted till my throat was sore.

General Meade, with a few members of the escort of which I was one, rode into the Confederate lines and to Lee's camp. The Southern commander had only a wall tent fly for headquarters. Longstreet was there and several others whom Meade had known in the old army. Meade and Lee conversed for a few minutes alone. In the meantime a sergeant of Meade's escort and a sergeant of Lee's headquarters guard entered into such a heated argument that the interference of several officers of both sides was necessary to prevent them from fighting to a finish.

As we were riding down the slope from Lee's bivouac, a weather-stained Confederate, wearing an old slouch hat, a short butternut jacket, and with a dilapidated blanket wrapped about his shoulders, shouted to Meade. The commander of the Army of the Potomac did not recognize the man who hailed him and who held out his hand, until the rebel said:

"Don't you know me, General? I'm General Wise of Virginia."

Then there was another handshake. Wise was the sorriest looking general I saw at the surrender. Lee and Longstreet and some of the others were clad in bright new uniforms, but Wise looked as though he had been rolled in the mud all the way from Petersburg.

After calling on Lee, Meade rode over to the Court House and congratulated Grant and Sheridan on the result. The Union generals seemed to enjoy the "love feast."

There was joy and gladness on all sides. A majority of the rebels who surrendered at Appomattox accepted the inevitable with better grace than could have been expected of them after the desperate resistance they had made. But when you put food into a starving man's mouth the chances favour his smothering his hatred if he has such feeling toward you.

"Dog gone it, that's splendid coffee," said a butternut clad veteran who shared my supper the night of the surrender. "You all overpowered us; we couldn't hold out on wind any longer. I like this meat; I tell you, it's good. I didn't know I was so hungry; I must have got beyond the hunger point."

Then came the order for the return. It was not "on to Richmond" this time, but "on to Washington." We all knew that the war was over—that Sherman would make short work of the Confederate Army in the Carolinas under Johnston.

When we mounted our horses and rode back toward Burkesville station, leaving the provost marshal and a small force at Appomattox to parole the prisoners, it was conceded by both Yankee and rebel that the Army of the Potomac and the army of Northern Virginia would never again meet as enemies on the battlefield. The boys in blue felt that they had fought a good fight, won a glorious victory, and could now return to their homes proud to have been permitted to suffer and do battle under the flag of the Union.

It was a happy army that faced about at Appomattox and took up the march for Washington. The bands played, and the victorious Federals sang. The bivouacs at night were camp meetings on a large scale. Somehow the boys did not need as much sleep as was required when in winter quarters. Discipline was relaxed, and colonels and corporals, captains and privates talked over the results of the last campaign without any "red tape nonsense," as the boys were wont to call a strict observance of military discipline when there was no fighting to do.

The song that was sung with the most expression on that homeward march, was a parody on "Dear Mother, I've come home to die," the last word being changed to "eat." Then there was that lively air:

When Johnny comes marching home again,
Hurrah, hurrah!
When Johnny comes marching home again,
Hurrah, says I;
The lads and lassies, so they say,
With roses they will strew the way,
And we'll all feel gay
When Johnny comes marching home.

On the road between Farmville and Burkesville station I dismounted at a farmhouse and asked a little negro boy who stood near the fence with mouth and eyes wide open, for a drink of water. The lad seemed to be frightened, and ran away around the house.

"You, Julius, come here!" shouted a middle-aged lady who stepped out on the *piazza*. She had overheard my request for water. The young darky returned at the lady's command.

"I'se 'fraid dese Yankees," he said.

"I don't think they'll molest you, Julius. Bring the gentleman a drink of water."

I was invited to a seat on the *piazza* pending Julius's expedition to the spring house, a rod or two back of the dwelling. He returned with a large gourd dipper filled with deliciously cool water. In the meantime three young ladies, daughters of the middle-aged lady, appeared on the *piazza* and were presented by their mother to the Yankee. Then Julius went to the spring to fill my canteen.

"I'm sorry we have nothing but water to offer you," said the mother.

The young ladies also ventured to speak.

"The two armies, ours and yours, just took everything in the shape of provisions on the place."

"Yes; and the soldiers found where we had stored a few hams and a sack of flour down in the woods."

"And they made out they came across the place accidentally like. I believe Jeb, a brother of Julius, told the Yankees where we had buried the box with the hams and flour, for he hasn't been seen on the plantation since."

"I am really sorry for you, ladies. I will speak to General Meade, and I am sure he will direct the commissary to supply you with something to eat."

"I think we can hold out for another day," said the mother. "My husband was in Longstreet's corps, and he said when he galloped by here the other day that the Confederacy was played out, and that if something providential did not turn up on the side of Lee's army they would all be gobbled up inside of ten days. His last words were: 'If you can save me a dish of meat of some kind till I get home, do it; it may save my life.'"

"And we're doing our best for papa."

"Yes, we are. When the last Yankees marched by on the way to the surrender, we found we had one goose left"—

"Yes; and we've got the goose yet, down in the cellar"—

"Now, Miss Emma, you have told a Yankee about the goose, and papa's chances for dinner when he comes home are mighty slim."

"Dear sir, you will spare us?"

"Mr. Yankee, let us keep our goose?"

"I know you didn't mean to rob us!"

"The goose is safe, ladies. Cook your goose for the family reunion, for I assure you that there isn't a man in the Federal army mean enough to steal a goose under such circumstances, especially now that the war is over."

"I feel relieved."

"Oh! so much."

"How kind you are."

"The Yankees are not so black as our papers have painted them. I'm so rejoiced to know that we can save the goose."

Just then Julius came bounding around the corner of the house. His hair fairly stood on end, and his eyes seemed starting from their sockets.

"Miss Julia! Miss Julia! Miss Julia!"

"What is it, Julius?"

"O, Miss Julia! Miss Julia!"

"Speak, you idiot!"

"De goose, Miss Julia, de goose! See dar, see dar! Look, dat Yankee gwine ober de fence yonder wid de goose you's a-keepin' for Massa Colonel Bob!"

Sure enough, Julius was right. While the ladies had been entertaining me on the *piazza* a straggling cavalryman had entered the yard. He had filled his canteen at the spring house. Then he interviewed Julius. Next he slipped into the cellar and raised a tub that was bottom-side up on the cellar bottom.

Under the tub he found the goose, which he seized by the neck. In a few seconds he had jumped over the fence to where his horse was standing, and without paying any attention to my shouts for him to "stop or drop that goose," the blue-coated robber put spurs to his steed and disappeared down the road.

The goose was gone. Colonel Bob's dinner was spoiled so far as that goose was concerned.

"Ladies"—

"Don't speak to me."

"Nor me."

"Nor me."

"Nor me."

"But I assure you"—

"Yes, you assured us a few minutes ago."

"I had misgivings all the time that Miss Emma would tell about the goose."

"But, mother dear, don't cry; I thought we could trust a gentleman."

"So we could, but we should have known better than to trust a Yankee."

I believe that I would have shot the bummer who confiscated that goose had he been within range of my revolver while I was under fire on that *piazza*. I never felt quite so mean in the presence of ladies before.

"Go and join your partner," said the mother.

"Leave us, sir!" chorused the daughters.

What a predicament for a youthful soldier. There I stood, despised and hated by four ladies with whom I had been apparently on good terms a few moments before. Had a band of bushwhackers opened fire on me at that moment I should have been happy again.

The bushwhackers did not come, but Julius did. I shall never forget Julius.

"Miss Julia, dis yere Yankee doan' know nuffin 'bout stealin' dat goose."

"How do you know, nigger?"

"Cos' what dat oder Yankee say."

"What did he say?"

"He tole me 'fi made de leas bit of holler so dat Yankee sittin' on de porch wid you all see he, he would don' cut my brack hed off wid he's s'od. Deed he did, Miss Julia."

"How did he know about the goose?"

"Spec I'se de nigger to blame. He axed me whar missus kept her pervisions, an' fo' I know'd what I do'n, I sav, 'Nuffin left but one ole goose, Massa.' Den he say, 'Whar dat goose?' an' what wor a poor nigger to do, Miss Julia?"

"We have done you an injustice, sir," said the mother, again turning to me.

"Pardon us, sir," said the younger ladies.

"Don't mention it, ladies. I am so glad that I am relieved from the suspicion of complicity in the stealing of that goose, that I would stay and help cook a dinner to celebrate Colonel Bob's return were it not for the fact that I must go on and report to General Meade."

We parted very good friends. A goodly store of flour, meat, coffee and sugar was sent to the ladies from the Union commissary department, and no doubt Colonel Bob reached home in time to share the rations with his charming family.

Although twenty-six years have come and gone since my experience on the *piazza* of that Virginia farmhouse, I cannot repress a feeling whenever I recall the circumstances, that I would be pleased to meet that "other Yankee" who did steal that goose and choke him till he cried "*peccavi!*"

CHAPTER 36

The Return March

The news of the assassination of Lincoln reached us at Burkesville Junction—the crossing of the Richmond and Danville and the Southside railroads—April 15, 1865. The terrible intelligence came over the military telegraph wire about midnight of the fourteenth, I think, but it was not promulgated to the troops until after reveille in the morning. Secretary Seward had been dangerously wounded by one of the assassins, and the Head of the Nation had been murdered by J. Wilkes Booth, who as he was escaping from the theatre at Washington where the President was shot, brandished a dagger on the stage and shouted, "*Sic semper tyrannis!*" and "the South is avenged!"

As the details of the dastardly plot were made known, the army was informed that the assassin intended to take the life of General Grant. Battle-scarred and stern-faced veterans who had fought from the first Bull Run to Appomattox turned pale and set their teeth as the dispatches were read to the men drawn up in line. It was difficult to believe at first that Abraham Lincoln, the great and noble and tender-hearted President whom we had seen only a few days before near Petersburg, was dead. Yet the sad news was confirmed as later dispatches came to hand.

The Union soldiers again began to look after their cartridge boxes. They knew not what to expect next. This was a new phase of warfare. But in spite of the declaration of the assassin that the South was avenged, a majority of the rank and file of Grant's army as they recovered from the first shock of the dreadful calamity, were ready to exonerate the men who had laid down their arms at Appomattox from any complicity in the plot that struck down the noble Lincoln at the very moment that the glorious sun of peace was rising above the dark clouds that had hung like a pall over the nation for four long years.

Lincoln was murdered on the fourth anniversary of the capture of Fort Sumter by the rebels. The traitors who directed the firing on the flag waving over that fortress four years before, and who had set on foot and carried forward the wickedest rebellion ever inaugurated, were responsible for the death of the martyr Lincoln and the thousands who fell on both sides of that sanguinary conflict.

A few days after the assassination we continued our march to Richmond, camping for a day or two in Manchester on the opposite side of the James. The ruin and havoc made by the rebels when evacuating their capital, subjected the inhabitants to great hardships. A large portion of the city was burned.

I witnessed the return of a veteran in butternut to his home in Richmond. He came down the hill from the State House and turned into a street leading toward the river. His right arm was in a sling. He had been wounded early in the morning of the day that Lee surrendered. The disbanded Confederate was literally in rags and the uppers of his shoes had seceded from the soles. Yet his face was beaming with joyful anticipation, for he was nearing his home.

But as he reached what had been the corner of another street and turned to the right, his serviceable hand was raised and his knees trembled as he looked in vain for the dwelling he had left when last he bade his little family goodbye and hastened away to help build the breastworks in front of Petersburg. The dwellings that had stood in that neighbourhood were now a mass of blackened ruins. The poor fellow sank down in the street and a coloured man hastened to his assistance.

"I declar, it's Massa John," exclaimed the negro as he raised the head of the soldier. "Doan' you know me, Massa?"

"Is it Pomp?"

"Deed an' 'tis Pomp, Massa."

"Where is your mistress and the children?"

"Dey's ober on the odder side de bridge, Massa; how glad dey'll be to see you. We all 'spected de Yankees dun kill you, shuah nuff."

Just then a woman came hurriedly from around the corner and stopped for a moment as she surveyed the scene before her.

"Who is it, Pomp?" she eagerly inquired, as she advanced toward the party in the street.

"Bress de Lawd, it's Massa John."

In another moment husband and wife were in each other's arms, their tears flowing freely.

Wounded confederate

"And the children, Mary?"

"Safe and well, praise God."

"Amen. Praise God you are all alive."

"But you are wounded?"

"Yes, clear; I'll be unable to use my right arm for a few months; but when it gets well we will rebuild the home which the Yankees have destroyed for us."

"But, my dear, our home was not destroyed by the Yankees. The city was fired by our own men as they left us. The fire was raging terribly when the Yankees came in and did all they could to prevent the spread of the flames."

"Is that so? Then I have fought for years, lost the use of my right arm and returned to find my home destroyed by order of one of our own generals. Surely, wife, the hand of God has been against the Confederacy. We were taught to believe that we were fighting for liberty, but we were mistaken. I love the stars and bars. I have fought and bled for our flag, yet I begin to feel that secession was not right. Our leaders were wrong, and it follows that we must suffer for it."

"What shall we do, John?"

"Do? Well, the outlook is not bright, I'll admit. But we'll not get discouraged. I have a brother in Boston who has money, you know, and I believe he'll help us out. He told me not to go into the Confederate army. He said we would get whipped, but I didn't believe it then. Brother was right, and I'll send him a letter next mail."

Then the wounded Confederate and his better half started off to meet their children at the house of a friend. I gave him the contents of my haversack and several other troopers who were with me also gave our late foe what they had with them.

"Thank you, boys; I'm glad it's over," he said, as he handed the provisions to Pomp, who "toted" it to their friend's residence over the bridge.

From Richmond we marched to Washington, enjoying the trip greatly. On the way we passed over many of the Virginia battlefields. Here and there farmers were ploughing and preparing to put in grain where the opposing armies had recently been in camp. The column was in the best of spirits. The war was over. Our side had gained the victory and we were homeward bound. As we came to the brow of Arlington Heights and caught our first glance of the Capitol in the distance, cheer after cheer was given. The bands played martial tunes and the rejoicing was general.

"The Goddess has been put on top of the dome," said one of the boys of Company I.

"Yes; but poor Taylor isn't with us to see the grand sight," remarked another.

We went into camp on Arlington Heights, and the bulk of the Army of the Potomac soon arrived. It was a grand reunion. The soldiers visited through the bivouacs and in Washington. Relatives and friends from home came down to see the boys and to congratulate the victorious army.

Then came the gallant army that had marched from Atlanta to the sea commanded by General Sherman. The two armies fraternized for the first time. And it was a glorious meeting. Volumes could be written of interesting incidents of those last days of army life around Washington.

Before the troops were disbanded they participated in a general review in Washington; the Army of the Potomac, May 23, and Sherman's army, May 24, 1865. It was the grandest military display ever seen. Orders for the review were promulgated several days in advance, and so thoroughly disciplined were the troops, that in all that vast aggregation of military organizations there was no break during the two days of parading. Everything moved with clocklike regularity.

The first day—Army of the Potomac day—found Companies C and D, First Massachusetts cavalry, in line before reveille. The boys had been all night polishing their sabres and other equipments. No one could sleep on such an occasion. We were to ride before the president, governors of loyal States and other dignitaries, and we were anxious to do honour to the event—the event of a lifetime.

I had the honour to be one of three soldiers of the escort to ride next to General Meade on the grand review. The general was the first military man to ride by the reviewing stand at the White House.

The headquarters flag of the Army of the Potomac was carried by a sergeant of our company. On the right of the sergeant, who was a few paces in the rear of General Meade, rode a trooper of Company D, and I rode on the sergeant's left; we were three abreast. It was a position of honour, and we felt it, although we did not appropriate to ourselves all the homage paid to the head of the column. We were willing to admit that some of the cheering was intended for the grand old hero of Gettysburg, George Gordon Meade.

As the escort and staff of the Army of the Potomac arrived at the Capitol building, thousands of schoolgirls dressed in white appeared.

The bands played "Hail to the Chief," and one of the prettiest of the larger girls came forward to present General Meade an evergreen wreath, beautifully festooned with roses, and neatly tied with satin ribbon. The general's horse "flaxed around" so that he could not reach the wreath, and he called me to receive it, which I did, and passed it over my shoulder, wearing it like a sash on the review. The bands played again, and we took up the line of march on Pennsylvania Avenue. On to the turn at the Treasury Building; another turn, this time to the left, and we were in front of the White House.

On either side the avenue was packed, and we looked into a great sea of faces all the way. And how the people did cheer and shout. Never was such another scene presented.

All the buildings along the line of march were decorated. Flags, banners and bunting waved from every edifice. Across the south face of the Capitol an inscription standing out in large letters declared:

The Only National Debt We Can Never Pay is the Debt We Owe To the Victorious Union Soldiers.

General Meade after passing the reviewing stand rode into the gate in front of the White House, dismounted and joined Grant and other distinguished people on the platform. The colour sergeant, the D Company orderly and myself remained mounted near the gate inside the yard, and witnessed the review of the gallant Army of the Potomac, sixty-five thousand strong, marching by, company front.

It was a magnificent spectacle. There we sat for six hours and more, as the proud Union soldiers marched triumphantly before the representatives of the government. So well planned was the movement of the troops, that some of the brigades, after passing the reviewing stand, marched to camp, were dismissed, and the soldiers returned to the city and joined the thousands of citizens witnessing the parade. And while the leading divisions were marching in review, some of those which came into column later in the day, were back in their bivouacs, cooking coffee for a lunch before falling into line.

The second day, May 24, Sherman's splendid army was reviewed. General Meade occupied a seat on the reviewing stand, and his two orderlies sat on their horses near the gate in the White House yard, as they had done the day before.

Sherman's "bummers" came in for a good share of the applause as they marched behind the regiments to which they belonged, and here and there a Georgia contraband also attracted attention. The review ended, we returned to our camp on the south side of the Potomac, on Arlington Heights.

June 2, 1865, came Grant's final order to the Union soldiers. It was read to the troops, and concluded as follows:

> In obedience to your country's call, you left your homes and families, and volunteered in its defence. Victory has crowned your valour, and secured the purpose of your patriotic hearts, and with the gratitude of your countrymen and the highest honours a great and free nation can accord, you will soon be permitted to return to your homes and families, conscious of having discharged the highest duties of American citizens.
>
> To achieve the glorious triumphs, and secure to yourselves, your fellow-countrymen and posterity the blessings of free institutions, tens of thousands of your gallant comrades have fallen, and sealed the priceless legacy with their lives. The graves of these a grateful nation bedews with tears, honours their memories, and will ever cherish and support their stricken families."

Chapter 37

Discharged From the Service

Here at Arlington Heights the squadron of the First Massachusetts Cavalry, Companies C and D, commanded by Capt. E. A. Flint, and on duty at headquarters Army of the Potomac, was mustered out June 29, 1865, by Capt. J. C. Bates, of the Eleventh United States infantry, chief commissary of musters, in compliance with special orders No. 24 headquarters cavalry corps, June 18, 1865. A few days later we were *en route* to the Old Bay State to receive our discharges at Camp Meigs, Readville. Many of the boys were so anxious to get home that they could not wait to have their papers made out, but left requests to have them sent on to them by mail.

I reached home a day or two after the Fourth of July. And what a reunion we had! All the family and many of the neighbours assembled to welcome the soldier boy. Of course I was a hero in the estimation of the good folks at home. I had yet seven months to live to reach my seventeenth birthday, but I had returned with a discharge which declared that "No objection to his being re-enlisted is known to exist."

In a marginal note it was stated that "This sentence will be erased should there be anything in the conduct or physical condition of the soldier rendering him unfit for the army."

Irving Waterman did not reach Berlin until two days after my arrival. He had remained at Boston to visit with one of the boys. My little sister Eva, when she saw me coming down the road without Irving, only waited to greet me with a kiss, and then started on a run for the home of Waterman's parents.

"My brother's come home!" she exclaimed.

"Praise the Lord!" shouted Mrs. Waterman.

"But your son didn't come."

"Didn't he—what's the matter?"

"He's dead."

"Dead? Irving dead—no, no! that can't be."

"But he didn't come, and he must be dead."

Mrs. Waterman headed a procession—a dozen or more—of men, women and children, who came up the street on a run. The news that Waterman was dead spread like wildfire, and soon a large number of villagers were at our house to hear all about it. Their alarm was changed to rejoicing when I assured them that Waterman was alive and well.

My little sister when she heard mother inquiring about Irving, and my reply that he had not returned with me, took it for granted that he was dead, and so hastened to inform Mrs. Waterman.

Late that night when the family separated to "catch a little sleep before chore time," as father put it, and I sank down into mother's best feather bed, and tried to remember the thrilling events in which I had participated since Waterman, Taylor and I started for that "shooting match," I felt that, after all,—

Be it ever so humble.
There's no place like home.

CHAPTER 38

A Regimental Reunion

And now, more than a quarter of a century after the restoration of the Union, how is it with the "boys"? Civilians—men who have been born since the firing on Fort Sumter—fail to understand why the war veterans should go out of their way, sometimes travelling across the continent, to attend a reunion of the regiment in which they served "Down in Dixie." I wish to take the readers who have followed the author from the Wilderness to Appomattox, to a regimental reunion before closing this book, to enable them to appreciate, in some degree at least, how much the veterans enjoy these fraternal gatherings.

Memory is often at fault in respect to incidents and dates. I had been under the impression that William Finney of Company I, First Massachusetts cavalry, was killed in the fight at St. Mary's Church, but a few years ago I had the pleasure of meeting my old comrade face to face in Boston.

I was sure that Finney started with us from Warrenton, when we set out on Grant's overland campaign, and that he was with us the first day in the Wilderness. Then I remembered that he was reported killed somewhere, and later there was a good deal of uncertainty as to his fate.

A few years ago while on a visit to Boston, I secured a copy of the muster-out roll of Company I, through the courtesy of Major Charles G. Davis, president of the regimental association.

On this roll I was surprised to find that William Finney was discharged "per expiration of term of service in Company C, First Massachusetts cavalry." I was all the more confident that the record was wrong as I was one of the Company I boys transferred to C troop when the survivors of our company were distributed among the other companies, and I could not remember that I had ever seen Finney at

Meade's headquarters.

October 30, 1889, I attended the annual reunion of the First Massachusetts cavalry association in the Lancers' Armoury, Boston. It was the first reunion of the survivors of my old regiment that I ever attended, and I was surprised to find such a marked change in the appearance of the old comrades. Of the one hundred and fifty members present, there were only five or six whose faces I could reconcile with the faces of the boys whose names they answered to. But a few minutes' conversation with them set matters right.

Among the survivors whose personal appearance had changed the least in the twenty-four years since the regiment returned from Appomattox to be mustered out at Readville, was Major Amos L. Hopkins, son of the late President Hopkins of Williams College. With the exception of taking on a considerable additional *avoirdupois* and a few good-natured wrinkles, the major had changed but little since that day in the fall of 1863, when I saw him for the first time in a recruiting office at Pittsfield.

The major's cousin, Edward Payson Hopkins, a student at the college, had recruited Giles Taylor, Irving Waterman and myself at Williamstown, and we were sent on to help fill the quota of Amos L. Hopkins, who had been commissioned a second lieutenant in August of that year, and was endeavouring to secure recruits enough to entitle him to a captaincy. I am glad to state that he was made a captain December 10, 1863, and just a year later he won the golden leaf of a major. His cousin, Edward Payson Hopkins, as has been stated in a previous chapter, was killed while leading his company in a charge at Ashland Station, May 11, 1864.

It is the wonder of the generation that has come to man's estate since Lee surrendered to Grant at Appomattox, that boys in the days of the war were considered capable to hold offices which on ordinary occasions, according to the general estimates, could only be filled by men who had had years of experience. Particularly does this apply to the boys who held commissions in the Union army. I thought of this at the reunion as I gazed into the still boyish face of Major Hopkins, and recalled how he had been a captain at eighteen, a major at nineteen, for a time in command of the regiment, and again adjutant general on the staff of Gen. Davies, our brigade commander. All of these positions he had filled with conspicuous bravery and efficiency.

The fact is historical; the war matured the boys wonderfully. A few months of active service at the front did more in this direction than could have been brought about in years of ordinary experience. As I recall it, the average age of the troopers of our battalion was not more than seventeen years. I think Major Hopkins graduated from Williams College the summer that he entered the army. Major Hopkins was wounded, and his horse shot from under him in the second day's battle in the Wilderness, May 6, 1864.

At the reunion the major related an incident of his experience on the battlefield that I remember to have heard at the time of its occurrence, but which, like hundreds of other events, had been forgotten until recalled by a comrade.

The major rode a splendid gray horse, and he was always a conspicuous figure when on duty. He had detailed from his company a jovial Irish lad as orderly—the regular army name for the position is dog-robber. The orderly cared for the major's horse and his own, blacked the officer's boots and did other chores for his captain. Major Hopkins told the story something as follows:

"At the time I was wounded my favourite horse was killed. The shell that ended the life of the animal damaged my leg so badly that I was carried to a temporary hospital just back out of range. While my wound was being examined by the surgeons, my orderly came along.

"'And is it aloive ye air, Cap'n?'

"' es, Pat; there's some life left in me yet, but my horse was killed.'

"'Arrah, Cap'n dear, it's too bad, faith, an' it is.'

"' But don't cry, Pat; the doctors will probably bring me through all right, though I may lose my leg.'

"'Sure, Cap'n, it's not the loikes of me what's crying for you or your leg, but it's too bad the poor horse was kilt, faith an' it is. He was a jewel of a horse; arrah, arrah. If it had been the other horse that had been kilt wid ye, it would have been all right, faith an' it would.'

"And though I was suffering great pain, I was compelled to join the surgeons in the laugh that followed."

I purposed when I set out for the reunion to request the secretary, Sergeant E. A. Smith of Somerville, to correct the records to show that Finney was killed at St. Mary's Church. I had been in the armoury only a few minutes, and was looking around for Company I boys, when Sergeant Charles H. Newton of Company C said to me:

"Here comes a member of I troop. Comrade Finney," addressing the newcomer, "this is Comrade Allen of your old company; it's his first meeting with us since we were mustered out."

"Why, yes, I remember Comrade Allen; you haven't changed any to speak of in all these years."

"And you are Comrade"—

"Finney; William Finney of Company I; don't you remember me?"

"I remember that we had a William Finney that was killed, or I thought he was, at St. Mary's Church."

"Well, I'm William Finney, what's left of me, and I was not killed at St, Mary's Church, but I came within an ace of being killed in the Wilderness, and while I was suffering in the Andersonville prison-pen, I sometimes wished that I had been killed instead of being taken prisoner by the rebels."

As Finney warmed up with his subject, I could see that there was some of the youthful fire left in him, although his hair was gray and his form was emaciated, the result of long suffering from rheumatism and kindred ills contracted in rebel prisons. But I had not seen him since May 6, 1864—more than a quarter of a century before the Boston meeting—when he was a dashing young trooper. As he continued the interesting story of his experiences, I became reconciled to his identity, and was rejoiced to know that he was still in the land of the living.

"It was the second day—May 6—that I was captured in the Wilderness," continued Finney. "Don't you remember how we were sent down the road on a gallop, to the assistance of a regiment in the woods.?"

"Yes, I remember it."

"Then we charged through a field; the rebels were behind a fence."

"That's so."

"And we charged and drove them back."

"Yes; we made it too hot for them."

"Then they were re-enforced, and came back yelling like demons."

"So they did."

"And they made it too hot for us."

"You're right, they did."

"And the recall was sounded by our bugler."

"And we fell back to a new line established on the road to Todd's Tavern."

"Yes; the regiment fell back, but I didn't. I staid there in that field."

"What for?"

"Because my horse was killed by a shell, and when he fell my right leg was under him, with my foot fastened in the stirrup. I could not free myself. The rebels swarmed across the field, and I was taken prisoner. My horse went down just as the recall was sounded, and do you know that all the time I was in Andersonville—seven months—I could hear that bugle-call ringing in my ears whenever I turned my thoughts to that bloody field in the Wilderness. It was the last I heard of my comrades for many months. I came to remember it as the bugler's farewell to me."

"Let's see, who was our bugler in the Wilderness?"

"I think it was Booth; don't you remember that rosy-cheeked boy who rode a white horse? If I'm not mistaken, he was Major Sargent's orderly the second day in the Wilderness."

"Yes, it must have been Booth. I wonder if he's dead?"

"I'd go many miles to see the bugler who sounded that call. But I have never seen him at any of our reunions, and the secretary could never find his address. Boy bugler Booth must be dead."

"Bugler Booth is alive," said a veteran with long hair tinged with gray, and who had been an interested listener to the conversation between Finney and myself.

"Do you know him?" exclaimed Finney.

"I do."

"Where does he live?"

"At No. 23 Bowery Street, Nashua, N. H."

"Is he ever coming to our reunion?"

"I can't say about future ones; he's here today."

"In this room?"

"Yes, in this room."

"Point him out to me—where is he?"

"Here; I'm bugler Booth!"

"What! You bugler Booth?"

"Yes, I'm bugler Booth."

"And you blew that recall in the Wilderness?"

"I did. I sounded the calls 'forward!' 'trot!' 'charge!' as we went in, and the recall when Major Sargent gave the order to fall back."

"Well, praise the Lord! Give us your hand, old boy. I'm so glad to see you. You've aged so I would never have recognised you."

"Nor I you. You're not the smooth-faced lad you were twenty-five years ago."

Tears were falling thick and fast from the eyes of the two veterans as they clasped hands with a grip that "*spoke louder than words.*" And what a look of brotherly love was mirrored in the eyes of each as they stood there face to face for the first time in so many years. Did the three survivors of Company I who attended the reunion of October 30, 1889, enjoy the occasion? What do you think about it, boys?

By a comparison of notes we found that at the date of the reunion Finney was proprietor of a grocery store in Brookline, a suburb of the "Hub"; Booth was doing well at Nashua, N. H., and the other survivor of Company I was serving on the staff of the Troy *Daily Times*. The reunion was a red-letter day in the history of each of the three.

And the banquet in the large hall of the armoury upstairs was a memorable event. War reminiscences and stories and songs of the long ago rounded out the programme. The comrade who had come from Troy, and who is now a local preacher in the Methodist Episcopal Church, was among those called upon to address the veterans. How his heart bounded with joy as he was enabled for the first time since the muster out at Arlington Heights in 1865, to look into the faces of the "boys" who had been his comrades from Boston to Appomattox, and renew the pledges of fraternal friendship.

But greater yet was the joy of that comrade that he was enabled to tell of his enlistment in the Grander Army that is marching on to victory under the banner of Prince Immanuel. In conclusion he said:

> Comrades, the Grand Army that saved the Union under the Hero of Appomattox is fast being mustered out. There is to be a reunion on the other side, boys. It will be for us all if we are faithful in serving the King of kings in this life. Let us close up the ranks, shoulder to shoulder, as in the days of old. Whosoever will may come and partake of the waters of life freely. Let me—as I would in the days of the war tell you of a spring of pure water—invite your attention to the words of the Lamb of God which taketh away the sin of the world: '*I am the resurrection and the life; he that believeth in me, though he were dead, yet shall he live. And whosoever liveth and believeth in me shall never die.*'
>
> Comrades, let us so live that when the last bugle shall sound, and all the hosts of God's grand army shall be gathered home, that we can say with the great Apostle to the Gentiles: ' I have fought a good fight, I have finished my course; I have kept the faith; henceforth there is laid up for me a crown of righteous-

ness, which the Lord, the righteous judge, shall give me at that day; and not to me only, but unto all them also that love his appearing,'

And the battle-scarred troopers said Amen.

OBITUARY

(From the Troy (N.Y.) *Times*, February 18, 1892.)
Today the remains of Irving Waterman, who died yesterday at Poughkeepsie, were brought to his late residence on River Street, in this city. The deceased was born in Berlin forty-seven years ago. He served in the First Massachusetts cavalry in the War of the Rebellion, and was first sergeant of a company in the campaign of 1865. He was only eighteen years old when he enlisted with three others at North Adams. Of the four, one, Lieutenant Edward P. Hopkins, son of a professor at Williams College, was killed while leading a charge at Ashland, May ii, 1864. Another, Giles Taylor, received his death-wound near Deep Bottom, July 28, 1864. The fourth comrade, Stanton P. Allen of the *Times*, survives. Mr. Waterman was injured in a runaway about two years ago, and his head was affected to such an extent that he was made insane. He is survived by a widow and two children. The remains will be taken Saturday to Berlin.

ATTENTION.

Down in Dixie is not a history of the War of the Rebellion; it is a grouping together, somewhat in chronological order, of Personal Recollections of events in which the writer participated during the great civil conflict. Incidents of soldier life, in camp and bivouac, on the march and on the battlefield, are given as they are recalled. The everyday affairs of the rank and file—how the soldiers lived, what they did in camp, how the privates saw things, and their share of crushing armed rebellion—have to a great extent been left unwritten. Little space could be devoted to them in histories of the conflict. Historians and military writers have gleaned for greater things. Yet these commonplace happenings were part and parcel of the herculean task of breaking the backbone of the Southern Confederacy.

Let it be borne in mind by any who may be inclined to criticise this volume in respect of inaccuracies of details or dates, that the book has been written from *personal* recollections and with only a few fragmentary war-time letters to supply missing links. The "Boys" of

1861-65 will bear testimony that *Down in Dixie* is a truthful account of events common to all who served in the Army of the Potomac, and as such it is believed it will please the veterans and be of interest to the general reader.

    Troy, N.Y., 1891.   S. P. A.

A Short History of the First Massachusetts Cavalry Volunteers
By Benjamin W. Crowninshield

When the war broke out, the North was by far less prepared for the struggle than the South. The two sections afforded a very different material from which to organise an army.

In the North, particularly in the East, the population of farmers and mechanics, devoted to peaceful pursuits, was unaccustomed to all manner of arms, and as a rule strange to any horse but a work-horse; and not one in a hundred a good rider, while a very large proportion had never fired a gun. Nearly all horses kept for pleasure were trotters used in harness and never mounted. In the South, every man and boy was familiar with all kinds of weapons, and especially skilled in the use of firearms. The entire population was used to horses, and all were good riders.

The regular army remained with all its organisation (except such officers as "went with their States" to the Confederate Army) with the North, and furnished the model for all three branches of the service. This model developed a steady infantry, a superlatively good artillery, never equalled in the South, and a cavalry better adapted to fight in line than the Confederate, which excelled in individuality, and consequently for scouting and irregular work. The Confederate cavalry was largely composed of Virginia regiments, who fought on their own soil and were familiar with the remarkable system of by-roads, and who furnished scouts, spies, and raiders on our lines of communication, of singular ability.

To the Federal Army were left the five old regular cavalry regiments, to which was added in April, 1861, a sixth. It was at first proposed to confine the cavalry of the Federal Army to these six regular regiments; and for good reasons, as things looked then. That was the time when many of those who ought to have known thought the war would be an affair of ninety days.

According to European ideas, a cavalry soldier is not supposed to be of any use in the field before a very careful training at a cavalry depot, lasting from one to training. two years; and his horse requires the same time, or longer. In many armies the horses are specially reared for cavalry service in immense breeding establishments by government, and in time of peace the cavalry is mounted exclusively on such animals. Each regiment has a depot battalion, where the men are drilled and horses prepared for service in the field. Such an establishment is thought indispensable. The regular cavalry of the United States has a cavalry depot at Jefferson Barracks, Missouri; but, owing to the great distance from where the cavalry is stationed, few horses are trained there, and the men are "licked into shape" in much less time than is the custom in Europe. The term of enlistment—three years here and at least seven in Europe—largely determines this, and the recruit has to learn his duty with his regiment principally. Fortunately, a large proportion of the enlisted men are veterans of many terms of enlistment.

At the beginning of the war it was impossible to properly train cavalry before putting it into the field, and consequently whole regiments of exquisite greenness were thrust into the Virginia mud in winter, there to try to learn, practically without a teacher, from books and hard knocks, in a few weeks or months at best, what in Europe in the best schools, under chosen instructors and on trained horses, years only can accomplish.

It cannot, then, be wondered at that the government hesitated to enlist *volunteer* cavalry, and only yielded when the battle of Bull Run had shown the hollowness of the ninety-day idea. Another obstacle was the enormous expense of equipping and maintaining cavalry.

The equipments for a regiment of twelve hundred men alone cost nearly $300,000, the officers' pay was greater than that of the infantry, and a larger number of artificers was necessary. It cost, in favourable times, probably fifty cents a day for each horse, and in inaccessible places three or four times that, for forage alone. It was obviously questionable whether at any expense an effective cavalry force could be evolved out of the peaceful Yankee citizen, unused to horses and arms, in any reasonable time. But mounted troops were a necessity, and with its lavish bounty the government did not shrink at the expense, nor hesitate at the difficulty of the task.

At first, the volunteer regiments were made up of the militia cavalry companies, both North and South; and all the companies in the first organised regiments bore high-sounding names, which, in the Federal service at least, were soon forgotten. In the Confederate cavalry the troopers generally owned their horses, and contracted for a certain pay (forty cents a day) to keep mounted. I can recall only one regiment in the Army of the Potomac where the soldiers owned their horses, the 3rd Indiana cavalry.

We find in a Southern book, McClellan's *Campaigns of Stuart's Cavalry*, the following *apropos* of horses and equipments:—

> A consideration of the difficulties under which the cavalry of the Army of Northern Virginia laboured will not be uninteresting to one who would form a true estimate of the services rendered by it.
>
> At the beginning of the war, the Confederate government, charged as it was with the creation of an army and of war material of all kinds, felt itself unable to provide horses for the numerous cavalry companies which offered their services, especially from the State of Virginia. Many companies, organized as cavalry, were rejected. With those that were enrolled the government entered into a contract, the substance of which was that the cavalrymen should supply and own their horses, which would be mustered into service at a fair valuation; that the government should provide feed, shoes, and a smith to do the shoeing, and should pay the men a *per diem* of forty cents for the use of their horses. Should a horse be killed in action, the government agreed to pay to the owner the muster valuation. Should the horse be captured in battle, worn out, or disabled by any of the many other causes which were incident to the service, the loss fell upon the owner, who was compelled to furnish another horse, under the same conditions, or be transferred to some other arm of the service.
>
> That the government should have adopted such a policy at the beginning of the war was a misfortune; that it should have adhered to it to the very end was a calamity against which no amount of zeal or patriotism could successfully contend.
>
> It is not in the spirit of unfriendly criticism that we today proclaim the unwisdom of such a policy. At the time, all acqui-

esced in it; the cavalryman most cheerfully of all. Virginia was full of horses of noble blood. The descendants of such racers as Sir Archy, Boston, Eclipse, Timoleon, Diomede, Exchequer, Red-Eye, and many others more or less famous on the turf, were scattered over the State. Gentlemen fond of following the hounds had raised these horses for their own use. They knew their fine qualities, their speed, endurance, and sure-footedness, and they greatly preferred to entrust their safety in battle to their favourite steeds rather than to any that the government could furnish. But the government might have furnished these horses at the outset, and by suitable activity it might have provided for replenishing the losses incurred in the service. The cavalrymen were kept mounted, but at an enormous loss of efficiency in the army, and by a system of absenteeism which sometimes deprived the cavalry of more than half its numbers. Why should it have been thought that the people of Virginia would hold back their horses, when they refused nothing else to the government?

The evil results of this system were soon apparent, and rapidly increased as the war progressed. Perhaps the least of these was the personal loss it entailed upon the men. Many a gallant fellow whose horse had been irrecoverably lamed for the want of a shoe, or ridden to death at the command of his officer, or abandoned in the enemy's country, that his owner might escape capture, impoverished himself and his family in order that he might keep his place in the ranks of his comrades and neighbours. Nor should it be a cause for wonder if this property question affected the courage of many a rider; for experience soon proved that the horse as well as the man was in danger during the rough cavalry *mêlée*. If the horse were killed the owner was compensated; but a wounded horse was a bad investment.

By far the greatest evil of the system was the fact that whenever a cavalryman was dismounted, it was necessary to send him to his home to procure a remount. To accomplish this required from thirty to sixty days. The inevitable result was that an enormous proportion of the command was continuously absent. Many of the men were unable to procure fresh horses within the time specified in their "details," and the column of "Absent without leave" always presented an unsightly appearance.

To punish such men seemed an injustice, and the relaxation of discipline on this point was abused by some with impunity. We have already seen that Fitz Lee's brigade, which should never have presented less than twenty-five hundred sabres in the field, was reduced to less than eight hundred at Kelly's Ford, on the 17th of March, and numbered less than fifteen hundred men at the time of the Battle of Chancellorsville, when many of the absentees had returned.

Great as was this evil among the Virginia regiments, it operated with tenfold force upon the cavalry of Hampton's brigade. Think of sending a man from Virginia to South Carolina, North Carolina, Georgia, or Mississippi, to procure a horse! Recruiting camps were established in Virginia and in North and South Carolina, and every means which the cavalry commanders could devise were used to ameliorate this state of affairs. But the inevitable tendency was downwards; and in the last year of the war hundreds of men were gathered together in the "Dismounted Camp," or, as the men called it, "Company Q," in the vain attempt to utilise good, but misplaced material. Special officers were appointed for these men, and the attempt was made to use them, dismounted, in various ways; but with no success. The men were disheartened. *Esprit du corps* could by no possibility be infused into such an assemblage. Every man looked and longed for the time when his horse might be returned from the recruiting camp, or when some other kind providence might remount him, and return him to his comrades. The penitentiary could not be more loathsome to him than his present condition, and yet even this was better than to give up all hope, and consent to a transfer to the infantry or artillery.

The want of proper arms and equipments placed the Southern cavalry at a disadvantage which can hardly be overestimated. At the beginning of the war the troopers furnished their own saddles and bridles. The English round-tree saddle was in common use, and sore-backed horses multiplied with great rapidity. After a time the government furnished an unsightly saddle which answered a very good purpose; for although the comfort of the rider was disregarded, the back of the horse was protected. Our best equipments were borrowed from our cousins of the North. The question of arming the cavalry was far more serious. Some of the more wealthy Arming of the Virginia counties armed their cavalry companies with pistols when they were mustered into service, but whole regiments were destitute of them. Breech-loading carbines were procured only in limited quantities, never more than enough to arm one, or at most two squadrons in a regiment. The deficiency was made up, generally, by Enfield rifles. Robertson's two North Carolina regiments, which joined Stuart in May, 1863, were armed with sabres and Enfield rifles. The difference between a Spencer carbine and an Enfield rifle is by no means a mere matter of sentiment.

Horseshoes, nails, and forges were procured with difficulty; and it was not an uncommon occurrence to see a cavalryman leading his limping horse along the road, while from his saddle dangled the hoofs of a dead horse, which he had cut off for the sake of the sound shoes nailed to them.

But in both armies the cavalry was a sort of *élite* corps, and men preferred to enlist in that branch, probably at the North because the would-be trooper preferred riding to walking, with perhaps an idea that at the end of a march his horse would be put up at some peripatetic livery stable. Certainly none had any definite idea of the duties.

The men were enlisted from all ranks of life with no reference to previous occupation and capability. No selection was even made according to size and weight, life. In Europe, except for the showy, expensive, and almost useless heavy cavalry which graces processions, opera-house entrances, imperial or royal drawing-rooms and staircases, and such pomps and vanities, a cavalry soldier must be light and active, and is especially selected for that branch of the service. An English authority. Beamish, says:—

> The men, therefore, intended for cavalry service should be selected with the utmost care respecting their disposition, size, and for vigour of constitution, and should, above all, be chosen from those who have been accustomed to horses from their youth, such as the sons of farmers, hostlers, and others who love horses, and are capable of taking care of them and likewise of the harness and equipments with which they are entrusted. From other men than these it is difficult, almost impossible, to form a good cavalry. What, for instance, can be expected from a stocking manufacturer, or a linen weaver, who considers the horse a wild beast? We all know that such men rarely have con-

fidence in their horses, but look upon them as their greatest enemies, against whom, for the future, they must struggle for their lives. They never learn to ride, never can preserve their balance, but hang on the horse like a senseless lump, which, in order to preserve its equilibrium, unnecessarily wastes a large portion of its strength, and on this account is soon wasted. The injudicious selection of men for cavalry may be productive of infinite mischief.

But such principles were ignored in the great United States Volunteer Army, and the men ranged from pigmy to giant, and there was never any authority for changing them, after enlistment, into other branches of the service, according to fitness. Even later in the war, when experience should have taught better, whole regiments were recruited after the same ideas; and as late as 1864 perfectly inexperienced company officers were put over them, and in some cases even the field officers were quite as ignorant as the men.

In the South things were better managed. The cavalry service was especially well organised. All Southerners were good riders, particularly those or the better class. A good horse was a gentleman's pride, and the more important the gentleman, the better his horse. Consequently, their cavalry combined the men of the best class, mounted on the best horses—in the early days of the war largely thoroughbred or very well-bred animals.

The officers were well-known men, of good social standing, and the field officers were many of them of the old regular United States cavalry, I have understood that a considerable number of the old cavalry veterans of the regular army went South with their officers in 1861. Thus at the very beginning the Confederacy had a large force of capital cavalry; every man a bold rider, well mounted, expert with revolver and rifle.

In one respect alone was the Federal cavalry superior, namely, in arms and equipments, for these were of the newest pattern. And yet even in this respect the advantage was questionable, for the government issued an overwhelming outfit. The poor soldier was oppressed with his trappings and arms, and mounted for a march with three days' rations for himself and his horse, with saddle and bridle, watering bridle, lariat rope and picket pin, nose-bag, carbine and its sling, revolver and its holster, ammunition for both in their receptacles, sabre and belt, he looked little like the trooper Détaille or De Neuville loved to

The Ideal Cavalryman

The real Cavalryman

paint. The most difficult thing a recruit had to do when ready for the march was to get in and out of the saddle, and a derrick, sometimes, would not have been a bad thing.

The regulars, arriving from their Western fields, were at first pushed into the field by companies. Reorganised later, they were so largely used as orderlies and headquarter guards as to seriously impair their efficiency. As regiments they were not brigaded until 1863, and were then small.

It has always seemed to me that they should have been filled up to the maximum and formed as a division, of three brigades of two regiments each; which should have held in check, if it did not destroy, the Confederate cavalry in those early days when volunteer regiments were no match for the rough riders of the South, who also possessed the immense advantage of "fighting upon their own dunghill."

The regulars, in larger or smaller detachments, during the first part of the war did brave work; but they were almost always used in small bodies, were usually outnumbered by the Confederate cavalry, and their efforts were frequently unsuccessful. At Gaines's Mills a most gallant charge was made by a small body of the 5th cavalry, a desperate diversion to enable a new line to be formed, which succeeded in its object at the expense of the cavalry, a gallant and heroic service.

The volunteer cavalry, until 1863, took the field usually as regiments attached to separate commands; and also, occasionally, by brigades. Under good commanders, notably under Buford, it did some handsome fighting. There was no cavalry bureau at Washington charged with its organisation and equipment, and particularly there was no general having command over the whole cavalry to direct its detail, and combine it for field work. Thus the regiments were not systematically recruited, or remounted as the horses became used up or killed. There was no combined movement of cavalry, and no separate cavalry organization. The officers commanding divisions and corps to which cavalry was attached seemed greedy for as large a force of cavalry as possible, and very commonly used it up with unnecessary and thankless work. There were many defeats, great discouragement, and demoralisation resulting from this abuse. As a rule, success attended the Confederates, and it seemed doubtful if volunteer cavalry in the Federal army was to be of any good.

Until the summer of 1862, in the Federal Army, the cavalry was groping about for its place in the field, the raid. while learning the elements of its duty. During the Peninsular campaign, under change of commanders, it did nothing to gain a name, being hardly mentioned in dispatches; while Stuart won a brilliant reputation by his march around McClellan's army, and originated the "raid" which afterwards became such a feature in every campaign. Pope, in his retreat, exhausted his mounted troops by hurrying them hither and thither in wild-goose chases. If his cavalry had been kept, on his flanks and always close to his enemy, he would not have lost sight of him, and eventually found him in his rear. This short campaign illustrates most forcibly what I insist upon,—that the Federal cavalry at that time had no general who understood its proper use. On the contrary, it was wasted and ruined in a service which stupidly not only gave it no rest to prepare for an emergency, but placed it where it could not even do good service. Lee used his intelligently, and with half the work it did not only good service, but gained a brilliant renown.

During the Antietam campaign the cavalry of McClellan's army did nothing; worthy of it. It moved aimlessly about. At the battle itself, about 8 a. m., the whole division crossed the Antietam on the Sharpsburg pike, and took a position close to Lee's centre, where he had concentrated about thirty-five pieces of artillery, with which, at times, without infantry support, he held the town.

Porter's entire corps, also, was within striking distance, but lay all day just out of fire on this road, and among the lost opportunities of the whole war none was more conspicuous than this. General Lee spoke of the Federal cavalry, "with a bravery worthy of a better cause" taking up this menacing position. Several times during the day the men mounted, and sabres were drawn, as all supposed, to charge, but the men were dismounted again without attempting anything.

The artillery fire of Lee's guns was fierce, and together with the fire of our own, of probably double the same number, across the Antietam Creek, the noise was infernal. This fire lasted all day, and this division of cavalry lay here accomplishing nothing, losing a few men by artillery fire. McClellan, by his inaction, permitted Lee to take troops from his right (while Burnside did *not* cross) to relieve his sorely pressed left. Lee. And then, after he had, with their help, stayed the adverse tide there, he took them and others back and fought Burnside's tardy troops when they did cross. On both right and left there were natural obstacles to McClellan's troops getting into position to attack, besides Lee's veterans. In the centre was no natural obstacle. The bridge was intact and securely held, the road excellent.

It led straight to Lee's centre. Moreover, it was already crossed by the cavalry, 4320 strong, and this force was within five hundred yards of Lee's centre, well protected by the ground, and all ready formed for battle. Antietam was my first large battle, and I vividly recall the crossing of the creek. We suddenly came into the artillery fire before reaching the bridge, and it seemed as if the whole ground was ploughed up by shells, and the air full of them. The bridge was particularly exposed. On it, as I crossed, lay the dead body of the colonel of the 4th Pennsylvania Cavalry and his horse. He had just been killed by a shell. The casualties were here numerous. But very soon after crossing, cover was found for the cavalry division, and could have been found for Porter's corps had it crossed, and a better place to put in troops was impossible. Attention has lately been called to this by an officer of the regular United States infantry, whose command was ordered out in front of the massed cavalry as skirmishers. He noticed the weakness of Lee's centre, unsupported by infantry, and the excellent opportunity to pierce it. He returned to General Porter and reported the situation in McClellan's presence, and entreated him to make the attack. At the moment Porter did not answer, but said later to McClellan, "Recollect, my corps is your only reserve."[1]

The morning after Lee had, with perfect success, crossed the Potomac, the cavalry rode down to the high river banks, looked across, stood and received the fire of twenty-seven guns in battery at Shepherdstown for a long time, and collected the very meagre leavings of Lee's army, a few abandoned wagons, a caisson or two, and other worthless trash. This was heralded in McClellan's dispatches as "the cavalry pursuing Lee's routed columns across the Potomac, with captures of guns," etc.

The day before (September 18), Lee's army was beaten, not routed, and a magnificent opportunity offered for a dashing commander to score a real victory, one that might have gone far to end the war. That day the whole army rested while Lee prepared to cross the river. How he must have rejoiced that the Federal commander was not an enterprising man!

During the rest of the autumn the cavalry of both armies was rendered almost useless by an epidemic, called "greased heel," among the horses. Yet Stuart, in whose command the same disease raged, managed to ride around McClellan's whole army, without any loss to his cavalry, capturing over a thousand horses and much other plunder, and causing our men no end of wild-goose chases; but, better than all that,

---

1. This story has been denied by General Porter, although asserted by others.

so adding to his already great prestige, that his cavalry was feared as masked batteries were at one time.

The following winter, in front of Fredericksburg, the Federal cavalry did picketing and scouting, not merely on the flanks of Burnside's and Hooker's army, but kept open and protected the rear and in fact all the country from Washington down to the Rappahannock, and all about Washington, a duty that required the utmost exposure, wear, and tear; and at the same time added nothing to the glory of that ill-used branch of the service.

In the spring of 1863 came a great change, which, for the Federal cavalry, might be called an emancipation. In February Hooker reorganized the entire Army of the Potomac. The cavalry was newly divided into brigades and divisions, better officered than before. Probably at no time during the war was the army in so good condition as in May, 1863. The cavalry had been ill-used during the winter, and the horses were not in good condition, but the discipline was first-rate, the regiments well officered, and fairly well drilled. While not in comparatively such good condition as the infantry, the cavalry had greatly improved, and wanted but a dashing general to win laurels.

General Stoneman was supposed to be such a man; but he made quite as marked a failure with the mounted troops as Hooker did with the whole army in the wretched battles about Chancellorsville. His carefully prepared raid came to naught. For this the exceedingly bad weather was largely to blame.

For nearly eighteen months the work had been scouting, picketing, and little encounters by companies or regiments, without any general leadership, without dash, enterprise, or success. How different in the Confederate cavalry! There, at the very outset, was an efficient force led to victory, and under such leaders as Ashby, Stuart, and Fitzhugh Lee, made to feel they could do anything. They twice rode round the entire Federal Army, in front of Richmond, and in Maryland, each time with perfect success, and almost with impunity, under J. E. B. Stuart, accomplishing excellent results in destroying and capturing, but particularly in learning that constant motion is the cavalry's forte, and boldness and audacity are its protection.

But the younger officers were getting to know their duties, and the troopers were becoming educated to their work, and in the spring of 1863, under a new leadership, the Federal cavalry first asserted itself against the Confederate troopers at Kelly's Ford, and showed itself at the Battle of Brandy Station, June 9, 1863, fully a match for Stuart s cavalry, and never afterwards proved a contemptible foe.

I do not intend to say there were not gallant fights made by some cavalry commands, but that on the whole the result was thus far unsuccessful and unsatisfactory. Stuart and Fitzhugh Lee and Hampton were constantly making successful raids upon the cavalry lines of pickets, and capturing men, horses, and wagons. They had the prestige, or, as it came to be expressed, "the bulge" on us.

The Battle of Brandy Station was a severe fight, in which the Federal cavalry, about ten thousand strong, crossed the Rappahannock on a reconnoissance in force, and attacked all Stuart's cavalry, of nearly the same strength, on his own ground. The artillery was freely used on both sides, and the number of guns was very nearly equal. After heavy and successful fighting all day, the enemy was put on the defensive, and made to develop his entire force, and even bring up his infantry. In the late afternoon our troops recrossed the river unmolested, having fully accomplished the object aimed at. There was more fighting than generalship. This was, for the cavalry, the turning point in the war.[2] The Confederates were never met before or afterwards in such force. They here lost their prestige and never recovered it.

In rapid succession followed severe contests of the cavalry, successful for the Federals at Aldie, Upperville, etc., June 17 to 22, and engagements of more or less importance daily all through the campaign. The cavalry of both armies was in constant contact.

Ordered by Lee to keep on his right flank, and unable to break through the Federal cavalry, Stuart rode round its rear and crossed the Potomac between it and Washington, and, severed from him by the whole Federal Army, only joined Lee at Gettysburg the second day of the battle.

General Lee has claimed that Stuart's absence caused him great inconvenience, and perhaps ruined his campaign of invasion. Stuart's historian indignantly denies this, and apparently gives good reasons. Be this as it may, it is sure that during this campaign, in a series of almost daily encounters, the Federal cavalry came out best, not without getting roughly handled at times, but always making itself respected; and up to July 3 kept Lee's cavalry separated from his army, and prevented their help when most needed by him.

During the rest of the summer after Gettysburg, and until the middle of September, nothing very important was accomplished by the cavalry of either army, although many encounters took place.

---

2. McClellan says "it made the Federal cavalry."

At Culpeper, September 13, on the advance, Stuart's cavalry was met and defeated, with a loss of three guns.

General Meade, in October, made his masterly retreat from the Rapidan to Centreville, followed immediately by an advance to the Rapidan. His cavalry in this retreat played a conspicuous part as rear guard; and on the advance cleared the way.

Later, in November, Meade crossed the Rapidan, and in the Wilderness met Lee at Mine Run in so strong a position that he declined to attack, and recrossed without fighting a battle. In this move his cavalry had several encounters, opened the roads in advancing, and brought up the rear in the retreat. It was well handled and beautifully manoeuvred, and won the admiration of all who saw it; but no chance for great distinction occurred.

This year developed the Confederate partisan. The flank of Meade's army and his long line of communication by the Orange and Alexandria Railroad were exposed to constant attack by Mosby's battalion, White's battalion, company H of the 4th Virginia cavalry,—the so-called "Black Horse Cavalry,"—and by other commands who operated in that district, where the men were at home. These attacks, which with little danger to the attacking force were very sure of success, caused the presence of a large body of Meade's cavalry at Warrenton and other points on his flank and rear, besides a cavalry brigade at or near Centreville. The Federal force accomplished little against Mosby and the other partisan battalions, but this service allowed something like rest to Meade's cavalry, and guarded the flanks and rear against any attack from regular Confederate troops.

Meade was not a believer in mounted troops, yet he used his cavalry better than any previous commander, and under him that branch gained largely in efficiency and prestige. Wintering in places where with the least wear and tear the flanks of the army could be protected, and at the same time the men and horses drilled, it improved by good care and good food during the winter of 1863-64.

Just before the campaign of 1864 opened, General Sheridan took command of the cavalry corps of the Army of the Potomac, reviewing each of the three divisions in turn. May 2, 1864, his cavalry crossed the fords of the Rappahannock, uncovered the roads on the south side, reconnoitred, and cleared the way until Meade and Lee were face to face. In doing this there was some severe fighting with Stuart's cavalry, in which the Federal cavalry invariably had the best of it.

On May 9, as the Wilderness offered no chance for mounted

troops, the raid to Richmond began, followed by a series of bloody engagements which ended at Yellow Tavern and Richmond. Stuart's cavalry was very roughly handled and he himself killed. This loss the Confederacy was never made good. There were enough good leaders amongst his generals, notably Fitzhugh Lee; but Stuart had been the leader for nearly three years. Nobody doubted his right to the place, and after his death nobody quite filled it. He died at a good time for his own fame, for not even he could have changed the inevitable result that followed. It is no discredit that it was so. The Confederate cavalry had fought long and well. The material for the rank and file was constantly deteriorating. Their prestige became always comparatively less as it increased on our own side. Now we had a leader, and not one only. From inferior grades had sprung up a plenty of able commanders of divisions, brigades, and regiments. Casualties in any rank, with a change of personnel, did not change the efficiency of organization.

The Confederate cavalrymen became better armed as the war went on, largely from captured weapons. Their fine, well-bred horses went, never to return, and in 1864 they were not so well mounted as their Federal opponents. Their granaries were laid waste, and a general decay set in that could not be stayed. All this was not without its consequences; and we find all through the rest of the war an almost invariable success attending the Federal cavalry in its battles.

Some reverses were inevitable. Success urges always to more dangerous deeds, and sooner or later to the impossible. Such was Wilson's raid to destroy Lee's south-western communication with Petersburg. Sheridan's Trevillian Station raid resulted in hard fighting and equal honours. It did irreparable damage to Lee's cavalry, for the losses of men and horses, particularly the latter, could not be replaced. The Federal cavalry accomplished little else that was tangible.

The desperate attempt of Early to make a diversion in favour of Lee, by invading Maryland, led to the Valley campaign, and Sheridan took with him the largest part of the cavalry, which in turn caused Lee to send most of his to oppose it.

Here was a better country for cavalry than we had seen before during the war, and here the supremacy of the Federal cavalry was most marked. Here, for the first time, did the cavalry attack infantry in line on a large scale. By small bodies this had been done before on both sides.

At the Battle of Winchester, the Confederate division of General Wharton was ridden over in perfectly open country by our cavalry, and almost the entire division—a small one—was captured. I will go into this somewhat in detail, as it has been often asserted that cavalry never during the war accomplished this feat.

At the end of August, 1864, Sheridan, in obedience to his instructions, had withdrawn his army to Halltown, near Harper's Ferry, on account of Anderson's division of Longstreet's corps coming to reinforce Early; the Confederate infantry was pushed close up.

While General Sheridan was at Halltown, he wanted to have prompt information of any movement of this division, and accordingly Colonel Lowell, in command of the "reserve brigade," ordered, in the early morning, an attack by two squadrons of the 2nd Massachusetts Cavalry upon the infantry pickets. The charge was successfully made upon what proved to be a South Carolina brigade, and the greater part of a regiment was captured most gallantly. The attack was made at the same hour and the same place on two successive days. On the 16th of September, the 3rd New Jersey Cavalry—a recently organised regiment—captured an entire infantry regiment (the 8th South Carolina of Conner's brigade, colours, colonel, officers, and men) in front of Winchester, on the Berryville pike. These small affairs were duly heralded, and inspired the cavalry with daring.

The Battle of Winchester was fought on the 19th of Battle September, Grant allowing Sheridan to attack Early, after going to meet him at Charlestown. Grant says, speaking of General Sheridan:

> I met him at Charlestown, and he pointed out so distinctly how each army lay, what he could do the moment he was authorised, and expressed such confidence of success, that I saw there were but two words of instruction necessary,—"Go in."

At this time. Early, with his inferior force, had his army spread out between Winchester and Martinsburg. His communications were upon a splendid road, the valley pike, and he could rapidly concentrate; but his extreme divisions were twenty-two miles apart.

Sheridan was at Berryville, eight miles from Winchester, his army well in hand and fortified with breastworks along part of the line. The road to Winchester was fairly good, but the Opequan, with steep banks on the east side, lay between, and had to be crossed. A difficult and narrow defile lay between the Opequan and Winchester, and it was not easy to rapidly concentrate in front of Winchester, though the distance was not so great as that of Early's most distant division from that place.

Sheridan previously sent all his cavalry but one division, which, protected the left flank, down to Summit Point, to cross there, and then march up the road to Winchester and come in on the enemy's flank. If his troops could get into position quickly enough, Early's divisions could be beaten in detail, and perhaps the greater part captured.

A very slight obstacle of water will cause great delay in crossing, and the little stream of the Opequan, not two feet deep, proved no exception.

Early soon found out what was going on, and for hours it was a race between the armies to get into position, one to attack and the other to defend Winchester. The ground becomes open and quite clear as the town is approached, and Winchester is surrounded by rising ground, which commands all the approaches. Here Early's infantry was posted. The battle was fought at most points in perfectly open country. The movements of the Confederate troops about the town could be plainly seen, as they were placed by the officers behind walls, and in some places were slight fortifications with artillery. This was the case where Wharton's division was in line, late in the afternoon. As the troops came up slowly, Sheridan, impatient of the delay, attacked with the 6th and 19th corps, before either Crook's 8th corps or the cavalry got on the field.

The attack was delivered just as Early had put his infantry in position. On his left he had placed Gordon's division in a piece of woods at a considerable angle with his front. The horse artillery was in battery on our right flank and poured in a very severe fire as our fine advanced. The 6th corps attacking on the left and centre was successful, with its 2nd division on the left. On the right the 3rd division, 6th corps, and 2nd division, 19th corps on the extreme right, were repulsed and had to retreat, but the enemy made no attempt to follow up his advantage at this point. The reserve, Russell's splendid 1st division, 6th corps, advanced and restored the 6th corps fine, Russell being killed; and on the right Dwight's 1st division, 19th corps, came into line and put things to rights there. Meanwhile, the 8th corps was coming up, and the cavalry in the distance was engaging Early's troopers. His flank being thus threatened by our cavalry. Early withdrew the horse artillery and Gordon's division, closing in nearer to the town.

Torbert, in command of the Federal cavalry, was driving Fitzhugh Lee steadily, slowly at first, then more rapidly, and when the attack in front of Winchester was renewed with the 8th corps, he came up in chase of Fitzhugh Lee, whose forces speedily and energetically retreated towards and through the town.

Our cavalry in pursuit, in line of battle, more or less disturbed by the speed of pursuit, came through the open fields until they suddenly saw in front of them Wharton's division of infantry in Hue, protected by a small fortification and by artillery. Instantly taking in the situation, they charged the line and carried all before them, riding over the opposing infantry and capturing many prisoners. I went over the ground the next morning at daylight, and carefully examined the place where this successful charge was made. Where Wharton's division had been in line was a slight hill sloping away north; a large house was on his right, and in front of it a small work, in which had been apparently two pieces of artillery. Wharton's infantry had been in line to the northwest from the house, facing about northeast. Their arms lay in piles, or windrows rather, where they had dropped them when the cavalry struck them.

The plain across which the cavalry had charged was dotted with dead horses, and many dead cavalry soldiers lay about; one, that I particularly noticed, because one half of his head was shot away down the line of his nose so cleanly that not a drop of blood was visible, lay just in front of where a gun had been. I judged him to have been killed by the last discharge of the gun, when the soldier was close to it, trying to capture it. An officer in Colonel Lowell's brigade says Colonel Lowell ordered him to charge this line of infantry and the guns, but before he could accomplish it,—having to collect his regiment,—another body of cavalry had done the work. Wharton's division at this time was the extreme rear guard, had been working hard all day, and was undoubtedly demoralised. Early's troops were going to pieces behind them. Defeat was inevitable and imminent. It was not a formidable force on account of these things. It was a small division in line of battle; a good line admirably situated to deliver an effective fire. Two guns were there and in use. But the cavalry saw them only to charge them instantly, and they did it well. In his book, *The Shenandoah Valley Campaign,* Pond says nothing of this.

We captured in the Battle of Winchester five guns, some colours, and about 2000 prisoners, chiefly of Wharton's division. Most of Sheridan's cavalry followed up that of the Confederate Army, and drove it up the little valley, or Page Valley, as it is called, and was not present at the Battle of Fisher's Hill, two days after Winchester, where Early's infantry and artillery were drawn up behind works. Averell's brigade, however, was there. In the afternoon he went into camp behind the right of Sheridan's line without orders, and when Sheridan, by a wonderful *coup d'œil*, had utilised his opportunity, turning a reconnoissance into a real attack, he sent for Averell to follow up the victory. Finding he had gone into camp, Sheridan relieved him on the spot.

Recalled to the main army, Sheridan's cavalry pressed Early back beyond Staunton, in a succession of eager but small engagements.

The Confederate cavalry, unable to cope with Torbert's bold riders, was reinforced by another brigade under General Rosser. Rosser on taking command boastingly proclaimed what he would do. What he did was to be fairly dashed out of the way, October 9, at the Battle of "Woodstock Races," as our men called it. His squadrons were ridden over and pursued twenty-six miles, at a gallop. Rosser's artillery was all captured entire, guns, horses, men, and even officers. Rosser's headquarter wagons were taken, or, as Sheridan reported it, "everything he had on wheels," and Custer came to headquarters wearing Rosser's best uniform.

Fitzhugh Lee was wounded at Winchester, and Rosser soon after assumed command of all Early's cavalry. He was not a West Point graduate,[3] but so well thought of that he was selected to fill Fitzhugh Lee's place, and was heralded by somebody at the South, in advance, as "the saviour of the valley." He kept this title afterwards, and I fancy it proved somewhat distressing to him.

One of the Confederate batteries captured at "Woodstock Races" had in it as a private soldier a West Point graduate, an old United States officer, who, at the breaking out of the war, went with the South. At first he had a high command. Rum ruined him, and his humiliation must have been complete as the West Pointers among Sheridan's officers recognized him that night, when dirty, hungry, a private, and a prisoner, he helped drive his own guns to his captors' headquarters.

General Early's own report to General Lee of this battle gives a pathetic account of his woes, and an excellent and impartial account of his cavalry. It is as follows:—

> This is very distressing to me, and God knows I have done all in my power to avert the disasters which have befallen this command; but the fact is, that the enemy's cavalry is so much superior to ours, both in numbers and equipment, and the country

---

3. Was at West Point about four years, and resigned on account of the war.

is so favourable to the operations of cavalry, that it is impossible for ours to compete with his. Lomax's cavalry is armed entirely with rifles, and has no sabres, and the consequence is that they cannot fight on horseback, and in this open country they cannot successfully fight on foot against large bodies of cavalry; besides, the command is and has been demoralised all the time. It would be better if they could all be put into the infantry; but if that were tried I am afraid they would all run off.

The Confederate cavalry was fairly used up and unable to take the field in any considerable force, and it made no show at the Battle of Cedar Creek, October 19, being brushed away almost ignominiously by Custer early in the day. Not so the Federal cavalry, who came into line with the infantry (Custer on the right and Merritt and Lowell on the left, the whole under General Torbert). On both flanks they fought infantry, and Lowell particularly put in his men mounted against Kershaw's division of Longstreet's corps, who were not merely in open country, but were protected by stone walls. For hours did our cavalry attack and keep back Kershaw's fine division, and they charged up to the stone walls, and here Lowell lost his life, and many brave officers and men were killed and wounded.

Charles Russell Lowell was a man made by nature for a cavalry leader. During the eight weeks of the valley campaign his command, the regular brigade of 1st, 2nd, and 5th United States, and 2nd Massachusetts cavalry, was almost daily engaged; and at one time for twenty-four consecutive days was in a fight of more or less importance. He had in the eight weeks no less than fifteen horses killed under him. What he did so conspicuously, all the rest did in high degree. The losses were severe, the glory great, the success splendid. Sheridan had picked Lowell out almost at once as an officer of exceeding merit.

Cedar Creek may be considered the end of this campaign, for no fighting of any importance followed.

In the spring of 1865 Sheridan's cavalry rode down to Grant before Petersburg, sweeping up all that remained north of the James, capturing the last guns left, and putting a military quietus on Jubal Early, General Lee's "bad old man," as he was called. His undoubted ability as a soldier, his perseverance and courage, deserved a better fate. We knew him as a hard fighter and good hater, and he is still irreconcilable.

Arriving before Petersburg, March 27, Sheridan was at once put on the left flank with his cavalry, and how he helped to push the Army of Northern Virginia to its fate is a matter of history. At the Battle of Five Forks the cavalry fought infantry, besides what remained of the Confederate cavalry.

In the final and successful attack in that battle, it was the 5th corps, particularly Ayres' division, that turned the flank of the breastworks, and made the victory complete; but on the front the cavalry, before the arrival of the 5th corps, drove all the Confederate troops behind their works and held them there; and later, at the final battle, rode over the breastworks and followed up the victory. General Pickett, commanding the Confederate infantry at Five Forks, said that while giving his final orders that day, just behind the breastworks, "a Federal cavalry soldier, mounted on a mule, jumped over the works and called on me to 'surrender, and be damned.'"

No one can doubt today, that the final surrender at Appomattox was due very largely to the cavalry, which constantly, during those splendid days, pressed against the Confederate Army in front, flank, and rear; never hesitating to inquire whether the force in their way was cavalry or infantry. Like the Irishman with his shillelah, "*they hit a head wherever they saw it.*"

It was only when General Lee found Sheridan's cavalry finally between his army and its supplies at Appomattox that he realised the end had come, and surrendered. Whether the cavalry directly caused the surrender or not, it is safe to say that the surrender would not have occurred then and there but for the boldness, dash, and perseverance with which Sheridan, with his splendid force, attacked Lee's army, and relentlessly followed his retreating columns.

ENGAGEMENTS OF THE FIRST MASSACHUSETTS CAVALRY.

The following table represents as nearly as may be the actions in which the regiment participated: —

Date.	Name.	Commander.
June 10, '62.	Johns Island.	Captain Sargent.
June 16.	James Island.	Captain Sargent.
Sept. 5.	Poolesville.	Captain Chamberlain.
Sept. 12.	Catoctin Mountain.	Colonel Williams.
Sept. 14.	South Mountain.	Colonel Williams.
Sept. 15.	Antietam Creek.	Colonel Williams.
Sept. 17.	Antietam.	Colonel Williams.
Sept. 19.	Potomac River.	Colonel Williams.
Sept. 21.	Potomac River.	Colonel Williams.
Sept. 28.	Shepherdstown, etc.	Captain Sargent.
Oct. 16.	Harper's Ferry and Smithfield.	Major Curtis.
Nov. 3.	Snicker's Ferry.	Colonel Sargent.
Jan., 1863.	Rappahannock Station.	Colonel Sargent.
March 17.	Kelly's Ford.	Lieutenant-Colonel Curtis.
May 1.	Rapidan Station.	Captain Gleason.
June 1.	Rapidan Station.	Lieutenant-Colonel Curtis.
June 6.	Sulphur Springs.	Captain Gleason.
June 9.	Stevensburg (Brandy Station).	Lieutenant-Colonel Curtis.
June 17.	Aldie.	Lieutenant-Colonel Curtis.
June 21.	Upperville.	Lieutenant-Colonel Curtis.
June 29.	Washington Cross Roads, Md.	Captain Crowninshield.
July 3.	Gettysburg.	Lieutenant-Colonel Curtis.
July 11–13.	Jones's Cross Roads, Md.	Captain Crowninshield.
July 16.	Shepherdstown (under fire).	Captain Crowninshield.
Sept. 13.	Culpeper.	Colonel H. B. Sargent.
Sept. 14.	Rapidan Station.	Colonel H. B. Sargent.
Oct. 12.	Sulphur Springs.	Major Sargent.
Oct. 14.	Auburn.	Major Sargent.
Oct. 14.	Bristoe Station.	Major Sargent.
Nov. 27.	New Hope Church (Mine Run).	Major Sargent.
Nov. 29.	Parker's Store.	Major Sargent.
May 5–8, '64.	Todd's Tavern.	Major Sargent.
May 9.	Chilesburg, Va.	Major Sargent.
May 10.	Beaver Dam.	Major Sargent.
May 11.	Ground Squirrel Church Bridge.	Captain Gleason.
May 11.	Ashland.	Major Sargent.
May 12.	Richmond (Meadow Bridge).	Major Sargent.
May 17.	Milford, Va.	Lieutenant-Colonel Chamberlain.
May 28.	Hawes's Shop.	Lieutenant-Colonel Chamberlain.
June 1.	Cold Harbor.	Lieutenant-Colonel Chamberlain.
June 2.	Near Cold Harbor.	Lieutenant-Colonel Chamberlain.
June 5.	Bottom's Bridge.	Lieutenant-Colonel Chamberlain.

DATE.	NAME.	COMMANDER.
June 10.	Old Church.	Captain Crowninshield.
June 11, 12.	Trevilian's Station.	Lieutenant-Colonel Chamberlain.
June 13.	White Oak Bridge.	Captain Crowninshield.
June 22.	Weldon Railroad (Williams farm).	Captain Crowninshield.
June 24.	St. Mary's Church.	Lieutenant-Colonel Chamberlain.
June 27.	Weldon Railroad.	Captain Crowninshield.
July 12.	Lee's Mills.	Lieutenant-Colonel Chamberlain.
July 28.	New Market (Deep Bottom).	Lieutenant-Colonel Chamberlain.
July 30.	Lee's Mills.	Lieutenant-Colonel Chamberlain.
Aug. 14-17.	Malvern Hill (Deep Bottom).	Lieutenant-Colonel Chamberlain.
Aug. 21-23.	Six Mile House, Weldon Railroad.	Lieutenant-Colonel Chamberlain.
Aug. 25.	Reams's Station.	Lieutenant-Colonel Chamberlain.
Sept. 16, 17.	Belcher's Mills.	Lieutenant-Colonel Chamberlain.
Sept. 29 (?)	Arthur's Swamp.	Lieutenant-Colonel Sargent.
Oct. 27, 28.	Hatcher's Run and Vaughan Road.	Lieutenant-Colonel Sargent.
Dec. 1, 2.	Stony Creek Station.	Lieutenant-Colonel Sargent.
Dec. 9.	Bellfield.	Lieutenant-Colonel Sargent.
Feb. 5-7, '65.	Dabney's Mills.	Captain Murphy.

Some of these engagements were small affairs, and indeed, in some of the large battles not enumerated here, the regiment was present, though not engaged, being held in reserve out of fire.

There were also other engagements where men of the regiment were under fire, and where some were included in a list of casualties, notably about Washington, in July, 1864, when all the dismounted cavalry was sent up and acted either as cavalry or infantry. As in this case, these men served under other officers than those of the regiment, and not as an organization, and as it is impossible to get particulars, such engagements are not included here.

While on picket, encounters would not unfrequently take place, of greater or smaller importance. Such are here reported, where the affair was of consequence enough to be called an engagement only; and yet it is difficult to draw a sharp line. The fact is, that "something was going on all the time" in cavalry. In winter, the raids into "Mosby's Confederacy" assumed large proportions, lasting sometimes many days, involving great exposure, and resulting in hard marching, freezing bivouacs, and some casualties, too.

Still, perhaps this list of engagements represents pretty nearly what was done by the regiment.

ENGAGEMENTS OF COMPANIES I, K, L, AND M, OLD THIRD BATTALION FIRST REGIMENT MASSACHUSETTS CAVALRY.

June 16, 1862	Secessionville, S. C.
	Morris Island, S. C.
	Fort Wagner, S. C.
	Siege of Charleston, S. C.
	St. John's Bluffs, Fla., Co. K.
	Jacksonville, Fla., Co. K.
February 8, 1864	Capture of Jacksonville, Fla.
February 8, 1864	Camp Finnegan, Fla.
February 8, 1864	Three Mile Run, Fla.
February 9, 1864	Baldwin Junction, Fla.
February 10, 1864	Barber's Ford, Fla.
February 11, 1864	Sanderson, Fla.
February 12, 1864	Lake City, Fla.
February 17, 1864	Callahan Station, Fla.
February 20, 1864	Olustee, Fla.
March 1, 1864	Cedar Run, Fla.
April 2, 1864	Eight Mile Run, Fla.
April, 1864	Palatka, Fla.
May 8, 1864	Bermuda Hundred, Va.
May 17, 1864	Drury's Bluff, Va.
1864	Harrison's Landing, Va.
June 10, 1864	Petersburg, Va.
June 16, 1864	Bermuda Front, Va.
August 14, 1864	Petersburg, Va.
August 16, 1864	Strawberry Plains, Va.
August 17, 1864	Deep Bottom, Va.
August 18, 1864	Furnell's Mills, Va.
August 27, 1864	Chapin's Farm, Va.
April, 1864	Hatcher's Run, Va.
September 29, 1864	Deep Bottom, Va.
October 7, 1864	Laurel Hill, Va.
October 13, 1864	Darbytown Road, Va.
October 27, 1864	Seven Pines, Va.
November 10, 1864	Charles City, Va.
December 21, 1864	Cumberland, Va.
April 2, 1865	Petersburg, Va.
1865	Harrison's Landing, Va.
April 6, 1865	High Bridge, Va.
April 9, 1865	Appomattox Court House, Va.

ALSO FROM LEONAUR
AVAILABLE IN SOFTCOVER OR HARDCOVER WITH DUST JACKET

THE LIFE OF THE REAL BRIGADIER GERARD VOLUME 1—THE YOUNG HUSSAR 1782-1807 *by Jean-Baptiste De Marbot*—A French Cavalryman Of the Napoleonic Wars at Marengo, Austerlitz, Jena, Eylau & Friedland.

THE LIFE OF THE REAL BRIGADIER GERARD VOLUME 2—IMPERIAL AIDE-DE-CAMP 1807-1811 *by Jean-Baptiste De Marbot*—A French Cavalryman of the Napoleonic Wars at Saragossa, Landshut, Eckmuhl, Ratisbon, Aspern-Essling, Wagram, Busaco & Torres Vedras.

THE LIFE OF THE REAL BRIGADIER GERARD VOLUME 3—COLONEL OF CHASSEURS 1811-1815 *by Jean-Baptiste De Marbot*—A French Cavalryman in the retreat from Moscow, Lutzen, Bautzen, Katzbach, Leipzig, Hanau & Waterloo.

THE INDIAN WAR OF 1864 *by Eugene Ware*—The Experiences of a Young Officer of the 7th Iowa Cavalry on the Western Frontier During the Civil War.

THE MARCH OF DESTINY *by Charles E. Young & V. Devinny*—Dangers of the Trail in 1865 by Charles E. Young & The Story of a Pioneer by V. Devinny, two Accounts of Early Emigrants to Colorado.

CROSSING THE PLAINS *by William Audley Maxwell*—A First Hand Narrative of the Early Pioneer Trail to California in 1857.

CHIEF OF SCOUTS *by William F. Drannan*—A Pilot to Emigrant and Government Trains, Across the Plains of the Western Frontier.

THIRTY-ONE YEARS ON THE PLAINS AND IN THE MOUNTAINS *by William F. Drannan*—William Drannan was born to be a pioneer, hunter, trapper and wagon train guide during the momentous days of the Great American West.

THE INDIAN WARS VOLUNTEER *by William Thompson*—Recollections of the Conflict Against the Snakes, Shoshone, Bannocks, Modocs and Other Native Tribes of the American North West.

THE 4TH TENNESSEE CAVALRY *by George B. Guild*—The Services of Smith's Regiment of Confederate Cavalry by One of its Officers.

COLONEL WORTHINGTON'S SHILOH *by T. Worthington*—The Tennessee Campaign, 1862, by an Officer of the Ohio Volunteers.

FOUR YEARS IN THE SADDLE *by W. L. Curry*—The History of the First Regiment Ohio Volunteer Cavalry in the American Civil War.

AVAILABLE ONLINE AT **www.leonaur.com**
AND FROM ALL GOOD BOOK STORES

ALSO FROM LEONAUR
AVAILABLE IN SOFTCOVER OR HARDCOVER WITH DUST JACKET

AN APACHE CAMPAIGN IN THE SIERRA MADRE by John G. Bourke—An Account of the Expedition in Pursuit of the Chiricahua Apaches in Arizona, 1883.

BILLY DIXON & ADOBE WALLS by Billy Dixon and Edward Campbell Little—Scout, Plainsman & Buffalo Hunter, *Life and Adventures of "Billy" Dixon* by Billy Dixon and *The Battle of Adobe Walls* by Edward Campbell Little (*Pearson's Magazine*).

WITH THE CALIFORNIA COLUMN by George H. Petis—Against Confederates and Hostile Indians During the American Civil War on the South Western Frontier, *The California Column, Frontier Service During the Rebellion* and *Kit Carson's Fight With the Comanche and Kiowa Indians*.

THRILLING DAYS IN ARMY LIFE by George Alexander Forsyth—Experiences of the Beecher's Island Battle 1868, the Apache Campaign of 1882, and the American Civil War.

INDIAN FIGHTS AND FIGHTERS by Cyrus Townsend Brady—Indian Fights and Fighters of the American Western Frontier of the 19th Century.

THE NEZ PERCÉ CAMPAIGN, 1877 by G. O. Shields & Edmond Stephen Meany—Two Accounts of Chief Joseph and the Defeat of the Nez Percé, *The Battle of Big Hole* by G. O. Shields and *Chief Joseph, the Nez Percé* by Edmond Stephen Meany.

CAPTAIN JEFF OF THE TEXAS RANGERS by W. J. Maltby—Fighting Comanche & Kiowa Indians on the South Western Frontier 1863-1874.

SHERIDAN'S TROOPERS ON THE BORDERS by De Benneville Randolph Keim—The Winter Campaign of the U. S. Army Against the Indian Tribes of the Southern Plains, 1868-9.

WILD LIFE IN THE FAR WEST by James Hobbs—The Adventures of a Hunter, Trapper, Guide, Prospector and Soldier.

THE OLD SANTA FE TRAIL by Henry Inman—The Story of a Great Highway.

LIFE IN THE FAR WEST by George F. Ruxton—The Experiences of a British Officer in America and Mexico During the 1840's.

ADVENTURES IN MEXICO AND THE ROCKY MOUNTAINS by George F. Ruxton—Experiences of Mexico and the South West During the 1840's.

AVAILABLE ONLINE AT www.leonaur.com
AND FROM ALL GOOD BOOK STORES

www.ingramcontent.com/pod-product-compliance
Lightning Source LLC
Chambersburg PA
CBHW030229170426
43201CB00006B/161